The Wife of Bath

Marion Turner [signature]

The Wife of Bath

A Biography

MARION TURNER

PRINCETON UNIVERSITY PRESS

PRINCETON AND OXFORD

Published by Princeton University Press
41 William Street, Princeton, New Jersey 08540
99 Banbury Road, Oxford OX2 6JX

press.princeton.edu

Library of Congress Cataloging-in-Publication Data

Names: Turner, Marion, 1976– author.
Title: The Wife of Bath : a biography / Marion Turner.
Description: Princeton : Princeton University Press, [2022] | Includes bibliographical references and index.
Identifiers: LCCN 2022026577 (print) | LCCN 2022026578 (ebook) | ISBN 9780691206011 (hardback ; acid-free paper) | ISBN 9780691206028 (ebook)
Subjects: LCSH: Chaucer, Geoffrey, –1400—Characters—Wife of Bath. | Wife of Bath (Fictitious character) | Chaucer, Geoffrey, –1400. Wife of Bath's tale. | Women in literature. | BISAC: LITERARY CRITICISM / Medieval | BIOGRAPHY & AUTOBIOGRAPHY / Literary Figures | LCGFT: Literary criticism.
Classification: LCC PR1868.W593 T87 2022 (print) | LCC PR1868. W593 (ebook) | DDC 821/.1—dc23/eng/20220608
LC record available at https://lccn.loc.gov/2022026577
LC ebook record available at https://lccn.loc.gov/2022026578

British Library Cataloging-in-Publication Data is available

Editorial: Ben Tate and Josh Drake
Production Editorial: Jill Harris
Text Design: Heather Hansen
Jacket Design: Heather Hansen
Production: Danielle Amatucci
Publicity: Alyssa Sanford and Carmen Jimenez
Copyeditor: Molan Goldstein

Jacket image: Lebrecht Music & Arts / Alamy Stock Photo

This book has been composed in Arno Pro

Printed on acid-free paper. ∞

Printed and bound by CPI Group (UK) Ltd, Croydon, CR0 4YY

10 9 8 7 6 5 4 3 2 1

for Peter and Cecilia,
who know the importance of painting the lion

Contents

Illustrations

Illustrations follow page 172.

Figure 1. The Wife of Bath in the Ellesmere Chaucer manuscript, c. 1400. EL 26 C 9, Egerton family papers. Copyright © The Huntington Library, San Marino, CA, 72 r.

Figure 2. The Pilgrimage Window, York Minster, early 14th century. Copyright © Taken by The York Glaziers Trust, reproduced by kind permission of the Chapter of York.

Figure 3. Vulva pilgrim brooch, Netherlands, late 14th or early 15th century. Copyright © Van Beuningen Family Collection, HP1, cat. no. 663, Inv. 2184.

Figure 4. The Ellesmere scribe comments on the Wife of Bath's Prologue, c. 1400. EL 26 C 9, Egerton family papers. Copyright © The Huntington Library, San Marino, CA, 63v.

Figure 5. The Egerton scribe comments on the Wife of Bath's Prologue, late 15th century. British Library Add MS 5140, 95r. Copyright © British Library / GRANGER.

Figure 6. The Egerton scribe comments on the Wife of Bath's Prologue, late 15th century. British Library Add MS 5140, 88r. Copyright © British Library / GRANGER.

The Wife of Bath

Introduction

It might have been my mother or it might
have been the Wife of Bath.

—HILARY MANTEL, *THE MIRROR AND THE LIGHT*, 595

Hilary Mantel's reference to the Wife of Bath, in her wildly popular 2020 novel set in the time of Henry VIII, makes two assumptions: first, that modern readers know who the Wife of Bath is; and second, that they understand what she might have signified in Thomas Cromwell's world. In this scene, Cromwell (Henry VIII's right-hand man) is telling his closest colleagues about how Geoffrey de la Pole will respond to interrogation, saying that he will endlessly obfuscate and will keep contradicting himself, saying something happened in October or March; in Sussex (far south) or Yorkshire (in the north); that the person involved might have been his mother or might have been the Wife of Bath. The implication is that Chaucer's heroine is as well known as the months or English geography or one's parents. And, although she is presented here as a foil to Geoffrey's mother, in fact the two women are rather similar. Margaret de

1

la Pole, suspected of treason to the king (and later executed for it), was a woman who, like Alison of Bath, challenged authority and went her own way, as many medieval women did.

Mantel correctly implies here that in the sixteenth-century *and* in the twenty-first, Alison of Bath was and is part of the cultural fabric of many English-speaking women's and men's lives. Why has this character from a fourteenth-century poem had such a dramatic impact across time?

The Wife of Bath is the first ordinary woman in English literature. By that I mean the first mercantile, working, sexually active woman—not a virginal princess or queen, not a nun, witch, or sorceress, not a damsel in distress nor a functional servant character, not an allegory. A much-married woman and widow, who works in the cloth trade and tells us about her friends, her tricks, her experience of domestic abuse, her long career combatting misogyny, her reflections on the ageing process, and her enjoyment of sex, Alison exudes vitality, wit, and rebellious self-confidence. Alison is a character whom readers across the centuries have usually seen as accessible, familiar, and, in a strange way, real. For many people she is by far the most memorable of the Canterbury pilgrims. Almost from the moment of her conception, she exceeded her own text, appearing in Chaucer's other writings (in a way no other character does) before being seized and appropriated by readers, scribes, and other poets alike. Over and over again, in different time periods and cultural contexts, readers see her as 'relatable' in certain ways, as a three-dimensional figure who is far more than the sum of her parts. She may be 'ordinary,' but she is also *extraordinary*.

However, Alison of Bath is not a real woman, nor was she based on a real woman, or created by a woman. She is not even a fully rounded, psychologically complex character in the same way that, say, Dorothea Brooke or Clarissa Dalloway are. But neither is she an eternal type, the principle of the feminine, an everywoman, Eve.

The Wife of Bath is, in some ways, a mosaic of many sources, all penned by men, most of them misogynist. Yet she does not come across as simply a jumble of the writings of Saint Paul, Jerome, Jean de Meun, and Walter Map. No one before Chaucer had turned the antifeminists' words around and against them as Alison does; no one had imagined a female character with this kind of wit, rhetorical technique, and personal experience going head-to-head with the most authoritative of authorities. Chaucer performed some kind of alchemy when he fused his cluster of well-worn sources with contemporary details and a distinctive, personalised voice and produced something— someone—completely new.

Indeed, before Chaucer, there had never been characters like this at all in English literature: characters from ordinary life who talk about themselves and their own experiences in detail, narrating personal histories and encouraging sympathetic response and identification. The emergence of this self-conscious, narrating 'I' figure was largely a new phenomenon in the late fourteenth century, as I will discuss in the first chapter. The fact that Chaucer developed this kind of literary narrator in the form of a confident, well-off mercantile woman who tells jokes, enjoys sex, and thinks for herself about the male canon and the exclusion of women's voices from it is astounding.

This book sets out to tell Alison's life story—from the earliest biblical sources to the present day—by asking two questions. Where does she come from, and what happens to her after her triumphant emergence in her prologue and tale? Undoubtedly Chaucer's favourite character, she has generally been his readers' favourite too (with some notable exceptions—such as the poet William Blake, who called her 'a scourge and a blight,' and the critic D. W. Robertson, who thought her 'hopelessly carnal and literal').[1] Her story is a story about class, gender, and narrative. Her unique position is derived not only from her sex but also from her background in trade and production (not land and ancient inherited wealth).[2] Things changed for women after the Black Death in England in very specific ways, and these material changes coincided with Chaucer's development of a new way of thinking about literary character. In literary terms, she is by far Chaucer's most developed example of a pioneering way of exploring narratives of the self; his confessional prologues are a distant ancestor of the soliloquy and the novel, forms that allow an author to stage a particular kind of revelation of the inner life.

What does it mean to write a 'biography' of someone who never existed? During the course of the first part of this book, I set the experiences of real, historical women alongside their fictional counterparts as part of an exploration of gender in history and culture. History and fiction cannot be straightforwardly separated in many of my sources. For instance, if we take a *historical* document—a petition presented to Edward III by the silkwomen of London in 1368—it is clear that there are *fictional* elements. The women declare that they have 'no other means of livelihood than their craft,' as they appeal for sympathy in their attempt to stop a rich Italian merchant pushing up the prices of material in London, presenting themselves as poor and desperate.[3] However, many silkwomen were wealthy business owners, often married to rich mercers, employing apprentices, sometimes owning other businesses and benefitting from inheritances. Late medieval London silkwomen included Agnes Woodhouse-Gedge, who inherited money and property from her brother, married a rich mercer, and owned a brewhouse in Peckham; and Isabel Bally-Otes-Franck, who married three mercers, had her own shop in Soper Lane, and was twice lady mayoress.[4] Similar women are almost certainly behind the 1368 text. The petition genre demands that they depict themselves as abject, in need of the king's support, when in fact some of them were substantial businesswomen with fingers in many pies. At the same time, the women also claim that they are motivated by concern for 'the king's special profit' and for the 'common profit of the realm,' while the threatening foreigner, Nicholas Sarduche, employs 'subtle operations.' They appeal to a widespread fear of foreign secrecy and selfishness, while associating themselves with the important contemporary value of 'common profit.'[5] There is clearly much that is fictional in this account.[6]

If we look at a *literary* text from around the same time—*Troilus and Criseyde*, a tragic romance set in the time of the Trojan War—Chaucer depicts a scene in which a group of women read a book (at the beginning of Book II). This scene tells us nothing about how Trojan women experienced texts or even about how Chaucer thought Trojan women experienced texts. Instead, it reflects the *historical* reality of how well-off Englishwomen in the fourteenth century read books. Criseyde and her friends and relatives are together, relaxing, while one reads aloud a romance (the quintessential medieval genre) from a medieval codex—it seems to be the twelfth-century *Roman de Thebes*.[7] The others listen, and then they discuss it. The terms used—'book' (86, 95) and 'romaunce' (100), as well as 'lettres rede' (103), indicating its rubrication—clearly evoke a medieval (not classical) reading experience.[8] This fictional scene is imbued with details that reflect historical reality, and it helps us to understand more about late-medieval reading practices and leisure activities.

At this time, we also see the emergence of autobiographical texts, and these texts have a particularly complicated relationship with fiction and with history. *The Book of Margery Kempe*, sometimes called the first autobiography in English and telling the life story of a woman who lived in the late fourteenth and early fifteenth centuries, is certainly based on the facts of her life, but is also modelled on other texts.[9] Margery's experiences often mirror suspiciously closely the experiences of saints and other holy women as she makes her life story fit into preordained paradigms.[10] For Margery, as for the silkwomen, her text passed through a male filter, as it was written down by a male scribe who had at least some control over its form and order.[11] Very often, in texts from these centuries, we see female experience expressed by a male voice. Fiction and fact are blended together and repackaged for us by male ghostwriters who often turn out to be unreliable.

In the first part of this book, I explore a whole range of evidence to try to understand where the Wife of Bath came from and how her first readers might have understood her and connected her to women they knew. In these chapters, I set the Wife of Bath in her late-medieval context, weaving together narratives of real women's experiences in post-plague Europe and the misogynistic literary stereotypes that shaped expectations of textual—and actual—women.

When he was creating Alison as a character, Chaucer's own skill and inspiration were powered by literary sources and by his historical environment, but the character came to full being in the mind of the reader, as I will discuss in detail in the first part of this book. In the second half of the book, the focus will shift to readers and reinventors across time who have remade Alison for their own historical moments.

In the centuries following Alison's emergence into literary history and into the consciousness of readers and writers, she has ventured far and wide. I explore, for instance, what Shakespeare made of Alison; the seventeenth-century imprisonment of printers who printed ballads about her; Dryden and Pope's efforts to make her less scandalous; her eighteenth-century journeys to the Continent, where Voltaire took her on, and across the Atlantic, where she went on the stage; communist readings of her in the twentieth-century; and twenty-first century reclamations of Alison by Black women writing postcolonial poetry and drama.

For many readers, the Wife of Bath became a shorthand for Chaucer, the most memorable aspect of his entire oeuvre. If we look, for example, at Ted Hughes's poem, 'Chaucer,' it is much more about the Wife of Bath than any other feature of Chaucer's writing.[12] It is fundamentally about Hughes's lover, Sylvia Plath, or his perception of Plath, filtered through his understanding of the Wife of Bath. Like many readers, Hughes uses the Wife of Bath as a way of thinking about his own life and desires. He describes a scene in a cow field near Cambridge, where Plath declaims the opening of Chaucer's General Prologue and then switches to reciting the Wife of Bath. Addressing Plath, Hughes says, 'Then came the Wyf of Bath, / Your favourite character in all literature. / You were rapt.' As she recites the Wife of Bath, she also, to Hughes, becomes a version of the Wife of Bath: she 'could not stop' talking (in case the cows panicked). We are given an image of a woman endlessly expressing herself, just as the Wife of Bath's Prologue is many hundreds of lines longer than any other *Canterbury Tales* prologue. Hughes writes 'You had to go on. You went on,' in a 'sostenuto rendering of Chaucer,' that became 'perpetual.' The tribute to her rhetorical power is prefaced with implicit references to sexual desire. The poem begins with Chaucer's address to springtime fertility, the piercing of the drought of March with April's sweet showers, and continues with a joyous reference to 'one of those bumpers of champagne / You snatched unpredictably from pure spirit.' Like Alison, Hughes's Plath is here vibrant, vital, appetite-driven, verbally powerful, and infinitely desirable.

The focus on Alison/Plath as speakers, commanding attention, is made funny, even mocking, given that the audience is bovine. Perhaps the cows represent male readers, incapable of appreciating her; perhaps we might read this as a comment on the 'natural' rhythms of Chaucerian metre; but there is also an implication that this is the sole kind of attention that female declaiming can command. She can only hold the interest of slow, lumbering beasts, and her position is undoubtedly silly. This somewhat uncomfortable, hesitant mockery of the female voice—listened to by an unintelligent, animalistic audience, finally driven off by a capable man (Hughes himself)—is a mild version of the discomfort that Alison has often provoked in her readers. When examining her adventures across time, it is striking that this is not a story of decreasing misogyny. Many twentieth-century responses, which often focused on her body and her sexual appetites in an extreme and caricatured way, were *more* misogynist than fifteenth-century engagements with Alison, which were often more concerned with combatting her rhetorical power. For many readers and rewriters, Alison has been a figure to be feared, hated, mocked, ridiculed, and firmly put in her place. Undaunted, she is still very much alive and well in literary and popular culture all over the world.

The Wife of Bath is one of only a handful of literary characters—others include Odysseus, Dido, Penelope, and King Arthur—whose life has continued far beyond their earliest textual appearances.[13] I can think of no other examples of this kind of character—a socially middling woman—who has had anything like Alison's reach, influence, and capacity for reincarnation.

The first ordinary middle-class woman in English literature has—like most women—had a great deal to do. Her extraordinary journey has, so far, spanned continents and centuries; and she has endured humiliations and attacks as well as celebration and almost incredible influence. This is Alison's tale.

PART I

Medieval Wives of Bath: Ordinary Women and English Literature

'Beaten for a Book': Literary Form and Lived Experience

The Wife of Bath was created at a moment in English history that saw extraordinary demographic change. Like the First World War, the plague was a demographic catastrophe that had the consequence of giving women greater opportunities in a time of labour shortage. The Black Death was an unprecedented and unparalleled event. Probably around a third of the population of Europe died in the first wave (1348–1349), and it returned periodically for the rest of the century. In the wake of the plague, there was more social mobility. Anxiety about wage rises was manifested in Statutes of Labourers, and sumptuary laws were passed to try to control the clothing that people wore. These attempts to prevent social climbing and class mobility failed, and the second half of the fourteenth century saw an increased loosening of feudal bonds and ideology, already on the wane.[1] Historians have discussed the fourteenth and fifteenth centuries as a 'golden age for women,' especially in London. While there are differing opinions, particularly about just how golden the age was and how long it lasted, most do agree that there was an increase in women's opportunities and status in England in the fourteenth and fifteenth centuries.[2] They had some economic power, as seen, for instance, in the formalisation of their right—whether single, married, or widowed—to trade as *femmes sole*, rather than under the governance of their husbands. This meant a woman could run her own business, be responsible for her own money and taxes, and train her own apprentices. Jointures developed, allowing a woman to own property jointly with her husband, so that she could bequeath it as she wished. In some cases we even see women disposing of jointly owned property against their husbands' desires.[3]

Chaucer witnessed the growing opportunities for women—and he himself had a mother who owned property and a wife who always earned her own money (she worked as a lady-in-waiting in great households). In the second half of the fourteenth century, there was a plethora of London-based poets from the middling orders writing in English, married, working in the city at paid jobs—rather than in monastic or courtly environments. Gower, Langland, and Hoccleve all fit this general model as well as Chaucer. Culturally, Chaucer was also strongly influenced by Italian humanism and its focus on ethics. As Chaucer's writing career progressed, and as he aged, he increasingly turned away from poetry that focused (sympathetically) on women as courtly marriage objects and towards poetry that portrayed women as intelligent, active, ethical forces in the world (women such as the 'loathly lady' in the Wife of Bath's Tale).[4]

The Wife of Bath shows us how literary forms and lived experience affect each other. Alison is neither a real medieval woman nor a figure made entirely out of textual stereotypes. Thinking about her involves considering the knotty relationship between representation and reality, the way that perception and ideological ideas about women impact upon the treatment of women in society—and vice versa.[5] As Georges Duby, one of the great historians of the Middle Ages, wrote: 'human beings do not orient their behaviour toward real events and circumstances, but rather to their image of them.'[6] To understand how experience and authority clash in her very creation as a character, we might explore how Alison herself graphically suggests there can be a link between written ideas about women and the physical, bodily experience of domestic violence. The 'book of wikked wyves' (685) does not appear until line 635 of her prologue, when she is telling us about her violent, misogynist, young fifth husband. Alison recounts briefly how Jankyn hit her because she tore a leaf out of his book, and that the blow deafened her (634–636). She then fleshes out the details: that she kept some independence after her marriage, but that her husband would preach to her about Roman marriages, Bible stories, and proverbs (637–665). The book then becomes the focus as Alison recounts its oppressive contents: anti-women, anti-marriage tracts by, for instance, Jerome, Tertullian, and Theophrastus (666–681). Jankyn gets great pleasure from luxuriating in misogyny; he reads it 'gladly,' 'for desport,' and laughs always when he reads it, which he does whenever he has 'leyser' (i.e., leisure [669, 670, 672, 683]). Alison digresses for her famous speech about institutional misogyny and the bias of the canon (688–696), asking 'who painted the lion?' (692) in order to point out that art is biased—humans tell a story different from that which the lion would tell, just as men's versions of life are different from women's. And women, like lions, have not had the chance to write stories. If they had, she says that they would have told of all the wickedness of men (693–696). When clerks are old and impotent, she claims, they sit down and write terrible things about women (707–710). Alison now returns to her story, how Jankyn every night would sit and read out insulting, aggressive stories about women (711–785). Eventually, when she sees he will never stop, she rips out three pages and hits her husband so that he falls backwards into the fire (788–793). He jumps up and hits her so hard on the head that she lies as if unconscious—and has genuinely been deafened (794–796).

Although the book only appears late in the prologue, and late in Alison's life, it is clear from the start that she is herself partly constructed out of the stereotypes in that kind of book, which tended to focus on many of the qualities that Alison delightedly demonstrates (She gossips! She drinks! She tells her husband's secrets! She looks for a new husband at her previous husband's funeral!). To a certain extent, she came out of that book *avant la lettre*. It is also clear, as already noted, that she is constructing her own arguments in relation to the arguments of men such as Jerome. The book of wicked wives—not Jankyn's specific book, but the weight of antifeminist literature—oppresses both female characters and real women. As Alison points out, because the pen has been so firmly in men's and not women's hands, there are no reasonable role models for women in literature or in life. She herself, as a literary character, is made out of male stereotypes. Medieval antifeminists would say that she demonstrates just how right they are about women; some modern feminists would concur that Chaucer stages her voice in such a way as to demonstrate women's traditional inadequacies.[7] But she steps outside these stereotypes in a metatextual moment when she declares her own awareness of the limitations of the canon—a moment at which she moves away from the texts of Jerome or Jean de Meun and instead uses a fable (who painted the lion?). The image of Jankyn and Alison sitting by the fire, reading a compendium manuscript of texts 'bounden in o volume' (681), injects another note of late-medieval 'realism' into the scene. In other words, it encourages us to think about what it might be like for an actual woman to sit there listening to terrible stories about women, hour after hour. After describing Jankyn's misogynist speech for seventy lines, Alison starkly states: 'Who wolde wene, or who wolde suppose / The wo that in myn herte was, and pyne?' (786–787). This is how it feels to be the recipient of unrelenting misogyny—unimaginable, unspeakable. It is also a moment in which this textual figure describes her memory and her emotions and invites the readers to enter into her world, to try to imagine what it is like to be her. Far more than an embodiment of antifeminist stereotypes, Alison and her text here encourage us to critique those source materials and to think about individual experience rather than official authority.

Crucially, and disturbingly, the book becomes the occasion for violence. Alison starkly tells us, 'I was beten for a book' (712). Life and texts, history and literature come together here. If we pretend that texts are wholly separable from life (authority from experience), that literary stereotypes have no connection to lived reality, we risk ignoring the violence that is enacted on bodies precisely because of what people have read in books. The way that women are treated in life is everywhere inflected by, as Virginia Woolf writes, the spectre of Professor von X 'writing his monumental work entitled *The Mental, Moral and Physical Inferiority of the Female Sex*.'[8] The Wife of Bath is many things, but one of those things is a representation of the dissonance between the reality of medieval women's experience on the one hand, and the textual misogyny that attacked women for perfectly normal behaviour (such as remarriage) on the other. These books of wicked wives were real medieval books:

compilations of misogynist tracts, to which Chaucer must have had access. When she describes the book, Alison first mentions three principal texts, those by Valerius, Theophrastus, and Jerome. Thirty-five extant manuscripts have been identified that contain Jerome's *Adversus Jovinianum* plus either Valerius or Theophrastus, with eleven that contain all three.[9] Real medieval widows, whose behaviour was entirely normal and in fact encouraged, still had to contend with books that insulted them in every possible way.

Indeed, we know from the writings of a real medieval woman that women were literally beaten because of books in the Middle Ages. In an extraordinary parallel with the fictional experience of the Wife of Bath, the medieval French author Christine de Pizan recounts an anecdote in which a husband reads the *Roman de la Rose* to his wife, and ends by attacking her violently. Christine tells of 'an extremely jealous man, who, whenever in the grip of passion, would go and find the book and read it to his wife; then he would become violent and strike her and say such horrible things as, "These are the kinds of tricks you pull on me."'[10] We see here how a fictional text can cause actual bodily trauma to women.

The first half of this book engages with the complex intermingling of textual sources and historical circumstances that lies behind the creation of the Wife of Bath. The first chapter describes how Chaucer invented the idea of literary character, exploring what it is that is so different about Alison compared to her predecessors and suggesting why she has been so fascinating to her readers. Each of the subsequent four chapters takes a different aspect of the Wife of Bath—her working status, her multiple marriages, her identity as a storyteller, and her proclivity for travelling—and discusses what that trait would have meant to Chaucer and his medieval readers. This was an audience accustomed to texts that classified people according to particular traits; they were familiar with interpretive schemes that assigned a whole set of characteristics to individuals depending on their job, or marital status, or set of relationships.[11] What did late-medieval writers and readers expect of the widow or the working woman, of the traveller or the storyteller? How did textual examples interact with the lived experience of medieval women? Each chapter looks at long-held medieval ideas about women, while also describing the lives of contemporary medieval women. The chapters are studded with mini-biographies of a wide variety of women, and they also encompass biblical types, art, pilgrim badges, misogynist satire, and poetic sources. Together, the chapters in the first part of the book seek to answer the question of how this revolutionary figure came into being at this extraordinary moment in history. Who and what was Alison of Bath?

CHAPTER 1

The Invention of Character

Jo March, Elizabeth Bennet, Jane Eyre, Scarlett O'Hara,
Becky Sharp, Pippi Longstocking and the Wife of Bath—women
and girls whom one can imagine being set into any time, or
location, and being just as entertaining, companionable and
prone to amusing, yet ultimately triumphant, misadventure
as they were in their original centuries.

—CAITLIN MORAN, *CAITLIN MORAN
ON BRIDGET JONES'S DIARY*

Alison of Bath is a middle-aged woman—a reasonably happy
older woman (even if she might prefer to be younger)—still
sexually active, still attractive, someone who works, goes on
holiday, and enjoys life. A woman like this could not speak in
texts before Chaucer's; her viewpoint was not seen as interesting. Moreover, she could barely even be spoken. In literature,
she hardly existed, just as (until very recently) once women
turned forty they mysteriously disappeared from Hollywood
movies and television newsdesks alike. More fundamentally
still, before Chaucer invented the Wife of Bath, there were no

characters at all with the particular kind of subjectivity and personality that she embodies. The characters that he created were different from those that had gone before and readers reacted to them differently, with deeply personal responses. As the epigraph to this chapter illustrates, readers often group Alison of Bath with characters from much later novels, as part of a set of women with whom many people identify and whom they see as representing something recognisable and vital. She lives for readers in a way that most characters do not.

Critics have lined up to tell us how different Alison is: 'a new kind of literary character . . . she has no literary antecedent'; a novel kind of figure 'whose sense of self dwarfs any tale she may tell or be a part of'; a pilgrim whose prologue calls up 'a distinct and memorable consciousness—one that exists, as we all do, in the dimension of time.'[1] In one of the most important books on character in Chaucer, Jill Mann suggests that the question of whether Chaucer was focused on 'life' or 'literature' sets up a false dichotomy. Of course he drew on multiple sources. But those sources were particularly rooted in contemporary social stereotypes—not timeless ones. Moreover, life and literature are not wholly separable in that readers are influenced by what they read, and perceive the people they know partly through the lens of what they have read.[2] More recently, in a brilliant discussion of character and Chaucer, Elizabeth Fowler focuses on the experience of character for the reader, writing about the ways in which poets put together flat images and details that combine to construct a sense of interiority and depth within the mind of the reader. Her argument is that Chaucer fundamentally changed what character could do: the *Tales* 'stretch and expand the capacities of the device of character,' and for Chaucer and the writers who have come after him, interiority could best be described and understood through literary techniques (rather than through religious practices).[3] In bringing together the conventional and the innovative, literature and life, the social and the personal, authority and experience (to quote the Wife of Bath's first words), Chaucer forged a particular way of representing personhood.

Where did this come from? It would be completely wrong to suggest that no one before Chaucer was interested in interiority. In some of the earliest texts written in English, we see fledgling and elliptical explorations of the complexities of self. This is particularly the case in short, elegiac poems that offer snapshots of emotions—poems including *The Wife's Lament, Wulf and Eadwacer*, and *The Wanderer* (these poems survive in a manuscript dated around 1000, *The Exeter Book*).[4] All of these poems meditate on memory, loss, and trauma. In the so-called twelfth-century renaissance, writers experimented with ways of writing about selfhood as the genres of romance and lyric offered new possibilities.[5] An increased interest in the private self was reflected in, for instance, the French romances of Chrétien de Troyes (written c. 1170–c. 1190) with their detailed depictions of the inner life. Religious art and writing focused more and more on human suffering, on identification with the human aspects of Christ, and on emotional responses to God. In 1215, when the Fourth Lateran Council established confession as mandatory, western European Christians were directed to think about their inner selves in systematic and rigorous ways. After this date, penitential handbooks (guides for priests that gave a taxonomy of sins) proliferated, as laypeople and clerics alike were encouraged to think more about the inner life and the nature of sin. Crucially, people also needed to talk about their behaviour, to analyse themselves and present themselves for judgement. While the rise of confession in some ways encouraged a codification of the self, it also enabled an increase in a

certain kind of self-awareness. There was thus a heightened interest in talking about oneself in the thirteenth and fourteenth
centuries, and literary confessions can usefully be seen in this
context. There was also a much longer tradition of confession
and self-examination in textual form—Augustine's *Confessions*
(c. 397–400) is a key example—and we might also think of texts
that dramatize an internal debate, such as Boethius's *Consola-
tion of Philosophy* (c. 524).[6] But it is particularly important that
in Chaucer's text, all kinds of very ordinary people are encouraged to express themselves and, in some cases, to reveal themselves to others—which places the prologues very much in the
context of late-medieval confessional structures.

The technology of confession fundamentally changed *how*
people thought about interiority, and confessional discourses
spilled into other kinds of texts.[7] In his continuation of *La
Roman de la Rose* (c. 1275), Jean de Meun, a cleric writing an
allegory, utilised confessional discourse particularly in his invention of La Vielle, the old woman on whom Alison was to be
partly based. While La Vielle lacks both the wit and vitality of
Alison and her moral understanding, she does introduce a
sense of the temporal self into the poem: she looks at her past,
she tells us about her experiences, she confesses. Unlike more
traditional allegorical characters, she has a past and a story, and
to an extent, she reflects on her life.

In the second half of the fourteenth century, English literature entered the age of the narrator. Chaucer was heavily influenced by the *dits amoureux*—love narratives—of Guillaume de
Machaut in particular, long poems that dramatized the relationship between a client and a patron through the eyes of the poet-
client figure.[8] These were poems about subjectivity, about the
personal feelings of those who had lost their love, about the biased
judgements of poets and of their superiors regarding who suffers

most in love, for instance.[9] Although the key poems in this tradition for Chaucer were 'judgement' poems, the point is not
that judgement can be absolute or reliable—these issues are,
essentially, beyond proof as they rely on personal feeling, on
experience, on how things appear to a contingent individual.[10]
That individual, the 'I' figure, tended to be a courtly male subject, heavily invested in the emotional life of a male patron.
While the *Roman de la Rose* too had explored the perceptions
of a subjective narrator, its allegorical nature blurred the idea of
the objective and the subjective.[11] In the fourteenth century,
the idea of literary subjectivity was much more fully developed.
Literature written in English saw a flood of experiential writing
from the third quarter of the century. Texts including Chaucer's
dream poems, Langland's *Piers Plowman* and the anonymous
Pearl are predicated upon the idea that narrators are subjective
figures, perceiving and experiencing events through their own
consciousness. In all of these poems, as in Machaut's, the degree
to which narrator and author can be separated is unclear.[12] And
Chaucer's narrators stand out as Chaucer brings a comic version of mercantile pragmatism into the world of courtly love
dream-vision.[13]

    This was a new literary world in which vernacular writers
were expanding the idea of what character—and particularly
narratorial character—could be and could do. Chaucer experimented with the experiential narrator in all of his narrative
poems, and in the *Canterbury Tales* he took those experiments
in a new direction. In the General Prologue, his narrator figure
enters into a version of free indirect discourse—a mode of writing in which the narrator appropriates the perspectives of the
characters. As the Chaucer figure characterizes each pilgrim, he
tends to describe them through their own eyes, giving us, for
example, a positive spin on various pilgrims' irregularities.[14]

When he came to write the 'confessional' prologues (those of the Wife of Bath, Pardoner, and Canon's Yeoman), Chaucer produced a group of first-person narratives of self: autobiographical narratives that foreground the perspectives of the characters, filtering their own experiences and then their stories through their own ostentatiously unreliable points of view. This sustained experiment in the invention of character was something wholly new in English literature.[15] Previously, when readers had sought to explore their inner selves, they had been encouraged to turn to religious texts—to identify with saints and Christ or to self-examine through penance. Chaucer wrested the control of the interior away from the authority of religious texts and located it in the secular realm.[16]

There are thirty-two pilgrims described in the General Prologue, including the Host (Harry Bailly) and the Chaucer-pilgrim. The Canon and the Canon's Yeoman arrive later. Twenty-three tell tales (the Chaucer-figure tells two tales). Many have shortish prologues, which contain personal information—complaints about their wives, spats with other pilgrims, or comments on other tales or on the tale-telling contest, for instance. Three pilgrims—the Canon's Yeoman, the Pardoner, and the Wife of Bath—are known as the 'confessional' pilgrims. These three have longer, self-revelatory prologues. The Pardoner's Prologue is 154 lines long (329–462). The Canon's Yeoman's Prologue is made up of 166 lines (554–719). The first part of his tale is also 'confessional' in style, comprising a further 252 lines (720–971). But the Wife of Bath's Prologue is a staggering 856 lines long. This alone alerts the reader to the fact that this is a different kind of character. Throughout the *Tales*, Chaucer treats her differently from his other pilgrims. She pops up at the end of the Clerk's Tale, when the Clerk ironically declares that he will sing a song 'for the Wyves love of Bathe' (1170)—in other words, for love of the Wife of Bath. There isn't anything else quite like this in the *Tales*, but we could compare it to other characters talking at various points in the text. More striking is her penetration into a different layer of fiction. One of the characters within the Merchant's Tale, Justinus, a character who should know nothing about Alison, refers to her as an authority, telling January that the Wife of Bath has 'Declared ful wel' on the subject of marriage (1685–1687).[17] This was only the beginning of Alison's long career as a bookrunner—a figure that escapes her own text.[18] Her next excursion was to get out of the *Canterbury Tales* to appear in Chaucer's *Lenvoy de Bukton*. In this short poem, Chaucer cites her as an authority figure, telling his friend to read the Wife of Bath ('The Wyf of Bathe I pray yow that ye rede' [29]) as a warning against marrying. Importantly, Alison has here become a text to be cited, an author. These things do not happen to any of the other pilgrims, and her long and varied life in other texts further demonstrates that her readers, as well as her author, saw Alison as different from Chaucer's other creations.

Readers of Chaucer have long had contrasting ideas about what his characters were. One school of thought held that they were rather like real people, and that Chaucer based them on historical individuals. J. M. Manly, for instance, maintained that various facts pointed to Alison of Bath having 'a real existence and to a personal knowledge of her by the poet,' adding that 'Chaucer writes as if he had seen her in her native place.'[19] A later critic, Donald Howard, emphasised the psychological realism of Alison, saying that in the cases of the Pardoner and the Wife of Bath, we 'see inside their minds.' He argues that Chaucer demonstrated 'an unusual kind of interest in women' and 'unusual insight into a woman's mind.'[20] Howard consistently suggests that 'women's minds' are essentially similar to each other but different from 'men's minds,' and indeed, as we shall see, many readers across time have treated the Wife of Bath as a representative of general womanhood, a principle of the undifferentiated feminine.

A group of critics got so carried away with the belief that Alison should be read as if she were a real person that they argued that Alison and her fifth husband, Jankyn, murdered her fourth husband.[21] Donald Sands wrote:

> She is not, it would seem, a psychotic, a schizophrenic, or a manic depressive—that is, a person suffering from personality disintegration and loss of contact with reality—but rather someone labouring under a character disorder which makes her acceptable to herself, but productive of conflict with others, a disorder which recent psychiatric texts label a sociopathic personality disturbance, an illness characterized by antisocial reaction, dissocial reaction, and usually addiction (in Alys's case, probably to alcohol).[22]

This kind of reading proceeds from the unspoken assumption that Alison has an existence outside the text—a backstory, a childhood, secret neuroses, thoughts and feelings that we can surmise. The idea that Alison is a copy of a real woman who lived near Bath, or that she is a person hiding her alcoholism, seems to me fundamentally to misunderstand what literature does and how Chaucer interacted with his literary heritage.

In contrast to these ways of reading character, many studies from the middle of the twentieth century focused on a formalist understanding of character: 'speakers are the effects rather than the causes of the language,' as character is an abstraction 'brought into being by the written or spoken words.'[23] To think about characters as akin to real people in some way was to fall victim to a naive, almost risible gullibility.[24] In studies of the Wife of Bath, many critics have focused on her textuality, suggesting that the plethora of literary antecedents reveals her unreality. Ganim sums up this approach: 'the Wife of Bath is a creation of the many anti-feminist tracts and discourses that she argues against.'[25] Ultimately, some critics argue that Chaucer's achievement 'derives less from the sympathetic observation of personality than from a magisterial and dispassionate deployment of inherited literary forms.'[26] Alison is words on a page—and those words are not even Chaucer's.

This too is a profoundly unsatisfactory way of thinking about Alison and is not true to the experience of the vast majority of readers, who do see her as more akin to a person than to a collection of words. Indeed, writing about literary character more generally, Brewer emphasises the importance of 'the apparent desire of many readers to imagine characters as in full possession of a deep interiority and a life which extends off-page, despite the patent counter-factuality of it all.'[27] In other words, of course characters are words on a page, but authors perform a magic that makes their readers work with the text to imagine something quite different. And in thinking about texts, we need to consider how they are worked upon by audiences. In an important book, *Why Do We Care About Literary Characters?*, Blakey Vermeule argues that 'the arts are the means by which humans orient themselves to other people's behavior.' Readers' empathetic reactions to literary characters lie at the heart of how we respond to fiction and, some would claim, are a crucial part of the ethical function of literature.[28] Texts are dynamic—they change when they are read.[29]

What was it like for medieval readers to encounter this innovative kind of character, depicted as a middle-aged, middle-class, sexually experienced, provincial woman? What kind of women might fourteenth-century readers have expected to find in texts? Readers of English texts might be familiar with romance heroines—women such as Goldeboro from *Havelock the Dane*, or Rymenhild from *King Horn*, or Herodis from *Sir*

Orfeo—in all cases princesses or queens, objects of sexual love and desire. They might know lyrics, which sometimes focused on more plebeian women, but characterised them by physical features and body parts, seen through the desiring eyes of the speaking male. One of the most famous of such lyrics in fact focuses on the body of another 'Alisoun.'[30] Readers might be familiar with guides for nuns and anchoresses, texts such as *Ancrene Wisse*, which encouraged women to channel their desires towards God, or with saints' lives, in which women are devout, idealised victims of torture and execution. In the dramatic upsurge in writing in English in the last quarter of the fourteenth century, a variety of female characters appear. In *Sir Gawain and the Green Knight*, one of the best of all medieval poems, there are three important female characters, all of them aristocratic. They are Guinevere, the queen, wife of King Arthur; Morgan la Fay, enchantress, sorceress, and half-sister of the king; and the nameless Lady, married to Lord Bertilak, an exceptionally beautiful temptress. The other female figure who watches over Gawain is the Virgin Mary. In another poem by the same author, *Pearl*, a female figure dominates: the Pearl-maiden is an innocent dead child, now a queen of heaven and a divine guide-figure. John Gower, writing at the same time as Chaucer, includes many (mainly classical) women in his long English poem, *Confessio amantis*, but they tend to be beautiful princesses or, occasionally, evil sorceresses, and their own perspectives are of little importance. He also includes an authoritative female guide-figure, Venus.

Langland, another contemporary of Chaucer's, sets his great poem partly in an urban, mercantile milieu and includes a range of different kinds of women—such as Lady Mede, part representation of Edward III's venal mistress, Alice Perrers, part allegorical figure for the circulation of money. He also gives us little vignettes of merchant women, such as Rose the Regrator, described by her husband, Covetousness, as tricking customers with inferior cloth and ale. She is an interesting figure, but not developed beyond a few lines or given a voice of her own. Medieval drama offers better examples of a variety of women speaking for themselves—though acted by male actors, and watched rather than read by the public.[31] In the cycle plays we do see female characters who are presented as more 'ordinary' women, despite their biblical origins—women such as Noah's wife, a stereotypical scold who refuses to get on the ark. These are 'types,' reminiscent of the typical targets of contemporary satirical texts in the genre of 'estates satire.'[32] They often fulfil an allegorical function, but their speeches do somewhat personalise and humanise them.[33]

In the continental poems that Chaucer read with such care and attention, the female figures again tended to be ideals such as Dante's Beatrice; aristocratic, beautiful women such as the female tale-tellers of the *Decameron* group; or the high-class lovers of romances and *dits amoureux*. Lower-class women featured as love objects or sex objects in the *pastourelle*, which typically staged a debate between a higher-class man and a shepherdess figure,[34] and in fabliaux, funny, subversive stories about mercantile adultery and the world upside down. In the *Roman de la Rose*, Chaucer encountered La Vielle, a former prostitute and bawd who does speak at some length about herself, but again is a 'type' figure in an allegory, representing an aspect of life/womanhood—she is a grotesque depiction of a cynical old age, an appalling old woman who was a stock figure from classical times. She was a crucial source for Alison, but I will discuss below how very different Alison is from her antecedent.

As vernacular literature had increasingly made room for subjectivity, that subjectivity had been heavily gendered. Lyric, romance, and the *dit amoureux* tended to focus on the male desiring subject, while women were the objects of male desire, often anatomised in detail. In general terms, men could actively represent and interpret, while women were represented and interpreted. Carolyn Dinshaw characterised this gendering of interpretation as 'sexual poetics,' a poetics in which readers, writers, and interpreters were assumed to be heterosexual males, while texts and women existed to be read, their mysteries penetrated by the active male.[35] Across time, in depictions of the act of reading itself, women were often used as metaphors for texts. Jerome, in an extended metaphor for translation, compares the pagan text to a slave-girl, stripped, shaved, and re-clothed by her captor.[36] Women were associated with deceitful rhetoric and ornament, figures of ambiguity and decoration.[37] For many patristic authors, women stood for the distractions of fiction: Augustine, for example, writes in the *Confessions* about his experience of being someone 'who weeps over the death of Dido dying for love of Aeneas, but not weeping over himself dying for his lack of love for you, my God, light of my heart.'[38]

Dido, in fact, represents one of the two types of women that were allowed space to speak in literary tradition.[39] Beautiful young victims of male violence or casualties of the march of history did have a voice. Ovid's *Heroides* (c. 16 BCE) dramatized the letters of abandoned women, and this influential text became a model for giving 'good,' suffering, badly treated women some kind of (male-authored) voice. Chaucer himself repeatedly allows Dido to tell her story, and he engages with the tradition of the *Heroides* in the *Legend of Good Women* and in other 'complaint' texts. He also, radically, extends the tradition to allow Criseyde, usually depicted as a promiscuous betrayer, to give her side of her story, and to present herself as a suffering woman, hemmed in by male violence and the inevitability of the fall of empire.[40] Indeed, she foretells that literary history will be biased against her and that (implicitly male-authored) books will 'shende' [destroy] her (*Troilus and Criseyde*, V, 1060).

The other kind of woman who reveals her experiences is the monstrous bawd figure, the terrifying old crone who is utterly cynical, lacks any attraction herself, and seeks to corrupt younger women and to deceive men. Ovid's Dipsas, from his *Amores*, is the key example here: she gives a long speech in which she lays bare her amoral views on how women should trick men. She is the main origin point for Jean de Meun's La Vielle. In the *Roman de la Rose*, La Vielle is an important figure in terms of what the text does with character: she speaks at length and autobiographically, somewhat stepping outside allegory to introduce a sense of temporality into the poem, although she remains profoundly limited as a figure. Dipsas and La Vielle are extreme projections of one imagined aspect of a woman; in no way do they represent an attempt to give women a real voice. Rather they are part of an antifeminist project to represent women's voices as terrifying, disgusting, and beyond redemption. Before Chaucer invented the Wife of Bath, there was no place in European literary tradition for a woman to speak out in this way who was neither a beautiful victim nor a hideous stereotype of an ancient procuress.

The other confessional pilgrims who are given a more developed subjectivity than the rest of the Canterbury characters are a working-class apprentice (the Canon's Yeoman) and a man perceived to have a deviant sexuality and who exposes the corruption of church practice through his own utterly amoral behaviour (the Pardoner). It is clearly significant that Chaucer chooses to give us insight into the mentalities of these marginal figures rather than selecting the Knight, for instance, or the Monk, Man of Law, Squire, or Merchant. But choosing Alison for his most sustained exploration of literary subjectivity takes his audacity to a whole new level. In his extraordinary experiments with character in the *Tales*, Chaucer deliberately picks people whose voices are in some way challenging to social norms, unsettling figures who undermine the relationship between servant and master, cleric and layperson, and woman and man. In his choice to make Alison of Bath into his most fully developed character, Chaucer decisively demonstrated his concern with breaking the moulds of literary history.

How, then, does Chaucer depict Alison's character, making her something far more than a mosaic of sources, despite her textual antecedents? What does he do in her long, autobiographical speech to get across the powerful sense of her personality that has had such a strong effect on readers across the centuries? How does he work such affective alchemy on his textual ingredients?

Let me quote a section from about halfway through her prologue to begin to explore this alchemy:

> But, Lord Crist! whan that it remembreth me
> (I think about)
> Upon my yowthe and on my jolitee,
> It tikleth me aboute myn herte roote.
> Unto this day it dooth myn herte boote   (reward)
> That I have had my world, as in my tyme.
> But age, allas, that al wole envenyme,
> (will poison everything)
> Hath me biraft my beautee and my pith!
> (has deprived me of my beauty and my vigour)
> Lat go, farewel, the devel go therwith!
> The flour is goon, ther is namoore to telle,
> The bren as I best kan, now moste I selle;   (bran)
> But yet to be right myrie wol I fonde. (469–479)

Memory, decay, death, hope, and change all pulse through these lines. In other words, they are suffused with an awareness of temporality, something that preoccupies most adults (and many children) to some degree. As a literary character—made out of words on a page—Alison teases us, tempting us to suspend that disbelief as she tells us that she does, in fact, have a past, and she also has a future. The lines oscillate between different temporal modes. The initial exclamation 'But, Lord Crist!' roots us firmly in the moment of her telling, while the second half of the line takes us to her memory, 'whan that it remembreth me,' and this memory of the past continues into the next line. In 471, we are brought back sharply to the immediate present with the powerful image of the memory tickling her heart's root. The present tense verb, 'tikleth,' evokes a sense of immediacy, but one of the things that makes this image so effective is that the idea of the root of the heart reminds us that our emotions, our consciousness, our sense of self is dependent on the past—on the metaphorical roots that symbolise our beginnings but continue to grow into our futures, just as roots keep spreading. The subsequent two lines again combine past and present. We are told, in the present, that 'unto this day' memory gives her rewards ('dooth myn herte boote'). The next line is the key line of the passage: 'That I have had my world, as in my tyme,' a lovely evocation of nostalgia, crystallised in her ownership of the space and time that she carved out for herself—*my* world, *my* time.

The speech goes on to bemoan age and decay, continuing to move between past and present tenses, and to use natural images—the pith and the flour ('pith' means strength or vigour, but its core meaning refers to part of a tree, plant, or fruit). Crucially, however, Alison does not dwell in self-pity, this is not a cry of irredeemable regret. She concludes by saying that she will still make the best of it—sell the bran—and that, in spite of everything, 'to be right myrie wol I fonde.' In other words, she is determined to be happy, to enjoy life, not to resign herself to despair and disappointment. The broad meaning of the verb she chooses—'fonde'—reflects her determination: 'fonde' means not only 'try, attempt,' but also 'seek, pursue,' and even 'enjoy,' or 'taste.'[41] She strives for happiness. Similarly, she tells us elsewhere that she will welcome a sixth husband (45)—her life, including her sexual life, is not over. This determination to be happy, to look to the future, to be optimistic, differentiates Alison sharply and decisively from figures such as La Vielle and Dipsas, who are defined by bitterness and cynicism. Indeed, it is notable that in the speech by La Vielle that forms the source for this speech, the speaker says nothing about the future at all—her speech is a visceral cry of regret for the pleasures of the past, lacking the complexity of Alison's words.[42] Alison, as many critics have noted, is a *vital* character.[43] That enthusiasm for living allows her to think hopefully about the future—and is a key part of what enables her to inhabit other texts across time.

Throughout her prologue, we see her in the process of re-membering.[44] The structure of the text mimics the movement of the mind, as she circles around memories and associations. Traumatic incidents and ideas keep resurfacing. We see this in the repeated references to the violence wrought upon Alison by her fifth husband. She mentions, in 506–507, that she still feels the effects of his violence on her body and will go on feeling it until her death. In 634–636, she returns to the subject, specifically referring to the occasion on which he hit her and deafened her. Thirty lines later there is another two-line reference to the incident—using the same verb 'smoot' and the same rhyme 'deef' and 'leef.' Alison returns to this in 712—'I was beten for a book, pardee!' But it is not until 788–828—the end of her prologue—that she tells the full story, the climax of the whole text. In a similar reflection of the insistence of trauma and oppression within memory, Saint Paul's aggressive text about virginity and marriage recurs over and over again in Alison's text; she cites 1 Corinthians 7 eight separate times in just over 100 lines.[45] (This is the chapter that begins: 'Now concerning the thing whereof you wrote to me: It is good for a man not to touch a woman.') Chaucer creates the impression of someone whose mind is battered by this text; it inhabits her thoughts however many times she twists it, comes to terms with it, or makes it suit her own agenda. It is something that she can't quite leave alone.

For the audience, the feeling that we are seeing a mind unfolding is one of the ways in which we create Alison as a character as we enter into the illusion of interiority. Readerly engagement is fundamental in making characters come to life, and Alison has consistently sparked such engagement from (most of) her readers. Her depth is also suggested by her emotions and by her moral sensibility. She tells us, for example, how wretched she felt within herself when her fourth husband was unfaithful, saying that within her heart she was tormented because he took delight in others (481–482). Towards the end of her prologue, after recounting in detail her fifth's husband's enjoyment of misogyny and the relentless emotional abuse that he unleashed on her, she says, starkly: 'Who wolde wene, or who wolde suppose / The wo that in myn herte was, and pyne?' (786–787). Her grief, humiliation, and misery, are unfathomable: here she tells us that others cannot grasp what is going on inside her. Again, Chaucer creates the illusion of depth, telling us that there are things going on beneath the textual surface, encouraging us to 'wene' and 'suppose'—that is, to think about, imagine—how she feels, as if she is a real person. This sense of a character is further developed by the revelation that she (in sharp distinction to her antecedents) has a moral sensibility.

Not only does she lament the existence of sin, but she also tells us that she abides by the rules—unlike her fourth husband she does not commit adultery but punishes him through flirtation: she explicitly tells us that she does nothing wrong 'of my body, in no foul manere,' but that simply by flirting, 'in his owene grece I made hym frye' (491–493). Here Alison is telling us about her past, and demonstrating her understanding of morality while also speaking in an idiosyncratic voice. The image, of making her husband fry in his own grease is brilliant: it refers to the common idea that he has made his own punishment—a rod for his own back. But the terms that she uses are sensory and homely; we imagine her cooking him over the stove. The language is also bodily in that we imagine a greasy, sweaty body—her husband's adulterous body—as something disgusting.[46] But Alison, as ever, does not dwell on horrible images of revenge. Instead, her voice turns to humour and comic optimism as, a few lines later she exclaims, 'By God, in erthe I was his purgatorie / For which I hope his soule be in glorie' (495–496). This is classic Alison: she pretends to justify punishing him by using religious terminology, but also hilariously claims that because she made his life so miserable, she may have helped him to go straight to heaven without further punishment after death.

Her funniness is one of the most striking aspects of her character and one of the most appealing things about her. In most modern editions, the Wife of Bath's Prologue and Tale come after the Man of Law's Tale. However, the evidence of the endlink to the Man of Law's Tale suggests that we 'should' have had the Parson's Tale at this point.[47] When we do get that tale, it is a long, prose tale, unrelentingly dour and serious, devoid of wit. The point is not that the Wife of Bath's Prologue is the opposite to this, rather that it does things differently—in that the demotic, funny style interacts with her understanding of the Bible, patristic authors, and the teaching of the church. Her prologue is a tale steeped in understanding not only of the writings of church authorities but also of (some of) their methods of argument: selective quotation, repetition, polemical language, rhetorical techniques. She acts here like an educated man, engaging with methods of argument usually seen as male.[48] So part of what she is doing is asserting that a different kind of person—non-clerical, female, unauthoritative—can debate the clerics and beat them at their own game. But she voices her views in a completely idiosyncratic tone. Alison's speech is noticeably colloquial, amusing, and accessible.

One of the most engaging aspects about her speech is her deadpan self-knowledge and willingness to laugh at herself. She does nothing to deny the church's belief that virginity is the best form of life; instead, she openly admits that she simply does not aspire to be the best: 'He spak to hem that wolde lyve parfitly; / And lordynges, by youre leve, that am nat I' (111–112). These are words that have to be heard: imagine her slowing down and announcing 'that—am—nat—I.' Alison does not want to be perfect; she just wants to live her life. She here pulls the rug from beneath the feet of her opponents by freely acknowledging many of their arguments and making the argument about something else—if she isn't doing anything technically wrong, why can't she be left alone? Why isn't it all right not to be perfect?

The way that she interacts with antifeminist argument is often key to her wit. *How* things are voiced makes a significant difference to how we receive them. The idea that widows are husband-hunting at funerals, for instance, was a misogynist commonplace. Matheolus asserts that 'While her husband lies on his bier and the wife is crying, she's also thinking ahead, thinking back, who to marry and how, once her three days are up.'[49] Similarly, Deschamps writes, 'as they carry the corpse to the grave, she'll be looking them over, trying to pick out who to have next.'[50] These bitter accusations are repackaged by the Wife of Bath, who blithely confides that, at her husband's funeral she was watching the young clerk, Jankyn:

> As help me God, whan that I saugh hym go
> After the beere, me thoughte he hadde a paire
> Of legges and of feet so clene and faire
> That al myn herte I yaf unto his hoold. (596–599)

Some readers see this kind of detail as demonstrating just how monstrous women are. But it is crucial for the reader's response here that we already know that the dead husband was adulterous, while Alison was faithful to him. Her (seeming) honesty about her inappropriate feelings also encourages us to be on her side; the detail she gives is funny because it is so out of place. To be at a funeral and examining the legs of a pallbearer is outrageous—and inappropriateness is at the heart of a great deal of humour.

The illusion of honesty that she cultivates through her assured performance is deeply appealing to many readers, who feel that they can see inside her head—and this becomes even more engaging when she voices things with which we can identify. For example, she states overtly that she hates the person who tells her of her vices, adding that many other people feel the same (662–663). Most people would agree; very few of us enjoy being told of our faults.[51] While this is undeniably true, it is also disarming for a character not to defend herself but simply to say how unpleasant it is to receive justified criticism. She seems to speak to us directly, to cut through what we expect.

Alison repeatedly assaults decorous expectations. She litters her speech with down-to-earth insults and exclamations. When performing for us the way in which she spoke to her husbands, her comments to them are interspersed with personal attacks: 'olde dotard shrewe!' (291), 'olde barel-ful of lyes!' (302). The insults often pair terms of respect with terms of contempt— 'Sire olde fool' (357) and 'leeve sire shrewe' (365), for instance— and they are part of her strategy of bringing down figures and works of authority. This is what she is doing, for instance, when she mentions Solomon, and then says she wishes that she were allowed 'To be refreshed half so ofte as he' (38). She suggests there is a double standard here, while also making the highly respected biblical authority seem undignified in his appetites, something reinforced by her subsequent imagining of the 'myrie fit' (42) that Solomon had on his first night of sex with each of his wives.

Her assault on authority is played out in many different ways throughout her irreverent and bold prologue. One of her strategies is to remind us of how relentless and unfair the misogyny to which she is subjected can be. Jankyn's comparison of her to Pasiphae (wife of Minos and mother of the Minotaur) is manifestly absurd (733–736). Taking one bizarre and extraordinary myth about bestiality and applying it to ordinary women—as Jerome also does—will strike most readers as a misuse of authority and a demonstration of the extremity and even desperation of misogynist arguments.[52] Alison's exhaustion is an exhaustion with which any abused group can identify—she sees that her husband will never finish reading this book and talking about how terrible women are (788). Throughout the prologue, Alison gets readers on her side partly by presenting herself as an isolated figure speaking out against a host of similar men, all of whom oppose her existence. The antifeminists are grouped together: 'Men may devyne and glosen' (26), 'men thanne speke' (34), 'Men may conseille' (66), 'men . . . in hir books sette' (129). Alison's 'I' is presented as the sole voice opposing these monolithic authorities.

While Alison's prologue is clearly the main location for the unfolding of her character, her tale is also significant. The *Canterbury Tales* are uneven in terms of precisely how each tale relates to its teller, and how much the voice of the teller comes through. In the case of the Wife of Bath's Tale, it is clear that the tale is closely connected to the teller. Chaucer takes a story that is, at its heart, about male virtue and heroism and turns it into a story about female virtue, ethics, the need for men to be educated and reformed, metamorphosis, female desire, and rape culture.[53] It is important—and for many readers, bewildering—to remember that Chaucer had himself been accused of 'raptus,' and had paid off his accuser, Cecily Champaigne, around a decade before he wrote this tale. In the past, some critics have argued that his obvious sympathy for women makes it impossible for him to have been a rapist, a line of argument that few would now find convincing. For many critics, it is crucial to acknowledge that Chaucer might have been a rapist; some assert that he certainly was. Others, however, believe that there are many ways of interpreting the scant evidence that survives: this case may have involved complex medieval wardship laws, for example. We don't know what happened—but we do know that Chaucer was closely involved in a lawsuit about violence against women.[54]

The story of the Wife of Bath's Tale has origins in two folklore motifs—the transformation of a 'loathly lady' into a young and beautiful woman, and the quest to find out what women most desire. These stories circulated in many languages and cultures, including in versions that are no longer extant.[55] The medieval versions that survive alongside Chaucer's are Gower's

'Tale of Florent' (almost exactly contemporary with the Wife of Bath's Tale), and the *Wedding of Sir Gawain and Dame Ragnall* (surviving in a late fifteenth-century version but perhaps circulating earlier or based on an earlier text).[56] In all three versions, a man is punished for something by having to find out what women desire; in each case he is given the answer by an ugly old woman whom he has to promise to marry (in the case of *Ragnall*, the sinner, King Arthur, has to hand over another man, Gawain, for marriage to the loathly lady). In the end, the lady transforms into a beautiful young bride. Beyond this, however, Alison's tale is radically different from the other versions. Perhaps most importantly, in the other two versions of the tale, the knight is a hero. In Gower's version, Florent's fault is that he has killed someone—but as he did this in a fair fight, it is not really a crime at all in the knightly world. In *Ragnall*, Gawain has done nothing wrong at all—the crime is Arthur's, and Gawain nobly agrees to take a punishment on behalf of his uncle-king. In both cases, the knight is presented as a victim: a lady, the 'slyheste' in the land, plots to trap Florent and put him 'to dethe'; Gawain sacrifices himself to save Arthur's life (350). In the end, in classic folktale and fairytale fashion, their virtue and suffering are rewarded, when they end up with a young, beautiful wife. In both cases, when the lady transforms, we find out that her real identity is youthful beauty, but she was transformed by witchcraft performed, significantly, by an older woman, her stepmother ('Florent,' 449; *Ragnall*, 692).

The transformation wrought on the core tale by Chaucer is connected to his intense interest in presenting Alison as a character with a literary subjectivity that affects and alters the story that she tells. In her version, the knight is not a figure to be admired. He is unambiguously guilty of a crime, and that crime is rape. From the beginning, we are presented not with a hero but with a villain—and this introduction turns the conventions of romance on its head. The knight does not rescue damsels and protect women—he is a threat to women, concerned only with his own ego and desires. This powerful restructuring of the story imposes a new coherence onto the plot, given that his punishment is to educate himself about female desire. While in the other versions, this aspect has no particular logic to it, in this version it is compelling: the knight has shown that he does not care at all about what women want, so now he has to spend his time thinking about it. Alison places the emphasis on female desire and female dignity, dwelling on the importance of men thinking about women as human beings whose interiority matters. It is also important to note, though, that the victim herself does not get a voice—male redemption remains at the heart of the story rather than female experience.[57]

Compared to other versions, Alison also presents the loathly lady with new emphasis. Unlike in the other versions, she is the ethical centre of the story, voicing a long speech about *gentillesse* and the fact that an old, ugly, poor woman can be a more moral and decent person than a young, handsome, rich man. Indeed, she makes it clear that birth and background have nothing to do with inner worth. Further, while the women in the other stories are young, beautiful women whose true essence had been hidden by witchcraft, this is not the case in the Wife of Bath's Tale, in which we are not told whether the beautiful and young or ugly and old identity is the 'real' one. The implication is that it is the inner self that matters, and that this woman might 'really' be old and ugly. (The film *Shrek*, which is based on the loathly lady story, takes this aspect of the tale further when Princess Fiona settles permanently in her 'ogre' appearance as her true identity.) Moreover, in the Wife of Bath's Tale, no mention is made of witchcraft. While the other two versions blame an older woman as the malicious cause of what has happened to the heroine, in the Wife of Bath's Tale the only criminal is the knight.

Part of Alison's project is to shine a light on the fact that there is usually no place in stories like this for reasonable older women—and certainly not for older women to have acceptable sexual desires, or to be the ethical heart of a story. The older woman in literature tends to be an object of contempt, ridicule, or fear. When she is sexualised, she is either a predator on young men, or a bawd, teaching young women or men how to get what they want.[58] As the other versions of this story show, older women also often appear as malign forces: the scheming grandmother who plots against Florent, or the witchy step-mothers who enchant the young virgins in both 'Florent' and *Ragnall*. In the Wife of Bath's Tale, the older woman is eloquent, reasonable, and ethical, and just as importantly, there is no evil old woman anywhere in the story. Significantly, while other versions dwell on every detail of the older woman's appearance, presenting it as utterly monstrous, Alison does no such thing. The initial description of the 'loathly lady' in 'Florent' includes seventeen lines of detailed description of her hideousness (280–296); similarly in *Ragnall* she is introduced with an eighteen-line catalogue of monstrosity (228–245). In stark contrast, Alison simply tells us that no one could imagine 'a fouler wight' (999) but gives us no further description at all. The ageing female body is not held up for ridicule and contempt; the storyteller does not encourage the reader to marvel at decay and old age.[59]

Given how different this tale is—not only from other versions but from the conventions of romance and folktale in general—it is evident that it is supposed to be read as Alison's 'take' on the subject, in keeping with her interest in repainting the lion.[60] Yet she also signals how hard it is to do that when operating within the constraints of pre-existing genres and literary structures. At the end of the tale, after all, the lady is indeed transformed into a traditional young, beautiful heroine, and she even becomes obedient to her husband, the (allegedly) reformed rapist. There are many things that are disturbing about this. One way of reading it is as a comment on the demands of genre: this is the only way that this story can end, with a 'happily ever after' marriage and the implicit promise of fertility, children, and the stable continuation of patriarchal society. The idea that Alison is framing this as a problem is suggested by the double ending of the Tale: she gives us the 'happily ever after' literary moment before immediately qualifying it by calling for a very different kind of relationship between the sexes both in her own life and in the lives of her audience:

> A thousand tyme a-rewe he gan hir kisse,
>
> > (one after another)
>
> And she obeyed hym in every thyng
> That myghte doon hym plesance or likyng.
>
> > (give him pleasure or enjoyment)
>
> And thus they lyve unto hir lyves ende
> In parfit joye; and Jesu Crist us sende
> Housbondes meeke, yonge, fressh abedde,
> And grace t'overbyde hem that we wedde;   (outlive)
> And eek I praye Jesu shorte hir lyves
> That nat wol be governed by hir wyves;
> And olde and angry nygardes of dispence,   (misers)
> God sende hem soone verray pestilence! (1254–1264).

The contrast is stark: in romance, we are presented with an obedient wife and a simple happy ever after; in life, Alison says, the ideal is that men will be meek, and men who will not be subservient to their wives should die quickly, perhaps of the plague. Here, this literary character opens up a fissure that seems to be between literature and life, between what 'they' do and what should happen to 'us'—though it is in fact between different layers of literature. Those layers are her own new kind of woman-centred, allegedly experiential narrative and the traditional genres of writing. Across the tale, she is making a plea for broadening our understanding of what kinds of women can play a part in literature, and what parts they might play. At the centre of her tale is the idea that an older woman can dispense wisdom as an ethical person, and that a woman can also have sexual desires, regardless of her appearance. This inversion of the norms of literature is so radical that one critic suggests that Chaucer here 'opens up new possibilities for literature, perhaps even for life.'[61]

As I have been suggesting, this complex relationship between literature and life is fundamental to understanding the innovations on which Chaucer is engaged. Chaucer is here using Alison as a vehicle for exploring the concept of what roles are available for women in literature, given the constraints of generic norms. The fact that she stages the *idea* of a conflict between life and literature serves to highlight the complexity of untangling the two realms: literature does not imitate life in a straightforward way, but nor does it operate in a hermetically sealed, separate world of fiction. In the *Canterbury Tales*, Chaucer was intensely interested in the grey area between what we might call realism and romance. Harry Bailly, the Host of the Tabard Inn, is not the historical Harry Bailly, but nor is he unrelated to him. Alison is not a woman that Chaucer knew, but nor is she simply a mash-up of La Vielle, the wandering woman from Proverbs, and Jerome's misogynist stereotypes. It is true that what we read affects how we live: reading over and over again about women behaving in a certain way can make readers perceive actual women through that lens.[62] But the converse is also true, in that we rely on our own experiences to make sense of the fragments of character that we glimpse in texts. When reading a text, we are given snapshots, and we use our own imaginations and our pre-existing knowledge to try to picture them more fully.[63] What the reader already knows—from life and from books—is crucial in determining how a literary character works on them. There is, then, an unspoken contract between poet and reader. Thinking about how character works, one critic comments that, 'As we are moved by poetry to imagine the human figure, we create ourselves and are created as persons.'[64]

Readers have always responded to Alison more passionately than they respond to any other Canterbury pilgrim. To comprehend how Alison was read by Chaucer's first readers, and why she made such a stunning and powerful impression, we need to understand not only the sources from which she was wrought but also the historical women and gendered structures of Chaucer's society. Each of the next four chapters takes an aspect of Alison and explores it through a variety of texts and evidence—starting with Alison's identity as a working and economically independent woman.

CHAPTER 2

Working Women

Women have always been poor . . . from the beginning of time.

—VIRGINIA WOOLF, *A ROOM OF ONE'S OWN*

While they have indeed (almost) always been poor, women have also always been economically active. Across Europe, women were prominent in many areas of production (such as agriculture, cloth-making, brewing, healing, and administration) from classical antiquity through to the Middle Ages.[1] Indeed, as discussed in the prologue to this part of the present book, many historians have argued that there was a golden age for women in the fourteenth and fifteenth centuries and a contraction of opportunities after that point.[2] Yet the bias of institutions and patriarchal history has tended to mask or obscure the economic importance of women across time. If we think about the Wife of Bath's ancestor, Saint Paul, most of us are far more likely to remember his statements about the desirability of women's subservience and silence than we are to recollect the crucial importance of working women in Saint Paul's first-century ministry and travels. The first convert to Christianity in Europe, for example, was a working woman, whose wealth helped to support Paul and his associates. Lydia was a business-woman from Thyatira, described as a 'seller of purple,' whom Paul encountered in Philippi, in Macedonia. As a seller of purple, Lydia made her money from trading in a dye made from the madder plant; she was a merchant. Acts of the Apostles describes the conversion and baptism of Lydia and her household, and her subsequent invitation to Paul, Silas, Timothy, and Luke to stay at her house. After Paul and Silas's later imprisonment, they then returned to the house of Lydia, which seems to have been their base.[3]

Educated, wealthy women were crucial to Paul's early mission. He sent the letter to the Romans to Rome with Phoebe, described as a 'diakonan' or deacon of the church, and as a 'prostatis' or helper/patron of many, implying that she too was a moneyed supporter of the church (Romans 16:1–2). The fact that she is not described as a daughter or wife or mother, but simply as herself, also suggests that, like Lydia, she is the head of a household, another economically independent woman.[4] Yet this kind of woman was not held up as a role model in the medieval church—rather, the most antifeminist quotations from Paul were repeated and excerpted, as if Christian women were always supposed to be silent, dependent, second-class citizens, when in fact one of the great attractions of early Christianity to women, slaves, and the poor had been its ideology of equality. Lydia, like Paula (Jerome's patron), is a hidden grandmother of the Wife of Bath.[5] Just as Woolf imagines Shakespeare's sister written out of history, so the history of these women—a successful independent trader and a wealthy, book-reading widow—was generally of little interest to the medieval compilers of books of wicked wives, who focused instead on the evils of women's speech, their untrustworthiness, and their sexual incontinence. Saint Paul and Saint Jerome, in their most extreme manifestations, became Alison's celebrated grandfathers while her grandmothers, both of whom facilitated these men's work and indeed bankrolled it, were buried in unmarked graves.

Alison too is a working woman. Indeed, working women found a host of new and more lucrative opportunities in the second half of the fourteenth century. In these decades a combination of factors produced a set of social norms that bolstered women's sexual and economic independence. This was not a time of equality between the sexes, but it is generally accepted that the Black Death inaugurated an era of new possibilities for women. They were involved in traditional female occupations, such as brewing, textile work, and service, and in more surprising occupations, as jewellers, artists, or founders, for example. They could join guilds and employ apprentices.[6] The nature of the evidence makes it impossible to discern precisely what proportion of women worked: for instance, married couples were assessed together for poll taxes and so the role of wives is often unclear, while we can get a clearer picture of the occupations of female heads of households (whose jobs ranged from tailors to chandlers).[7] More generally if a woman's work was seen as assisting her husband, that work might be entirely elided from any record. In Chaucer's London world, however, it is evident that women played a major part in the economy, both at the bottom end as servants and in low-status occupations and, in smaller numbers, at the top end as merchants and wealthy investors. Between these extremes were women who worked with their husbands and who, in the event of their becoming widows, were competent to take over the business. The Wife of Bath was born in the later fourteenth century partly because of the development of the so-called European marriage pattern (discussed in detail below) which came with a complex set of norms around paid work, individual choice, and modes of lifestyle and inheritance. A figure such as Alison could not have emerged in the literature of societies that had radically different expectations of women's sexual and economic roles. In this chapter, I will discuss the lives of working women and women with economic independence in the later Middle Ages, arguing that Alison only makes sense as a character in the specific environment of post-plague northern Europe.

One of the first things that we learn about her, in her description in the General Prologue, is that she is a clothmaker: 'Of clooth-makyng she hadde swich an haunt / She passed hem of Ypres and of Gaunt' (447–448). In other words, she is so skilled at clothmaking that she surpassed the famed clothmakers of the Low Countries. While occupations such as weaving and spinning are traditionally associated with women throughout history, this reference has a specific and commercial tone. England's only major economic product at this time was wool: English sheep were the foundation of the country's wealth and power.[8] Throughout the later Middle Ages, the politics and economics of the wool trade were fraught and complicated, as English merchants sought a monopoly and the monarchy tried to profit by giving special privileges to different groups, especially Italian merchants.[9] For many years Chaucer worked as the Controller of Customs at the Wool Quay in London; his life was closely intertwined with the complexities of the wool trade.

Wool was used to make cloth, and the clothmakers of the Low Countries were renowned for their skills. Flemish weavers were encouraged to come to England, and these immigrant workers then became the targets of xenophobic violence in the Great Revolt of 1381. Clothmakers within England had an advantage over those on the Continent, in that they could buy the wool at a cheaper price, and making and selling cloth could be very profitable.[10] In the later fourteenth century all of the most successful female merchants in Exeter, for example, were cloth merchants; a historian notes that these wealthy women were also all widows—though women were also often employed in the less lucrative parts of the manufacturing process.[11] There was a great deal of cloth manufacture in the Avon valley, near Bath, an area conveniently close to the wool areas of the Cotswolds and the Mendip hills. Alison is presented as someone who is making money in a crucial part of the economy of the later fourteenth century, supervising the manufacture and sale of cloth—she is a person of stature.[12]

Her economic independence has also come through inheritance from her husbands—in other words, she has benefitted from the relatively progressive inheritance laws and customs of the time. (This sharply differentiates her from prostitute/procuress antecedents such as Dipsas and La Vielle.) Grouping her first three husbands together, Alison tells us, 'They had me yeven [given] hir lond and hir tresoor' (204), and repeats a few lines later, 'they hadde me yeven al hir lond' (212). The implication is that all of these men have been able to will their land and wealth freely to Alison, so with each widowhood she became personally richer, and an ever-greater prize on the marriage market.[13] When she falls crazily in love with her fifth husband, she makes the disastrous decision to give up her economic independence: 'And to hym yaf [gave] I al the lond and fee / That evere was me yeven therbifoore. / But afterward repented me ful soore' (630–632). The story of the first part of their marriage is the story of her struggle to reverse this decision. Jankyn's aggressive misogyny and obsession with his 'book of wikked wyves' leads to Alison's attempted destruction of the book and their physical fight, complete with her accusation that he has murdered her to gain unfettered possession of her land. They reconcile when he gives her back her economic control: 'He yaf me al the bridel in myn hond / To han the governance of hous and lond, / And of his tonge, and of his hond also; / And made hym brenne [burn] his book anon right tho' (813–816). Having control over her husband's tongue and hand—symbolising speech and behaviour—is presented as the consequence of, or as secondary to, having governance over the house and land. Having power (governance) over the marital property seems inevitably to confer power over the marital partner: economic power is the foundation of other kinds of power in marriage, Alison suggests. The Wife of Bath's argument is not identical to Woolf's famous belief that a woman needs a room of one's own and five hundred pounds a year.[14] But the fundamental premise *is* the same: women can have no likelihood of autonomy if they are economically dependent on men.

The Wife of Bath's Prologue also more generally reflects a world in which women worked. There are several references throughout the prologue to the kind of household in which Alison and her succession of husbands live. She mentions 'our mayde' (241), her 'norice' [nurse] (299), and 'my chamberere withinne my bour' [my chambermaid within my bedroom] (300). This is a world of female wage labour, a household in which several women are employed for varying tasks. In later-medieval England, girls often left home to work elsewhere for a few years to earn money before (in many cases) marrying and setting up a new household.[15] This social model was radically different from a social model in which girls married early and entered their husband's family home, a standard practice in many medieval (and later) cultures but largely confined to the very highest echelons of northern European societies.[16] In some contemporary societies, wealthier households relied on slave labour to do the service work of the household and look after the house and the older generation. Tuscan society, for instance, depended heavily on slave labour after the plague, and a decree on 2 March 1363 permitted the unlimited importation of foreign slaves to Florence.[17] One list of the slaves sold during the latter decades of the century includes 357 names: the vast majority (329) were women or girls, almost all of whom were between the ages of twelve and thirty.[18] The casual references to servants in the Wife of Bath's Prologue in fact remind us of the economic opportunities for girls and women at this time in England. The high proportion of wage labourers in northern European society at this time is striking. While around 50 percent of the population of England across the fourteenth and fifteenth centuries were wage labourers, the equivalent statistic for China during the Ming dynasty (1368–1644) is 1–2 percent.[19]

Going into service was one key way of entering the labour market for English girls, and both opportunities and wages increased after the Black Death. In 1377, 38.2 percent of households in York had servants, and 31.9 percent of the adult population was in service.[20] Across the post-plague decades, there was a noticeable influx of labour into the cities, especially female labour as women came to urban centres as apprentices or servants.[21] The idea of service as a life-cycle phase allowed young people—both men and women—to earn money before they set up their own household, with a partner of their choice. It also helped to create an environment in which lifelong single women proliferated, in sharp contrast to other contemporary societies—for instance, in southern Europe, or in European Jewish communities.[22]

The late-fourteenth-century poem 'How the Good Wife Taught Her Daughter' can be seen in this context.[23] This is an advice poem from a woman to her daughter, and it is predicated on the idea that the parent and adolescent child are separated:

that the daughter is making her way in the world, away from her parental household, a situation unthinkable in many societies. The poem is not wholly chronological, but to a certain extent the early part of the poem depicts a situation in which the girl is single and may be receiving offers of marriage. Later in the poem, the girl is married, and then a mother herself; eventually she is imagined passing on the advice to her own adolescent daughter. In the first part of the poem, the mother envisions a situation in which the girl is approached by a suitor, and she urges her to show him to her friends, and not to go anywhere with him where they might fall into sin. It seems clear that the mother is here warning her daughter about situations in which she might find herself, now that she is no longer under the parental roof. Felicity Riddy has suggested that there might have been readers of this poem who resisted, who did exactly what it warned against. These girls led 'risky, unconventional, and adventurous lives' and, having left their villages and moved to town, now went to taverns, worked for a living, chatted to men, laughed in church, and did all the things that the good wife warns against.[24] The maids of the Wife of Bath's Prologue remind us that Chaucer lived in a world in which women did not tend to move seamlessly from daughter to wife, from parental to marital home—a large proportion of women worked for at least a part of their life cycle, and this work often involved living in their workplace, out of the overt control of their parents. Being a servant might not seem desirable to many of us today, but the opportunity to earn money gave women choices that their counterparts in southern Europe, for instance, tended not to have to the same extent, and shifted the generational and gendered balance of power somewhat. Both job opportunities and wages increased noticeably in Chaucer's lifetime, due to the seismic economic effects of the Black Death.

Historians and economists have coined the term 'European Marriage Pattern' to describe a largely northern European trend in which women had choices about whom to marry, tended to marry relatively late, had few children, and set up new households upon marriage (rather than living in extended families with in-laws).[25] This pattern went alongside significant participation in the labour force by women and high levels of numeracy and literacy.[26] Arguably, these marital and economic trends led to the rise of Europe—in other words, women's roles and their participation in the labour force were catalysts for the striking development of northern Europe in the centuries following the Black Death. The authors of a book about this marriage pattern argue that 'This story of female empowerment, therefore, is crucial for understanding the specific developmental path of the Western European economy, which resulted in the Industrial Revolution of the late eighteenth century,' suggesting that the high level of female agency that the European Marriage Pattern facilitated enhanced economic growth.[27] While this marriage pattern had previously been the marriage pattern of the poor—who tended to have more choice over their marriage because little money or land was at stake—after the plague, the pattern expanded quickly, responding to dramatic new opportunities in the labour market, opportunities that came with high wages. It thus became the norm in northern European societies.

A number of conditions enabled this development of both marriage trends and working patterns. In earlier centuries, as the church became more involved in marriage practices, opinion varied as to the foundations of marriage: the church increasingly emphasised the importance of both parties consenting to the marriage as the fundamental part of matrimony, with consummation as a secondary aspect.[28] This weakened the power of girls' fathers in particular, and of patriarchy more generally. This focus on consent was less commensurate with traditions in southern Europe than with those farther north, and was less accepted in the south as a result. The rights of girls and women to give or withhold consent was a crucial step in allowing them to have autonomy over a range of life choices, and in removing them somewhat from parental authority. As a child is not able to make those choices, this emphasis on consent also encouraged later marriage. The northern European habit of neolocality—forming a new household at the point of marriage—also tended to delay marriage, as men and women needed to earn money to provide for that household. Women were incentivized to work both before and after their marriage, as they had rights to money and property under inheritance law. In southern Europe, parents married off their daughters young, and those women were less likely to work both because they had more children and because they tended to have rights only to their own dowries after their husband's death—they could not benefit from their own work.

In Northern Europe, where general patterns of female wage earning, later marriage, and fairer inheritance laws already existed, the Black Death acted as a catalyst for the expansion of the European Marriage Pattern, so that it became standard for all groups except for the very rich. Recently, economic historians have argued that in the later Middle Ages, the EMP developed particularly strongly in England and the Low Countries.[29] The years immediately following the catastrophe of the plague saw a dramatic drop in population, a surging economy, and rising wages.[30] Men and women—but particularly women, according to some data sets—migrated from the countryside to towns, and commanded better incomes than they had been able to in earlier years.[31] Women had a new economic power. Fascinatingly, in some jobs there seems to have been no gender pay gap at this time in England and other northern European countries, and women also worked in a wide range of jobs.[32] The conditions that I have been describing had a host of knock-on effects: couples had fewer children and focused more on educating and training those children, allowing a move away from Malthusian society to a more skilled and economically productive society.[33] This was not a feminist utopia, and historians disagree about how long these conditions lasted, but there is widespread agreement that in the second half of the fourteenth century many English women had more choices and more autonomy than they had at other points in history or in other places.[34] This changing economic world with its specific valuation of women's labour and protection of their inheritance rights and their marriage choices is a crucial context for the invention of the Wife of Bath.

Chaucer's world was full of working women, from his own wife, who earned a regular salary from her roles in great households, mostly as a lady in waiting to Constance of Castile, wife of John of Gaunt, to the *femmes sole* who traded under their own authority in London. Women undertook a wide variety of jobs, but were most commonly employed in trades relating to victualling, including brewing, and in trades related to textile work or clothes production.[35] Sometimes we find women in surprising occupations, such as Isabella de Morland, one of four master parchment makers in the late fourteenth century, or Agnes Bookbynder, working in Norwich in 1374–1375.[36] Medieval women drove oxen, worked as blacksmiths, and owned ships.[37]

One of the most famous of medieval women, Margery Kempe, was an ostentatiously working woman. Kempe was born around 1373 and married around twenty years later. We know a great deal about her because of *The Book of Margery Kempe*, which she dictated to scribes much later in life, in the 1430s. Early in the book, she describes her attempts to set up businesses, probably in the late fourteenth or early fifteenth century. She tells us that she started her first business out of pride and covetousness, because she 'ever desired mor and mor.'[38] Kempe set herself up as a brewer and became one of the greatest brewers in Lynn for a few years, until she began to make huge losses, because she lacked experience ('ure'). The yeast kept collapsing on her ale, and so she abandoned brewing and apologised to her husband for not having listened to his advice. However, Kempe adds that, 'yet sche left not the world al hol, for now sche bethowt hir of a newe huswyfré,' and set up a horse mill. The language that she uses here to describe setting up a business is significant: she describes working as refusing to leave the world, and she also calls her jobs 'huswyfre,' as if these jobs are particularly women's work. Brewing in particular was usually the province of women at this time, although milling did not have gendered associations in the same way. The second business venture also fails, as horses and servants alike refuse to work for Margery, who interprets the problems that beset her as God's punishment for 'hir pride, hir coveytyse, and desyr that sche had of the worshepys of the world'. Women's engagement in the world—'huswyfre' that keeps them from leaving 'the world al hol'—is rewritten as a sinful submission to greed and vanity, as Kempe prepares to enter into her identity as devoted bride of Christ.

Women without Kempe's religious vocation felt no such anxiety about paid work, and widows in particular often continued to run their husband's business and to train the household apprentices. Matilda Penne, for instance, continued her husband's work as a London skinner after his death, preparing and selling furs throughout the 1380s, until her death in 1392–1393. This was specialist work, involving inspecting and purchasing skins, often from Hanseatic merchants, supervising their preparation, selecting and matching them, and making linings. Matilda's competence is suggested by the fact that another skinner passed on an apprentice to be trained by her, by the fact that she successfully ran the business for twelve years, and by her wealth at her death. Matilda worked closely both with men (especially her nephew, Peter Herlawe, the main beneficiary of her will) and with women. She asked to be buried not next to her husband, but 'in front of the Cross where I am accustomed to stand,' in an interesting depiction of herself as independent. Her will mentions twenty men and twenty-three women, with substantial bequests going not only to relatives but also to fellow widows and neighbours, including Margery Twyford and Joanna Carleton, presumably friends who formed a crucial community for Matilda.[39]

Further up the social scale, women worked in complicated and skilled roles, administering massive estates, dealing with staff, agriculture, household management, complex accounts, provisioning, and even armed disputes. Women of this class were expected to be able to administer lands, especially when their husbands were away (for instance in the city, or at war) or if they were widowed. Throughout their lives, high-class women needed a wide range of skills. Christine de Pizan writes about this in detail in a northern French context, in *The Treasure of the City of Ladies* (1405). In a chapter addressed to ladies who live in manor houses or castles, she describes some of the abilities that they should cultivate. These women will be 'in charge' of all the 'bailiffs, provosts, administrators and governors' and they must be able to offer 'protection' to their men. As a result, such a woman 'should be well informed about and apprised of the legal aspects and local customs'; she must be 'kind, humble, and charitable' to good neighbours and employees; and she should 'work with her husband's counsellors.' Indeed, while she needs to be the person in charge, Christine also emphasises that the lady must make it clear that she listens to the 'wise old men,' so that 'no one may say that she wants to do everything her own way.'[40]

If it comes to it, a noblewoman should be able to command an army. Christine writes that she 'ought to have the heart of a man, that is, she ought to know how to use weapons and be familiar with everything that pertains to them,' and goes into detail about the necessity of being able to launch an attack, to defend one's lands, and to make sure the garrisons are sufficient. Such women need to speak 'authoritatively,' with 'eloquent words,' and 'to understand all the workings of the administration.' Christine goes on to discuss the fact that women need to understand money: they must use all their skills of persuasion to encourage their husbands 'to discuss their finances together' and to live within their income. Women need a detailed understanding of finance and the law: 'It is proper for such a lady or young woman to be thoroughly knowledgeable about the laws relating to fiefs, sub-fiefs, quit rents, *champarts*, taxes for various causes, and all those sorts of things.' Further, they should familiarise themselves with agriculture, down to 'which way is the best for the furrows to go according to the lay of the land.' It is clear that Christine is advocating extremely hands-on governance; rich, privileged women are expected to be fully involved in the details of running an estate, as well as understanding (and directing) the big picture.[41]

Her advice is not fanciful and is equally applicable to the English context. Some of the great ladies of the later Middle Ages were exceptionally competent administrators, formidable

politicians, skilful legal adversaries, and ruthless military strate-
gists. In other words, they were expected to do everything that
men could do.[42] Alice Chaucer, duchess of Suffolk and granddaughter of the poet, took on all of these roles with aplomb.
Having benefitted from all three of her marriages, when she was
widowed for the third and final time in 1450, Alice was an extremely rich woman. Her third husband, William de la Pole,
duke of Suffolk, left her a jointure in most of the vast de la Pole
lands. In his will, he wrote that 'above al the erthe my singular
trust is moost in her,' and, in a letter to his son, urged him to
'obey alwey hyr commaundementes, and to beleve hyr coun-
celles and advyses in alle youre werkes.'[43] His implicit trust in
his wife was amply rewarded. Over the next twenty-five years,
Alice looked after these estates with a single-minded focus, and
indeed she expanded her landholdings further, deploying aggressive tactics in East Anglia. She lent money to the Crown,
and ended up with lands in twenty-two counties. William's trust
in his wife, and his encouragement of his son to see his mother
as a competent governor and as his best adviser, was not unique.
Similarly, John Paston III addressed his mother, Margaret, saying, 'Modyr . . . ther is neyther wyff nor other frend shall make
me to do that that your comandment shall make me to do, if
I may have knowlage of it,' adding that 'I nevyr contraryed
thyng that ye wold have doon.'[44]

Alice Chaucer was widely seen as someone of political influence and importance. Of course women could not sit in Parliament at this time, but that did not mean that they lacked political power. Alice was married to William de la Pole for almost
twenty years, during which time she partnered him in many
political activities. For instance, she joined him in escorting
Margaret of Anjou from France to England to marry Henry VI
and be crowned queen—William himself having acted as proxy

in the wedding ceremony in France.[45] In the second half of the
1440s, William became the king's chief advisor and was soon
the focus of widespread discontent.[46] Accused of treason in late
1449, William was exonerated by the king but banished for five
years. As he set sail from England, his ship was intercepted and
he was summarily executed at sea on 2 May 1450, after a mock
trial. Alice was now on her own, with a young son, and was
herself a political target. It is clear that rebels and parliamentar-
ians alike viewed her as a political force. That summer, a major
rebellion rose, led by Jack Cade. When the rebels entered London they set up a commission of 'oyer et terminer' (a standard
legal instrument in the Middle Ages, but usually in the hands
of the government) at which they indicted a number of traitors.
The list specifically included Alice: along with several others,
the 'ducissa Suffolchiae' is accused 'de proditione in Gwyhalda
Londoniae' (of treason at the Guildhall of London).[47] It was
not only the rebels who viewed her with suspicion. In November that year, the Commons introduced a bill to Parliament,
demanding the dismissal of twenty-nine people from the king's
entourage. Only one person on this list was a woman—Alice
(named second on the list, after the duke of Somerset). The
Commons asked that these individuals be banished for life
from Henry's presence and be banned from coming within
twelve miles of the king. Ultimately, Henry nominally agreed,
but excepted lords and 'certain persons [. . .] who have been
accustomed to wait continually upon his person'; it seems clear
that Alice was not banished and continued to be an influential
presence at court.[48] However, she also had to contend with a
trial for treason. There are puzzlingly few sources for this trial,
but William of Worcester's chronicle, *Annales Rerum Anglicarum*, tells us that 'In eodem parliamento ducissa Suffolciae
acquietata est per pares suos' (In the same parliament, the

duchess of Suffolk was acquitted by her peers [i.e., by the Lords]).[49] While all this was going on, she was also battling attacks on her estates as the retainers of the duke of Norfolk, emboldened by the fall and murder of Suffolk, sought to capitalise on their advantage and take control of more of East Anglia.

Alice, however, was not a woman to allow the murder of her husband and her own trial for treason to keep her down. When her son's marriage to Lady Margaret Beaufort was set aside by the king in 1453, so that he could marry this important heiress to his own Tudor relative, Alice negotiated with Richard, duke of York, and acquired Elizabeth of York (sister of the future kings Edward IV and Richard III) for her son's bride in 1458. Although she and her family lost the role of Constable of Wallingford in 1450, she had personally regained the role before 1455, when she was asked to keep the duke of Exeter in custody there.[50] She continued to work to maintain and expand her possessions and her influence. Indeed, it is in the 1450s and 1460s that we really see her mettle and her political acumen. As a widow, whose husband had been disgraced and murdered, and whose son was still a young child, she was clearly vulnerable. In East Anglia, the de la Poles were embroiled in various land disputes with the duke of Norfolk and with others, including Sir John Fastolf. Alice regrouped and, as Helen Castor has commented, demonstrated that with her 'shrewd political brain' and 'formidable talents,' she was 'more than a match for the duke of Norfolk' and her other adversaries.[51] For instance, her husband had claimed the manor of Dedham in 1447, but it had returned to Fastolf. In 1461, she seized it again by force. A few years later, she negotiated secretly with two different groups, doublecrossing the archbishop of Canterbury in order to claim the manor of Hellesdon. The Paston letters are full of references to Alice, sometimes termed 'the old lady,' and her threats.[52]

Her political talents are particularly demonstrated by her negotiation of the complex allegiances of the Wars of the Roses, at their height in the years of her widowhood. Indeed, she frequently managed to be in favour with both sides and maintained her elevated position throughout these turbulent years.[53] Related to both Lancastrians and Yorkists through her Beaufort connections, she was able to place her son at the heart of the Yorkist regime, although her husband had been the principal advisor of the Lancastrian Henry VI.[54] Indeed, having escorted Margaret of Anjou to England as queen, Alice took on the role of Margaret's gaoler in 1472, now that she was a trusted ally of Margaret's enemies. Into her old age, Alice was still an impressive political operator, doing everything that a male landowner would do, including marshalling military force to take over properties and maintaining diverse alliances in changing political waters. The only difference was that she, in fact, did it better than most of her male contemporaries. Great ladies were expected to work.

Further down the social scale, working women were employing somewhat different tactics to help them to survive, relying on solidarity and on mutually supportive organisations that were sometimes set up on the basis of gender. In 1368, a group of women in London who worked in silk came together as an informal guild to protest against the behaviour of an Italian merchant who had bought up all the silk in the city to sell at punitive prices (as mentioned in the introduction to this book). As a group, these women submitted a bill to the mayor, Simon de Morden, and a petition to the king, Edward III. These complaints focused on the behaviour of Nicholas Sarduche, for price-fixing and driving up the price of silk from fourteen shillings to eighteen shillings per pound. The most interesting aspect of the case is that the women were acting together and demanding the protection of the law and the government of city and realm. They described themselves collectively and emphasised that Sarduche's behaviour threatened the 'common profit' of the country.[55] Hundreds of years later, Woolf imagined women who worked together—Chloe and Olivia, who liked each other, and shared a laboratory—suggesting that women's friendships or working partnerships are largely absent from literature.[56] The medieval historical record, however, gives us glimpses into exactly this kind of relationship: women working together and relying on each other for mutual support. Many silkwomen employed apprentices; Alice Claver even left her successful business to her favourite apprentice, Katherine Champion.[57] While the Wife of Bath does not tell us about working relationships with other women, her friendships— with maids, her niece, and her two 'gossips' or best friends—fill her prologue. Most threatening to patriarchal society, her relationship with her friend replaces a hierarchical relationship with a male priest, as her friend, another Alison, knows her 'Bet than oure parisshe preest' (532). Alison plays on fears of female conspiracy when she recounts her mother's advice (582, 589–590), and her friend's complicity in her flirtation with Jankyn (who lodges at her friend's house, 534–555). Relationships between women underpin the lifestyle that Alison describes.

The kind of mutual support depicted in the silkwomen's petition is not unique. At various points in documentary records we see glimpses of women employing each other and working together. There are even some fascinating references to women employing other women for roles connected to writing and affiliated trades, precisely the area in which women were most likely to be silenced by the overwhelmingly male machinery of book production. Matilda Penne, for instance, left a small piece of silver and mazer in her will to someone called Petronilla Scriveyner—Petronilla the scribe.[58] We know nothing else about this woman, but the rarity of female scribes makes it particularly interesting that Matilda seems to have employed one, perhaps for her accounts and bookkeeping. In another striking example, Christine de Pizan writes in her *Book of the City of Ladies* (pt. 1, chap. 41, 76–77) about Anastasia as the best miniaturist and manuscript decorator in Paris.

These references are especially notable given that we struggle to hear women's voices precisely because they were not in charge of the machinery of writing and document production. Margery Kempe's *Book*—sometimes called the first autobiography in English—was written down by male scribes, and critics cannot easily unpick the different voices in the text. Matilda Penne's will, or the petition of the silkwomen, would have been written down by male scribes and according to forms derived by men.

Only occasionally do we hear directly from women. When Christine de Pizan tells us about her experience of becoming a working woman—indeed, becoming a paid writer—she refers to it as involving a sex change. In the *Mutacion de Fortune* (1403), she gives an account of her life, describing her education, marriage, and widowhood. After the death of her husband, when she had to fend for herself and make money as a writer, she writes about:

> […] qui je suis, qui parle,
> qui de femelle devins masle
> par Fortune, qu'ainsy le voult; si me mua et corps
>   et voult
> en homme naturel parfaict;
> et jadis fus femme, de fait homme suis, je ne ment pas
>   (139–147)

(Who I am, who speaks, who from female became male by Fortune, who willed it so; she changed me both body and face into a perfect natural man; while I was formerly a woman, I am in reality a man. I do not lie.)[59]

She describes this sex change literally: she became stronger, her voice deepened, her body became harder and more agile. This change is depicted not as transvestism but as a physical sex change. In other writings too, she tells us that widows need 'the heart of a man' to survive (*Treasure of the City of Ladies*, pt. 2, chap. 9, 110).

For all the ubiquity of the working, affluent, relatively independent woman in the later fourteenth century, she was still seen as masculine, as gender-fluid. Women were a crucial force in the economy in the years following the Black Death, but the very power that economic independence gave them—the power to choose whether and whom to marry, the power to escape parental control, the power to spend their own money—was profoundly threatening to the idea of female inferiority and subservience promoted by men such as the clerical authors of books of wicked wives. For Alison of Bath, economic independence is absolutely fundamental to her identity and to the authority that she wields: the property that she inherits, gives away, and finally reclaims is at the heart of her story. The world that she lives in—a world of female inheritance possibilities, comfortably well-off widows, and mobile working women—is very much a post-plague, northern European world. Alison needs to be read in that historical and geographical context.

CHAPTER 3

The Marriage Market

[L]et other pens treat of sex and sexuality;
we quit such odious subjects as soon as we can.

—VIRGINIA WOOLF, *ORLANDO*

If readers only remember one thing about the Wife of Bath, it is usually that she had five husbands. Indeed, her story begins when she is twelve (Wife of Bath's Prologue, 12), and Chaucer births her at this age because this is the age when a girl could enter the sexual economy. Canon law permitted girls to marry at twelve, boys at fourteen.[1] At twelve, Alison embraces the identity of wife, no longer under parental authority. Across time, the point at which girls become sexually available is generally the point at which they become interesting to writers. While the 'wife' in Alison's informal title could simply mean woman, for her it certainly also invokes the specific identity of married woman, a player in the marriage market. Any guide to the sources of the Wife of Bath will tell you that La Vielle from the *Roman de la Rose* is the principal model for the Wife of Bath as a character. This sexually experienced older woman instructs

a young man in the arts of love and lays bare the wiles of women
in this deeply misogynistic and problematic poem. But the key
difference between Alison and La Vielle is that while Alison is
a serial wife, La Vielle is an old prostitute turned bawd-duenna
figure. Alison's respectable status, as someone who does nothing illegal, nothing even outside church or civic norms, makes
her a very different figure from Jean de Meun's old woman. This
fundamental difference has tended to be underplayed in critical
history, but it is a crucial aspect of what Chaucer was doing in
his creation of Alison.

Widows made the world go round in fourteenth- and
fifteenth-century England, through their circulation of wealth.
These women were important, widely respected, and protected
by law. Chaucer and his readers knew many much-married
women, and such women suffered no diminution of respect.
But the historical reality of wealthy widows, both mercantile
and noble, contrasts dramatically with textual traditions about
much-married widows. And these traditions are fundamental
to the formation of the Wife of Bath. In the first sentence of her
prologue, she tells us that she has had five husbands, beginning
her marital career when she was twelve years old (Wife of Bath's
Prologue, 4). That summary of her marital life would not have
seemed absurd to Chaucer or his audience. But she then goes
on immediately to remind her audience that the church fathers
had, historically, attacked remarriage specifically. The story of
her life begins not with a discussion of childhood, or virginity,
or her first marriage. Instead of launching into chronology, she
begins with a theme, engaging with her long-term identity as
much-married widow, an identity which she might have entered into before she was even a teenager, as Alice Chaucer was
to do a few years later. For the first time in English literature, a
historically recognisable woman from the middling ranks of

society (albeit a very textual one) is given voice; we are shown her perspective on the church fathers' misogyny, and specifically their antagonism to remarriage. They say, she tells us, that she shouldn't exist. But she will not be silenced. She foregrounds the nature of her response to her encounter with men such as Jerome as the clash of experience and authority (Wife of Bath's Prologue, 1)—real life and books. Alison refuses to be the kind of woman praised by Jerome, whom Dorigen then echoes in the Franklin's Tale (1436–1456): these are women who do not want to live after their husband's death, or who would rather die than remarry.[2] Jerome and Dorigen's list of such women includes Alceste, Penelope, Laodamia, Portia, Artemesia, Rhodogune, and Valeria. While a powerful textual tradition eulogised these wives as ideal in their extreme fidelity and chastity—one was famous for killing a maid who suggested that she remarry—the reality of Chaucer's world was very different in the expectations it had for widows and in the lifestyles that it valued.

A quick look at the vocabulary used to describe widows demonstrates just how different the position of a woman such as Alison was in comparison to her predecessors in some earlier cultures. The Middle English 'widow' refers to a woman whose husband has died (or, sometimes, a man whose wife has died). The Hebrew *almanah* means literally 'silent one,' while the Greek *chera* means 'woman without'—with its implications of being without not only a man, but money and status too. Both words reflect the fact that these women were economically and legally vulnerable.[3] The Latin *vidua* means 'deprived of' and referred to a woman without a man, whether divorced, widowed, or never married. All were grouped together in a position of lack.[4] This is in sharp distinction to the late-medieval widow, who had specific rights and protections in English law.

When a girl such as Alison entered the marital state, at the age of twelve, it was fairly likely that she was embarking on a career of serial wife- and widowhood. The inheritance laws of late-medieval England made widows attractive marital prospects and made remarriage appealing for the widows themselves. By the second half of the fourteenth century, under the common law, widows kept a third of their husband's property for life (or a half if there were no children). Mercantile women tended to do even better. In London, for instance, a widow was entitled to live in the marital home for life, or at least until remarriage—whereas under the common law, she only had the right to stay there for forty days. A London widow could also keep a third of her husband's moveable goods for her lifetime.[5] A further third of the property was divided amongst all children equally (there was no primogeniture). Widows usually gained the wardship of their underage children (and sometimes of their husband's underage children by previous marriages) and could profit from their inheritance until the children came of age.[6] Mercantile widows, then, received a generous inheritance, and they kept it if they married again. The existence of dower (the property that a widow inherited from her husband if he predeceased her) as well as dowry (the property that a woman took to her marriage) allowed widows to be independent, all the more so as they also had the right to stay in the family home. Contrast this, for instance, with the situation in much of southern Europe, where dowry, but not dower, was common. Furthermore, in Florence, a widow's dowry would either be returned to her birth family or kept by her husband's family—she did not receive it in her own right. Her husband's family offered strong inducements to the widow to stay with them: if she did return to her natal home with her dowry, she was not allowed to take her children with her. The children remained with her husband's family and were therefore deprived of their mother's dowry as well as her care. As a result remarriage of widows was much less common.[7]

Chaucer and his associates, friends, and relatives were very familiar with the legal and social status of widows in the mercantile city. Marrying five times was not an outrageous idea. An example of a very respectable, middle-class woman's marital career in Chaucer's city reveals the social and sexual norms of the day. Margaret Stodeye was the daughter of John Stodeye, one of the most important members of the London elite in the mid-fourteenth century.[8] Alderman of Vintry Ward (where Chaucer and his family lived), Lord Mayor, and member of Parliament, this wealthy vintner, who bought property from Chaucer's parents, was certainly well known to the poet.[9] John increased his wealth and status further through his own marriage to Joan Gisors, co-heiress of John Gisors (III), another London vintner. John and Joan Stodeye had four daughters, exceptionally eligible girls in the merchant class of London. By late 1370, Margaret had married John Berlingham, a mercer and rising London politician and administrator. The marriage was very helpful socially and financially for Berlingham, whom we now see associating with his eminent father-in-law and increasingly dominant brother-in-law, the future mayor Nicholas Brembre, whose rise was facilitated by his marriage to Margaret's sister Idonia. However, Margaret was widowed after about five years. Berlingham died in 1375, leaving Margaret with two children, Thomas and Idonia, and pregnant with a third. That same year, or possibly early the following year, Margaret married for a second time, to John Philipot—who was himself now on his third wife. As Margaret had married for the first time in 1370, she was probably by now in her early or mid-twenties. No one expected her to remain single, or thought it unseemly for

a pregnant widow to be the subject of marriage negotiations.[10]
Quick remarriage was very common—Chaucer's own mother
had been widowed sometime after January 1366 and was married again before June.[11] At this point, Margaret was in fact an
even more appealing marriage prospect than she had been first
time round: now she had her inheritance from her first husband and was about to receive her massive inheritance from
her father, who died in 1376.[12] Her brother-in-law Brembre had
also been furthering his wealth and influence, and marriage
with Margaret cemented Philipot and Brembre's close ties.[13]
Margaret was married to John for over eight years. During this
time, Philipot was mayor of London and a member of Parliament; he also was one of the three merchants who were
knighted for their role in riding with Richard II to negotiate
with the rebels in 1381.

When Philipot died, in 1384, leaving Margaret a widow once
again, he left her an enormously rich woman, giving her all his
lands and tenements within the City of London for her life.
After her death, some of these were to pass to his children, but
others were to be given to the city, their profits to be used especially for public health (conduits and latrines).[14] It is interesting
that he wanted to delay his charity in order for Margaret to
maintain herself in luxury. Margaret's third husband was John
Fitznichol, another widower, to whom she remained married
until early 1391. That same year, she married her fourth husband,
Adam Bamme—by December that year he was petitioning the
king on behalf of his new wife's stepson from her previous marriage.[15] This marriage lasted the same kind of length as all of
Margaret's marriages—six years this time. Again, Margaret had
the experience of being wife to the mayor of London, one of the
most important men in the city. Margaret and Adam had a
child, so she was not beyond her forties at this point. When he

died in 1397, however, Margaret decided she had had enough of her career as wife, a career that had seen her amass more and more land, wealth, and prestige. Presumably now approaching the menopause, she took a formal vow of chastity before Bishop Braybrook of London, making it absolutely clear that she was no longer in the business of marriage.[16] Having held the position of wife, with short breaks in between husbands, for nearly thirty years, she now began a thirty-four-year widowhood. She continued to amass wealth, especially as she, along with her sister Joan, inherited the rest of the Stodeye fortune when their other two sisters (widows of Brembre and another wealthy Londoner, Henry Vanner) died without children. The remarkable inheritance laws of London were in many ways more favourable to widows than they were to sons, for instance.

Urban widows were not the only attractive prospects in the marriage market, although they were particularly well protected in law. Two of Chaucer's own relatives negotiated the complexities of multiple marriages in aristocratic circles, in the decades after his own death. His granddaughter, Alice, is well known as one of the most powerful women of the fifteenth century, as discussed in the previous chapter. Her exact contemporary was Katherine Neville, the daughter of Chaucer's niece, Joan Beaufort (herself the daughter of Chaucer's sister-in-law Katherine Swynford and John of Gaunt).

Like Alison of Bath, Katherine was married at around the age of twelve, and gave birth a year later.[17] Although this was legal, it was rare for girls to marry and give birth at such a young age. Katherine's father, Ralph Neville, had paid a vast sum (3,000 marks) to secure the wardship of John Mowbray, son of the disgraced duke of Norfolk, in order to marry him to Ralph's own daughter. Ralph also secured the wardship of Richard of York, whom he married off to another of his daughters, Cecily—so it was not only girls who were vulnerable in the marriage market.[18]

Katherine joined the household of Henry V's queen, Catherine de Valois, and in 1425, when the dukedom was restored to her husband, she became the duchess of Norfolk. Her husband left her all of his Axholme lands in a will made in 1429; in a subsequent will made on the day of his death in 1432, he left her extensive valuables and a life interest in lands in Axholme, Yorkshire, Sussex, and the Gower peninsula and made her his chief executor. Her next marriage is a little mysterious: she seems to have been single in autumn 1440, and in 1442 was fined for not having acquired the necessary royal consent for her marriage to Sir Thomas Strangways. However, by August 1443, she had had two children with Sir Thomas, he had died, and she was married to a third husband—John Beaumont. Either her second marriage had been kept secret for some time or at least one of their children was illegitimate. Her third husband was killed in battle in 1460, and now, given that Katherine was sixty years old, we might expect her to have entered into the comfortable role of dowager widow, as Margaret Stodeye had done at a considerably younger age. But widows followed different paths, and the truly scandalous part of Katherine's life was yet to come. In 1465, she married for a fourth time at the age of 65. Her groom was Sir John Woodville—the teenage brother of the queen. The queen, Elizabeth Woodville (herself a widow when she married Edward IV) was an ineligible match, in birth, political allegiances, and wealth, and her relatives needed quick promotions in court. One explanation for this marriage, then, is that Katherine was exploited—this marriage gave the young John Woodville immediate access to wealth and lands, and the Woodvilles were getting what they wanted at this time. That may be true. But the explanation is not wholly satisfactory. Katherine, after all, was the king's aunt, sister to his mother. It seems unlikely that a woman with such connections could be forced into a marriage widely seen as repellent and distasteful, even 'diabolicum.'[19] Although in fact she outlived her fourth husband by many years, the odds were that she would die relatively soon, and that he would not long be able to enjoy her wealth, which would pass to her children. Perhaps they *wanted* to marry each other—for sexual or other reasons. Such things do happen, albeit rarely. The marriage lasted four years, until the fortunes of the Wars of the Roses turned, and John Woodville was executed. Katherine was now a widow for the fourth time—and, like the Wife of Bath, she had married a younger man and outlived him. She was still alive and active in 1483, when she attended the coronation of another nephew, Richard III.

Like Katherine Neville and Alison of Bath, Alice Chaucer was launched onto the marriage market as early as possible—in fact, earlier than the law allowed.[20] Again, women's right to inherit was crucial in her background: Thomas Chaucer, Geoffrey's son, had been rewarded for his service to and relationship with John of Gaunt with a lucrative marriage to an heiress, Maud Burghersh.[21] Their only child was Alice. She seems to have been married off at around the age of ten, and widowed by age eleven. It is highly unlikely that this was a consummated marriage, but as a child widow she nonetheless inherited both land and goods from her thirty-five-year-old husband. If he had not died, she would, of course, have been obliged to consummate her marriage, with a twenty-four-year age gap. She did not marry again until she was about seventeen, when she married Thomas Montagu, earl of Salisbury. When she was widowed, seven years later, she received half of his goods, as well as 1,000 marks in gold, 3,000 marks in jewellery and plate, and the revenues of his Norman lands. Alice was now a very rich, childless woman, twice widowed, and still in her early twenties. No one would expect her to remain single, and indeed she continued to move upwards in the marriage market. Having already progressed from a baronet to an earl, she now married another earl, who was to become a duke. She was licensed to marry William de la Pole, earl of Suffolk—the husband closest in age to herself—in 1430. Their marriage lasted around twenty years; again, her husband left land on extremely favourable terms for Alice: in particular she held jointure of most of the extensive de la Pole estates. William de la Pole was impeached and ignominiously killed, but Alice managed to secure her inheritance. She now enjoyed a further twenty-five years of widowhood, during which time she vastly increased her own wealth and political influence, was a creditor to the Crown, and became a noted businesswoman and politician.[22] As Margaret Paston, another formidable woman (whose family was embroiled in property disputes with Alice), wrote, she was 'sotill, and hath sotill councell wyth here.'[23] Her subtlety and acumen were similarly acknowledged by her husband, whose letter of advice to his son urges him to rely on her intelligence and good council.[24] Privileged wealthy widows were powerful and respected figures in the medieval polity.

For most twenty-first-century readers, the early emphasis in the Wife of Bath's Prologue on defending remarriage seems to reveal attitudes no longer prevalent—today, in most cultures it would seem very odd to question the morality of a widow remarrying. But in Chaucer's circle too, it would be odd. Alison excavates old-fashioned attitudes, the beliefs of some (not all) of the early church fathers, promulgated in her time by misogynist books that had little connection to lived experience. As Mary Carruthers has argued, the audience would recognise 'the common truth of what she is saying,' and the legitimacy of her ridiculing clerical teaching on remarriage.[25] In her first sentence, she tells us that she has married five times 'If I so ofte might have ywedded bee' (Wife of Bath's Prologue, 7)—reminding us that there are some who would challenge the idea of marrying more than once. In her second sentence, she says that she has been told that as Christ only went to one wedding, that was a sign that people should only marry once (9–13). Her third sentence again reminds us of a biblical anecdote: the occasion when Jesus met a Samaritan woman, and 'spak in repreeve' (16) of her, saying that she had had five husbands, and that the man that 'hath' her at that moment 'Is noght thyn housbonde' (19). Alison follows this by saying, 'What that he mente therby, I kan nat seyn' (20), then asking why the fifth man was not her husband, questioning how many husbands were allowed, and criticising men's desire to interpret, to 'glosen' the Bible (26). Alison then returns to biblical texts that she sees as unambiguous, the command to 'wexe and multiplye' (28) and the command to leave father and mother and go to a wife (31)—emphasising that God says nothing about bigamy, or indeed octogamy (33).

There is a lot going on in these lines. The story of the Samaritan woman is clear in the Bible. It comes from John 4:

> Jesus saith to her: Go, call thy husband, and come hither. The woman answered, and said: I have no husband. Jesus said to her: Thou hast said well, I have no husband: For thou hast had five husbands: and he whom thou now hast, is not thy husband. This thou hast said truly. The woman saith to him: Sir, I perceive that thou art a prophet. (16–19)

In other words, she has been married five times and is now living with a man to whom she is not married. Augustine understood this, writing that, 'this woman truly did not have a husband then; but she was cohabiting with some man in an illicit relationship, an adulterer rather than a husband.'[26] He was primarily, however, interested in the exegetical interpretation of this scene, positing that the five husbands represented the senses, while others had suggested that they stood for the five books of the Pentateuch. Tertullian argued that Jesus was in fact condemning multiple marriages.[27] Jerome compounded this error, by writing that Jesus 'castigavit' (reproved) the woman for claiming to have a sixth husband—an invention with no basis in the Bible.[28] Is the Wife of Bath misunderstanding scripture, copying Jerome, or parodying Jerome? The comments that she 'kan nat seyn' what it means and that 'men' 'glosen, up and doun' these lines suggests she is poking fun at Jerome's interpretation—which is not just contorted but evidently wrong. Indeed, in the service of rhetoric, Jerome said many things in his *Adversus Jovinianum* that he knew were wrong.[29] The comment about octogamy also directly references Jerome.

To understand the debate about remarriage we need to see it in a long context. In the Bible, Jesus says nothing against remarriage. Saint Paul advises widows to stay single, as he is himself, but makes it clear that there is nothing wrong about remarriage: 'A woman is bound by the law as long as her husband liveth; but if her husband die, she is at liberty: let her marry to whom she will; only in the Lord' (1 Corinthians 7:39). In the same chapter he also advises: 'But I say to the unmarried, and to the widows: It is good for them if they so continue, even as I. But if they do not contain themselves, let them marry' (8–9). Paul's general attitude to marriage should be seen in the context of his focus on changing attitudes to the body and to women in particular amongst pagan communities. Paul was preaching in a world in which female infanticide was practised, and in which male promiscuity and polygamy was standard behaviour. Women were devalued and insistently sexualised. While Paul no doubt had many reasons for his beliefs, partly he was differentiating the new sect from previous belief-systems through its focus on the dignity of the human body—and the Christian focus on the vulnerable at this time made it particularly attractive to women, the poor, ethnic minorities, and slaves. Galen noted that one of the very odd things about Christians was that they were not promiscuous.[30] While Paul's misogyny has been much discussed, his decrees that women should be silent in the churches (1 Corinthians 14:34), that it is better to marry than to burn (1 Corinthians 7:9), and that women should be subject to their husbands (Ephesians 5:22) are not the whole picture, as mentioned in chapter 2. Indeed, Phoebe was not told to be silent in the church: Paul sent her from Cenchreae to Rome as his representative to explain his words in the churches (Romans 16:1–2).

Biblical misquotation and partial quotation dominates medieval misogynist texts. Just as Jerome selectively quoted those parts of the Bible that suited him, so Alison quotes the half of verses that suits her best: 'man shal yelde to his wife hire dette' (130)—whereas the context of this quotation makes clear that it is all about mutuality, rather than one sex yielding to the other ('Let the husband render the debt to his wife, and the wife also in like manner to the husband. The wife hath not power of her own body, but the husband. And in like manner the husband also hath not power of his own body, but the wife' [1 Corinthians 7:3–4]). Paul is more complex than either the church authorities or Alison implies.

Jerome's misogyny, and specifically misogamy, was far more extreme and more notorious in the Middle Ages than Paul's. Jerome's writings are at the heart of Jankyn's book of wicked wives, and of numerous similar real medieval collections. In excerpted and compilation form, his monstrous text was wildly popular. As his recent editors have commented, today, most people would see Jerome as 'animated by a nearly neurotic horror of female sexuality' and as 'incapable of sustained and systematic logical argumentation' in the *Adversus Jovinianum*; moreover, even in his own day, the text 'became a serious personal embarrassment' to Jerome.[31] It is also important to remember that he wrote this repellant tract in the spirit of satire, which thrives on extreme opinions. His attitude to remarriage is also worth looking at in the context of his own life. Alison refers to him as a 'clerke at Rome' (673), reminding us of a specific moment in Jerome's life.[32] When Jerome was in Rome, he formed a lifelong tie with a rich widow, Paula, and with her daughter, Eustochium. In 385, scandal forced Jerome to leave Rome: he was accused of sexual impropriety and of legacy-hunting—that is, of trying to gain women's money, and specifically widows' money. He went to Palestine, and Paula followed him. Jerome and Paula remained close companions for the next twenty years, while Paula funded the building of a monastery for Jerome and a convent for herself. She also financed Jerome's commentary and translation work, while she herself studied the Bible in its original languages. Of Jerome's surviving 123 letters, 36 percent were addressed to women.[33] It is clear, then, that wealthy widows were not only sought as wives—their money had a number of uses, and it was undoubtedly in the interests of a man such as Jerome to secure that wealth for the church, or his own part of the church, rather than encourage its circulation through further marriage. Of course, that is not to say that Jerome did not have multiple motives—some acknowledged, others unacknowledged. But the historical context of Jerome's attitude to widows throws particular light on his invective against remarriage.

While some authorities such as Tertullian condemned remarriage, others, such as Augustine, supported it. The standard view in late-antique times was that remarriage was not desirable but was permitted. Marriage was not really a church matter at this time: it was only later that marriage became a sacrament. In the twelfth and thirteenth centuries, when marriage became the seventh sacrament, canon law generally took the position that remarriage was acceptable and that there was no distinction between second or subsequent marriages. The nuptial blessing was reserved only for first marriages—although in practice priests seem to have found ways to give subsequent marriages the approval of the church.[34] Moreover, it is clear that widows did not feel obliged to consider their first marriage as superior to their subsequent marriages—throughout her long widowhood, Margaret Stodeye styled herself by the surname of her second husband and asked to be buried next to her fourth.[35] The realities of late-medieval English marriage norms were quite different from those imagined in books of wicked wives, papal decrees, or canon law. Experience, in other words, challenged authority.

In giving a literary voice to a much-married woman, a voice that did not simply ventriloquise a straightforward misogyny, Chaucer created a literary space for a figure who was socially central in his world, but textually marginalised. In the later Middle Ages, when a married woman did write a text, printers hurried to change her into something else. Henry Pepwell printed a much-truncated and edited version of Margery Kempe's book in 1521, as part of a devotional anthology. In his description of who she was, he turned Margery—a married woman who had fourteen children, was plagued by fantasies about male genitalia, imagined love-making with Christ, and wrote in explicit and traumatising detail about marital rape—into a walled-up nun, saying in his preface to the book that she was a 'deuoute ancres' (devout anchoress).[36]

But the fact that middle-aged women's experiences of marriage were not normally seen as material for literature was precisely what made such a figure interesting to Chaucer. At the heart of the *Canterbury Tales* is the idea of interruption. We repeatedly hear an authoritative voice challenged by the kind of voice that isn't usually given the opportunity to speak—in life or in literature. This most famously happens in Fragment I of the *Tales*. After the General Prologue, the Knight (highest representative of the second estate, those who fight), tells his high-style tale. The Host wants the Monk (highest representative of the first estate, those who pray) to follow, but instead the Miller—low-class, drunk, and vulgar—mounts a verbal revolution, refusing to stay in his place, refusing to wait his turn, refusing to keep quiet. He insists on telling his brilliant tale, and the whole idea of hierarchy disappears as, for the rest of the fragment, the pilgrims make their own decisions about tale-telling—and two more low-class speakers follow the Miller with their own fabliaux (vulgar, low-style, comic, carnival tales). After Fragment I, the ordering of the rest of the *Canterbury Tales* is uncertain. Chaucer died leaving an unfinished text, and internal manuscript evidence makes it clear that he changed his mind at various points about the order of tales, and about who was going to tell which tale. But it is evident that at one point— and this may have been his final intent—Chaucer had the idea for a parallel pattern of authority and interruption. Fragment II opens with the Host inviting the Man of Law, a respectable urban figure, to tell a tale. Chaucer seems to have changed his mind about which tale the Man of Law was to tell—first, the prose Melibee, later the story of Constance's journeys to Syria, Northumberland, and back to Rome. At the end, the Host suggests that a clerical figure tells the next tale (this time not the

Monk but the Parson). However, someone interrupts, and (in the key Ellesmere manuscript and in most modern editions) the next tale is told by the Wife of Bath.[37] The identity of the person interrupting is not clear. It has been erased in manuscripts, and is variously the Shipman, Summoner, or Squire. Yet the person speaking—who refers to their 'joly body,' says they do not wish to hear a cleric 'glosen' the gospel, and adds that they will not talk in 'queinte' terms or in Latin epithets— certainly sounds like the Wife of Bath.[38] (One school of thought, and set of editors, places the Shipman's Tale—which was originally intended for the Wife of Bath—next in the collection.)[39] This, then, is a textual mess, but it is clear that at one point Chaucer envisaged a scene in which the Man of Law's Tale is 'supposed' to be followed by the Parson according to the Host's plan—but the Wife of Bath, mirroring the Miller, inserts her own voice instead. This is the order that modern editions tend to replicate. The Wife of Bath, like the Miller, exemplifies Chaucer's specific interest in bringing to the fore voices that are not usually given the opportunity to speak, in emphasising the rights of all, or almost all, to have their stories heard.[40] Both characters also demonstrate Chaucer's interest in enabling these less authoritative voices to speak instead of clerics (Monk and Parson). As we shall see, readers have often seen affinities between the Wife of Bath and the Miller: in one early-twentieth-century play they even end up married.[41]

The multiple interruptions of the Wife of Bath's Prologue foreground very clearly how problematic it was for a woman—even a respectable, wealthy, mercantile widow—to speak in the world of authoritative texts, given the force of the books of wicked wives stacked up against her. Those interruptions come exclusively from male clerics: the Pardoner (169–193) and the Friar

(835–862). The Friar then draws in the Summoner and the Host, who maintains her right to speak. No other pilgrim is interrupted so much. The insertion of the Wife of Bath's voice into *textual* culture is startlingly novel. But in everyday life, it would have been entirely normal for a man such as Chaucer to encounter, to respect, and to listen to much-married, economically powerful urban women.

CHAPTER 4

The Female Storyteller

'Women can't write; women can't paint.'

—VIRGINIA WOOLF, *TO THE LIGHTHOUSE*

For me, the most arresting moment of the Wife of Bath's Prologue comes at line 692, when she asks her audience: 'Who peyntede the leon, tel me who?' In this crucial question, she undoes the authorities that have dominated her prologue, and that dominated medieval clerkly and courtly literature, simply by pointing out that they are biased and unreliable. At this extraordinary moment, she makes her audience aware that the canon is not impartially selected or objectively authoritative. On the contrary, only one sex has had the opportunity to tell its own story.

Alison refers to the male-centric nature of the canon through a reference to one of Aesop's fables. The way that she chooses to interpret the story of the man and the lion was unprecedented. The versions of 'the man and the lion' most familiar to a late-medieval reader were those that were taught in the schoolroom, such as Avianus's Latin translations. In Avianus's rendering, a noble 'venator' (huntsman) was engaged in a long dispute with a lion, when they saw a tombstone. On this monument, a sculptor had carved an image of a lion 'flectentem colla' (bowing its neck in submission) and 'in gremio procubuisse viri' (prostrate in a man's embrace). The man uses this image to tell the lion that he should not be proud, as this sculpture demonstrates that the lion is killed by the man. The lion responds that humans are absurdly overconfident if they think that it is reasonable to use 'artificis . . . manum' (an artist's hand) as a witness. He points out that if lions were able to engrave, then the sculpture would show the man being devoured by the lion's jaws. The overt moral is that art is unreliable, that artists will be biased towards their own kind.[1]

Alison's exposé has remained resonant and relevant right up to the present day, although of course there have been changes and improvements in the status of women's writing. In Jane Austen's *Persuasion*, Anne Elliot closely echoes the Wife of Bath's concerns, when she says, in response to Captain Harville's comment that every book that he has ever opened has demonstrated woman's inconstancy: 'if you please, no reference to examples in books. Men have had every advantage of us in telling their own story. Education has been theirs in so much higher a degree; the pen has been in their hands. I will not allow books to prove anything' (chap. 23). Perhaps the most famous passage in Virginia Woolf's *A Room of One's Own* tells the story of Shakespeare's imagined sister, Judith, a woman of equal talents to himself, suggesting that it would have been impossible for a female Shakespeare to get her voice heard. Woolf writes that, 'a highly gifted girl who had tried to use her gift for poetry would have been so thwarted and hindered by other people, so tortured and pulled asunder by her own contrary instincts, that she must have lost her health and sanity to a certainty' (64). In recent years, many writers have discussed the ongoing bias towards male authors, looking at (for instance) the proportions of male and female writers put forward for literary prizes, the overwhelming preponderance of male protagonists in prize-winning books, and the relative space given to male and female writers and reviewers in literary publications.[2]

Many medieval churchmen suggested there was an inherent antipathy between women and books, characterising women as frivolous, stupid, bodily, and domestic, in contrast to serious, intelligent, cerebral, and intellectual books. A key example of this occurs in Richard de Bury's *Philobiblon* (The Love of Books), written circa 1345, in which the books themselves castigate priests who live with women, claiming that those women attack the books and want to swap them for clothes and fabrics, seeing them as superfluous. While the idea underpinning this is that women are unintellectual and impede men's commitment to books and study, the attack on women also in fact makes clear precisely why women might be quite right to despise most books. The *Philobiblon* calls woman 'a biped beast,' worse than 'the asp and the basilisk' and admits that 'the inmost hearts' of books are indeed antipathetic to women, holding up the profoundly antifeminist Theophrastus and Valerius as exemplary texts.[3] It is thus perfectly possible to read against the overt meaning of this text, and to see that it is the books' uniform anti-women bias that is the real problem—not the alleged unintellectual bias of women.

In the twelfth century, a female author, Marie de France, wrote a version of the 'man and the lion' tale and added a new element—but that element was class rather than sex. In her rewriting, the man is a 'vileins'—an ordinary man—while the lion has noble lineage. The man shows the lion the painting of a man killing a lion, and the lion takes him to an emperor's palace to

show him a treacherous baron being thrown to a lion. The lion
then takes the man to a desert and defends him against another
lion, thus demonstrating his own nobility and *gentilesse*. Marie
then tells us, in her moral, that we should not pay attention to
paintings or to fables—they are 'mencuinge' (lies) and 'sunge'
(illusions). Like Avianus, she focuses on the unreliability of art,
undercutting its authority, but she also reminds us that the creation of art is dependent on power of various kinds.[4]

These fables were so well known in the later Middle Ages
that the Wife of Bath need only briefly refer to the lion to recall
the story to the minds of her audience. But in linking the story
to misogyny and openly articulating the gendered problems of
the canon, the Wife of Bath does something quite new. She brilliantly places her reference in the middle of a discussion of
clerks' hatred of women, and specifically of wives. After detailing
her husband's 'book of wikked wyves'—containing the very authors praised by the *Philobiblon* ('Valerie and Theofraste' is
Jankyn's name for his book)—she says that 'it is an impossible /
That any clerk wol speke good of wyves' (688–689). She then
asks, 'Who peyntede the leon, tel me who?' (692), making it
clear to us that when reading books of wicked wives, we must
think about the motivations and backgrounds of the authors.
In her next, emphatic sentence, she imagines an alternative
canon:

> By God, if women hadde written stories.
> As clerkes han withinne hire oratories,
> They wolde han written of men moore wikkednesse
> Than al the mark of Adam may redresse. (693–696)

Her initial 'By God' strongly inserts her own voice into the narrative, reminding us that she is indeed telling her own story. She
goes on, through her hypothetical 'if' and her subjunctive

'wolde han,' to fantasise about a different system, a world in which women are able to write stories with as much freedom and prestige, and with as much access to an audience and to the technologies of book preservation and production, as clerks. Importantly, Alison is not here setting women up against men; rather she is setting women up against one particular group of men—clerks. These men are cloistered in chapels, dedicated to the church and, while they may indeed have been promiscuous in youth, they are (by the time they are writing against women) impotent. The kind of clerk she has in mind, 'may noght do / Of Venus werkes worth his olde sho' (707–708). His attempt at sex, in other words, is worth less than an old shoe and he is embittered by his own inadequacy. Again, the immediacy of her tone—'worth his olde sho'—insistently reminds us that this is her own voice, that a female character is bucking the trend and telling her own story at luxuriant length.

How unusual was it in the later Middle Ages for a woman to write, to tell stories, or to involve herself in textual culture? How might a contemporary audience have responded to this aspect of Alison—the female storyteller? David Wallace has suggested that Chaucer's interest in female eloquence is the most 'singular' aspect of his writing.[5] Throughout the medieval period, northern European women were profoundly engaged in textual culture: we see them as patrons, book owners, letter writers, translators, commentators, and collaborators; at times they appear working in book production as scribes and illuminators.[6] But while anonymous may indeed often have been a woman, as Woolf argued, female writers tended to lack the authority necessary to be recognised as named authors.[7] When they did put their own names to texts, those names were systematically erased in ingenious ways.[8] Particular anxieties coalesced around educated women who were not virgins, women who had entered the sexual economy *and* aspired to be authors—from Heloise to Margery Kempe.

Chaucer's own world was overshadowed by various female patrons, although he himself was a poet who largely avoided direct patronage. Philippa of Hainault, queen of England for the first twenty-five years of Chaucer's life, came from a cultural centre and was an artistic and literary patron, credited by Froissart as having created him as a poet.[9] The court of Edward and Philippa, strongly influenced by Hainault literary culture and promoting poets from Philippa's homeland such as Jean de la Mote, was a key environment for Chaucer's early poetic development.[10] Chaucer's earliest extant poem, *The Book of the Duchess* was written to commemorate the death of Blanche of Lancaster, who may have patronised him in some way. Later in life, Chaucer makes a reference to Anne of Bohemia, when his avatar is ordered to present the *Legend of Good Women* to 'the queen / [...] at Eltham or at Shene' (*Prologue to the Legend of Good Women*, F version, 496–497). Nicola McDonald has written compellingly about the ludic world of poetry and sexual play at Anne and Richard's court, a world in which risqué jokes, poetic riddles, and fun was the norm, a world presided over by women.[11] Contemporaries of Chaucer such as Joan de Bohun owned and commissioned books—Hoccleve's *Complaint of the Virgin* was dedicated to her—and her daughters headed cultured, book-owning households. One daughter, Mary, who married Henry Bolingbroke, owned a French Lancelot and Psalters; the other, Eleanor, who married Thomas of Woodstock and became duchess of Gloucester, bequeathed many books to her children, including books of romance, a mirror for princes, and religious books. Another late-fourteenth-century duchess, Isabel of York, left a book by Machaut and another about 'launcelot' to her son; while in the early fifteenth century, Elizabeth Berkeley commissioned a translation of Boethius.[12]

Chaucer's niece Joan and his granddaughter, Alice, are fascinating examples of privileged medieval women who engaged with literary culture in socially acceptable ways. Joan Beaufort was the youngest child of John of Gaunt and Katherine Swynford and was therefore the niece of Chaucer's wife, Philippa (Katherine's sister). Joan's second husband, whom she married in 1396, after the pope and Parliament had agreed to legitimise Joan and her brothers, was Ralph Neville, earl of Westmorland. Joan had connections with many important late-medieval writers, both secular and spiritual. She was given a copy of an English Gower book—presumably the *Confessio amantis*—in 1430. Joan also owned a book containing *The Chronicles of Jerusalem* and *Le viage de Godfrey Boylion*, which she lent to Henry V. In 1426, she inherited a book called *Tristram*, a romance, possibly in English. Joan was also a patron—or a potential patron—of Thomas Hoccleve, who dedicated a book of his poems to her. This book—written in Hoccleve's own handwriting—still exists, comprising a set of poems known as the *Series*.[13] It is a particularly fascinating sequence, beginning with autobiographical poems that describe in detail his own mental health, recounting a breakdown and period of recovery. At the end of the final poem in the book, the *Tale of Jonathas*, a stanza addressed to Joan appears:

> Go, smal book / to the noble excellence
> Of my lady of Westmerland / and seye
> Hir humble seruant / with al reuerence
> Him recommandith vnto hir nobleye
> And byseeche hire/ on my behalue and preye
> Thee to receyue / for hire owne right

And looke thow in al manere weye
To plese hir womanhede / do thy might.
humble seruant
to your gracious
noblesse
T. Hoccleue[14]

Hoccleve clearly hoped that Joan could help him and indeed he may well have already received encouragement from her. He here uses a well-known trope, deployed by Chaucer at the end of *Troilus and Criseyde*—'Go little book!'—to send the book as his intercessor, beseeching Joan to read without bias, 'in al manere weye.' Elsewhere too we see Hoccleve imagining a female audience for his poetry: earlier on in the *Series*, when he mentions his patron, Duke Humphrey (Joan's nephew and brother of Henry V), he draws a sketch of a scene in which Humphrey would show his books to female friends. Hoccleve writes that as Humphrey likes 'For his desport and mirthe, in honestee / With ladyes to haue daliance,' therefore, 'this book wole he shewen hem par chance' (D 703–707).[15]

Joan also may have owned manuscripts containing spiritual texts; the evidence for manuscript ownership is not always secure but it is probable that she owned a manuscript of Richard Rolle's *Meditations on the Passion*. This early-fifteenth-century manuscript contains her name, albeit in a later hand.[16] Most interestingly of all, we know that Joan personally spent time with one of the first named female writers in English—Margery Kempe. Joan met Margery around 1413, when she summoned her and, according to Margery's *Book*, was pleased with her. Margery quotes a priest who interrogated her, claiming that he said that Joan 'liked your words,' but he then criticised her, alleging that she advised Joan's daughter, Lady Greystoke, to leave her husband (chap. 54). This meeting took place decades before Margery dictated her book, but it is nonetheless fascinating that Joan, a learned, book-owning woman went out of her way to meet a woman who was herself knowledgeable about scripture and religious writings and was to go on to become an author. The specific accusation to which this meeting gave rise is entirely predictable: when women get together, they can't be trusted, they conspire against men, they encourage the breakdown of patriarchal society.

Joan's first cousin, Thomas Chaucer, was part of the same group as she throughout their childhoods although he was a decade or more older. The Chaucer, Beaufort, and Swynford children spent a great deal of time with Gaunt's legitimate Lancastrian children, including the future Henry IV, and there is evidence of tie upon tie between these half-siblings and cousins. While Joan's children included book-owning women—such as Cecily, duchess of York and the mother of Edward IV and Richard III; Anne, duchess of Buckingham; and Katherine, whom we met in the previous chapter, with her teenage husband—Thomas's daughter, Alice, the only grandchild of the poet, was also a noted cultural patron.[17] Alice owned many books, some religious, some literary; and a signed note survives in which she requests that her books be moved from a closet near the ground, where they are at risk of damage, to somewhere safer, a testament to her personal concern about her books.[18] Similarly, the fact that one of her books is described as 'clasped with latoune newe' demonstrates that the book has been used and repaired, that she is reading and taking care of her books. Her 'literary' books that we know about are an interesting selection. Later in her life, in 1466, a set of books was moved from Wingfield, the Suffolks' ducal seat, to Ewelme, Alice's natal and preferred home. This group included seven literary books. These were a 'quare of a legend of Ragge hande' (a saint's life, either written in uneven handwriting, 'rag hand,' or about the female educator, Saint Radegund); a French version of the 'quaterfitz Emond,' a *chanson de geste* concerning Charlemagne; Vincent de Beauvais's *De morali principis*; the *Ditz de philisophus*, a book of philosophy in French translated by Guillaume de Tignonville; Lydgate's translation of the *Pelerinage de la Vie Humaine*; Christine de Pizan's *Citee des Dames*; and finally a French book of 'temps pastoure' which may have been Christine de Pizan's *Le Dit de la Pastoure*.[19] This is an eclectic mix of French and English; of genres including romance, philosophy, saint's life, and allegory; of established and contemporary texts.

Alice also had personal connections with poets, most notably Lydgate. She commissioned his 'Virtues of the Mass': the manuscript in Saint John's College, Oxford, includes this dedication: 'Hic incipit interpretatio misse in lingua materna secundum Iohannem litgate monachum de Buria ad rogatum dominae comitissae de Suthefolcia' (Here begins the interpretations of the mass in the mother tongue according to John Lydgate, monk of Bury, at the invitation of his mistress the countess of Suffolk).[20] Indeed, her connections with Lydgate may have been fairly substantial: he had written a balade for her father, Thomas, in the early part of the fifteenth century, and was a careful reader and imitator of her grandfather. Lydgate manuscripts bearing the marks of ownership of Alice's second and third husbands may in fact have a closer connection with Alice herself, and she may have introduced the poet and/or his works to Salisbury and Suffolk.[21]

Alice was also a donor to Oxford University, which was only a few miles from her beloved home at Ewelme where she promoted the education of the young by founding a school. Four days after her husband's murder, the university wrote to her calling her 'oure ryght especiall benefactrice and singuler lady.' In 1454, a letter from Oxford thanks her for her gifts of books and gold, and for a grant of twenty pounds to be used toward the construction of the Divinity School. Another letter of thanks survives from 1461, acknowledging Alice's 'nobill and notabill geffts.'[22]

It would be extraordinary if this educated, literary woman did not know her grandfather's poems, although we do not have direct evidence of this. Some critics have stated that she 'no doubt' had an excellent copy of the *Canterbury Tales*; others have even implied a possible connection between the most famous of all Chaucer manuscripts—the Ellesmere Chaucer— and Alice and William de la Pole.[23] It would be fascinating to know what Alice and other early women readers thought of the Wife of Bath, but the evidence is lacking. We do know that women were always part of Chaucer's audience, and that women (including Lady Margaret Beaufort, mother of Henry VII and granddaughter of Chaucer's wife's nephew, John Beaufort) owned *Canterbury Tales* manuscripts in the fifteenth century, but the conversations that such women had about Alison are, unfortunately, lost to us.[24]

We have ample evidence, then, of women's interest in books: of their sponsorship of authors, their owning and reading of books, and their engagement with literary culture. But there is far less evidence of named female authors working in medieval Europe. As critics such as Diane Watt have shown, this is partly because women's texts were often overwritten and appropriated by male authors, while the women were 'dismissed as unworthy authors, and their roles in the production of literary works were overlooked, ignored, and forgotten.'[25] Women in general simply lacked the authority to be seen as 'authors'— the gatekeepers of authority. Alison herself does mention one well-known female author, but mentions her as one of the writers included in the book of wicked wives, a proponent of misogyny, or misogamy. That writer is Heloise: 'Helowys / That was abbesse nat fer fro Parys' (677–678). Alison also mentions Trotula—an eleventh-century female writer and doctor, who wrote gynaecological treatises, although there is no evidence that Chaucer knew her writings.

Chaucer may have known about Heloise and her writings from other sources too, but he certainly knew them from the *Romance of the Rose*. Jean de Meun includes her as an example cited by the Jealous Husband, a character imagined and mocked by the Friend. This Jealous Husband gives an impassioned series of examples against marriage—placing the arguments of Heloise, and the story of her relationship with Abelard shortly after the story of Valerius, told by Walter Map (the book of wicked wives is known to Jankyn as the book of 'Valerie and Theophrastus'). In the *Romance of the Rose*, Heloise is characterized as 'intelligent and well-read,' a woman who 'busied herself with her studies' and demonstrated 'erudition.' At the same time, Jean de Meun emphasises the fact that Heloise was against marriage and argued strongly against marriage when her lover, Abelard, wanted them to marry. The Friend says that Heloise 'understood feminine ways for she had them all in herself' and that only her unique erudition (he says, 'I do not think that there has ever been such a woman since') enabled her 'to conquer and subdue her nature.' He tells us that Heloise thought that sexual pleasure was greater when rare and when the relationship was not changed by issues of 'lordship and domination,' and that she wanted Abelard, and also herself, to be able to study and not to be tied down.[26] Heloise is thus presented as one of the group of philosophical misogamists.[27]

The story that lies behind this version was first told in letters written by Abelard and Heloise in the twelfth century, including

Abelard's *Historia Calamitatum*.[28] The story of their scandalous relationship and its brutal ending became notorious. Abelard, a famous scholar and cleric lodging at the house of Fulbert in Paris, began tutoring Fulbert's young niece, Heloise, already renowned as a great intellectual, and they began a passionate sexual relationship. When the rumours about their relationship became widespread, and Heloise was pregnant, Abelard rushed her out of Paris, disguised as a nun, to stay with his relatives, where she gave birth to their son. Heloise's relatives pressured Abelard to marry her and, while he was willing, she was firmly against the idea, despising the institution of marriage and the idea of their living a domestic life with what she perceived to be an inevitable attendant intellectual deprivation. Abelard insisted, and they married, with the proviso that the marriage should remain secret. Fulbert, however, started to tell the news around the city and to make various threats, and Abelard now removed Heloise to live in the convent of Argenteuil. Fulbert believed that Abelard had abandoned Heloise, and he sent his henchmen to punish Abelard: they viciously attacked him, castrating him. In the wake of this atrocity, Abelard became a monk and Heloise a nun, although she remained plagued by her sexual desires and frustrations. Later, Abelard gifted a convent to Heloise and her nuns, and they exchanged a series of letters.

Heloise emerges from her letters, and from the letters and descriptions of others, as a complex and fascinating character. She is not the kind of proto-feminist that some modern readers would like to find. In one letter to Abelard, for instance, she dwells on the horror of what was done to Abelard, blaming herself, and quoting misogynist parts of the Bible:

> What misery for me—born as I was to be the cause of such a crime! Is it the general lot of women to bring total ruin on great men? Hence the warning about women in Proverbs:

'But now, my son, listen to me, attend to what I say: do not
let your heart entice you into her ways, do not stray down her
paths; she has wounded and laid low so many, and the strongest have all been her victims. Her house is the way to hell,
and leads down to the halls of death.' And in Ecclesiastes:
'I put all to the test . . . I find woman more bitter than death;
she is a snare, her heart a net, her arms are chains. He who is
pleasing to God eludes her, but the sinner is her captive.'
(Letter 4, p. 66)

She goes on to cite a well-worn list of examples of temptress
women from the Bible, such as Eve, Delilah, and Job's wife. But
much of the time, she suggests that the problem is not sexual
desire or indeed the sexual act—their real mistake was marrying, something which she always resisted and to which she
never wanted to consent. Heloise insists that she always 'preferred love to wedlock and freedom to chains' and that she preferred to be a 'concubine or whore' than a wife. Addressing
Abelard directly, she insists, 'I never sought anything in you
except yourself' (Letter 2, 51). While at some points in the letters she accepts the idea that fornication is sin, her principal
focus is on marriage as a constraint and as something that is
detrimental to those who want to experience a life of the mind.
Abelard, after his castration and turn towards a life of devotion,
echoes this, emphasising to Heloise that she can now 'turn the
pages of sacred books' instead of having to deal in 'the obscure
degradations of women's work' (Letter 5, 84). Heloise's sexual
longing reverberates throughout her letters, as she tells Abelard
that her mind 'still retains the will to sin and is on fire with its
old desires,' saying that she thinks constantly of the 'pleasures
of lovers,' which she can hardly 'shift from my memory' (Letter
4, 68). Heloise emerges from her letters as a woman who wants

a life of study but also a sexual life, a woman who despises the institution of marriage and the dull rules of morality that regulate society. In texts such as the *Romance of the Rose* and the fictional book of wicked wives, she is cited as a kind of authority—but gains that status because of her anti-marriage and (to a certain extent) anti-women views.

This is, however, only a partial view of Heloise, a highly-educated intellectual, whose letters demonstrate an exceptionally sophisticated ability to craft elaborate prose and to make skilful arguments, a writer well-versed in classical and biblical traditions and in the art of letter-writing. Constant Mews has noted that since Jean de Meun's interpretation of Heloise and Abelard, writers have tended to focus on their love affair at the expense of understanding them as thinkers who were 'preoccupied by issues of language, theology and ethics'; Barbara Newman characterises the letters as texts fundamentally about 'conscience and consciousness.'[29] In Heloise's own lifetime she was recognised as a scholar and author. Abelard tells us that when he first met her she was already 'most renowned throughout the realm' because 'in the extent of her learning she stood supreme' (*Historia Calamitatum*, 10). Peter the Venerable said, much later, that in her pursuit of learning she had 'surpassed all women ... and [had] gone further than almost every man.'[30] Hugh Metel wrote to Heloise, saying that 'by composing, by versifying, by renewing familiar words in new combinations,' she had 'overcome womanly weakness' and 'hardened in manly strength.' Metel's comment is especially interesting because it acknowledges Heloise as an accomplished wordsmith and poet.[31]

Yet the fact of Heloise as an author has met with consistent and sustained resistance. The skewed view of her began with Jean de Meun who, although he acknowledged her intellect, was principally interested in her anti-marriage views and her personal history. But it was in more recent centuries that historians, clerics, and critics cast doubts on her authorship altogether. Nineteenth-century editions of the letters left Heloise's name off the title page, and men began openly claiming that Heloise had not written the letters at all, suggesting that they were composed by monks. One scholar, Etienne Gilson, lecturing in the 1930s, argued that Abelard and Heloise were metaphors for Christian theology and the pagan world.[32] John Benton, in the 1970s, first suggested that all the letters were forged and then changed his mind to state that both sides of the correspondence were penned by Abelard, who wanted to demonstrate 'the carnal weakness of a woman without proper male direction.'[33] Indeed, there was a wave of critics 'preoccupied with putting women in their place,' whose denial of Heloise's well-attested authorship was grounded in profoundly limited and misogynistic ideas about what a medieval woman might have thought and written. One male critic took a slightly different tack, saying that the issue of whether or not Heloise wrote the letters is 'minor' as it only relates to 'the history of women' or, in fact, 'the history of sensibility.' This is an extraordinary dismissal of the importance of women's experience and an equally breathtaking consignment of female experience to 'sensibility.'[34] In fact, as Barbara Newman has magisterially demonstrated, there is no reason whatsoever to doubt Heloise's authorship, which is attested in all the manuscripts and which was not doubted by contemporaries, who revered her writing skill.

Indeed, there is good reason to suppose that a swathe of further letters and poems was also penned by Heloise. The *Epistolae duorum amantium*, a set of more than one hundred letters and poems, may represent Abelard and Heloise's early correspondence.[35] The surviving manuscripts are from the late fifteenth century, and the topic of love between an older male teacher and a young female student was (depressingly) a popular one in the art of letter-writing tradition.[36] However, not only is the language and knowledge of texts consistent with a twelfth-century date, there are also specific aspects of the texts which make them 'fully consistent' with authorship by Heloise and Abelard. In a fascinating argument, Constant Mews has shown, for instance, that the female writer's use of the term 'guttula scibilitatis' (a droplet of knowability) takes a distinctive neologism used by Abelard (scibilitas) and blends it with an image from the *Song of Songs* to create an image of knowability trickling from the honeycomb of wisdom. Mews suggests that it would be 'far-fetched' to imagine anyone other than Heloise developing Abelard's language in this way.[37] More broadly, the letter writer's use of sources such as Cicero, Ovid, and the Bible is in keeping with Heloise's later writing influences. Further, the development of the idea of 'dilectio'—love that operates through an act of choice—as something that can be manifested between men and women (Cicero had seen it as only relevant to male relationships) is entirely consonant with Heloise's philosophy of love.

The troop of nineteenth- and twentieth-century men who battled hard to crush the idea of Heloise as an author was driven by an assumption that medieval 'women did not write—in spite of ample evidence to the contrary.'[38] Across time, similar attempts to silence or limit the voices of female authors are evident when we look at other women too. The most famous English medieval female author is Margery Kempe, who dictated her autobiographical book in the 1430s. When Wynkyn de Worde chose to print it in 1501, he printed a radically cut and changed version, removing all the more personal and interesting parts of the text, and turning it into a standard—and short—selection of devotional musings, titled *A shorte treatyse of contemplacyon taught by our lorde Ihesu*. As we saw in the previous chapter, Henry Pepwell went even further when he reprinted the text in 1521, turning Margery into an anchoress.[39] Margery's life was dominated not only by her rootedness in the sexual economy but also by extravagant travel, as far afield as the Holy Land: the idea of her as an anchoress, who by definition stays in one place, is absurd. The early printers thus made Margery 'safe,' by turning her into the kind of woman who *was* allowed to think and write (a devout anchoress), and giving her the kind of subject matter that was acceptable for a woman to consider. When her book was discovered during a raucous game of ping-pong in the 1930s at the Butler-Bowdens' stately home, critics were dismayed by what she was really like, and her rehabilitation was a long time coming.[40] Debates continue to rage about whether or not she can 'really' be considered an author given that she dictated her book.

The female author who is most similar to the fictional Alison in her interest in challenging the male-centric canon is a woman who was Chaucer's contemporary and whose life and circle overlapped with his in many intriguing ways. Christine de Pizan is one of the most interesting medieval women and one of the most original and versatile medieval writers. Born around 1364 in Venice, she spent most of her life around the French court, moving to Paris as a young child when her father got a job with Charles V as an adviser and astrologer. Christine was a well-educated girl, whose father in particular encouraged her studies. She married in her teens and had three children. When Christine was in her early twenties, her father died and, a couple of years later, she was widowed. As her brothers had moved to Bologna, Christine, aged about twenty-five, was now left with three young children, her mother, and other dependents; she was harassed by lawsuits and denied the money that she was owed. Her response was to decide to provide for herself and her family by becoming a professional writer—a truly audacious and extraordinary decision. Her literary output over the next few decades included the *Book of the City of Ladies*, the *Book of the Three Virtues*, a (commissioned) biography of Charles V, a series of attacks on the *Roman de la Rose*, and the first poem about Joan of Arc. Many of her texts include some autobiography, and they also frequently include defences of women and discussion of the misogyny of literary culture.[41]

Like Alison of Bath, Christine directly addressed the bias of the canon, most notably in the arresting scene with which she opened the *Book of the City of Ladies*. She described the origins of the book, imagining a scene in which she was sitting in her study, surrounded by books, reading a volume by Matheolus. As she read, she began to wonder why so many men wrote terrible things about women, why so many authorities seemed to speak 'with one voice' in their utter condemnation of the whole female sex. Christine thought about herself and about all the women that she knew, and could make no sense of this, finding no evidence from her personal experience that women were the kind of creatures depicted by authoritative texts— but assuming that the writings must be correct. Three ladies (Reason, Rectitude, and Justice) now visited Christine and comforted her, explaining that women have been attacked so unfairly and for so long because there has been no one to defend them. Women have endured 'the countless verbal and written assaults that have been unjustly and shamelessly launched upon them,' while no one has written texts to give the other side of the story. Now Christine is being asked to do that, to write about women who are 'of good reputation and worthy of praise.' Her task is to build a city of ladies, an edifice in which women can be kept safe from attack, and that can oppose the formidable architecture of misogyny.[42]

Christine's concern with the painting of lions is seen elsewhere in her writings too—indeed issues of gendered authorship are a constant preoccupation for her. In the *Epistre au Dieu d'Amours*, for instance, Cupid asserts that clerkly authors did not know much about women. He goes on to state: 'Should it be said that books are filled with tales / [of misogynist teachings] ... / To this I say that books were not composed / By women,' adding, 'If women, though, had written all those books / I know that they would read quite differently.'[43] This is fascinatingly similar to Alison's argument—she too blames the bias of clerks, explicitly comments that women have not had the chance to answer, and says that if women had written stories, they would have said very different things.

Both Alison and Christine are oppressed by the same set of antifeminist—and specifically misogamist—authors, including Walter Map, Theophrastus, and Jerome, as well as Matheolus. The umbrella text that channelled a great deal of misogyny and cast a shadow over so much late-medieval culture was the *Roman de la Rose*. The Wife of Bath's Prologue is partly a struggle with the *Roman*, an agon in which Alison takes La Vielle and performs a version of her, with knowing and witty panache, with feeling, and with humour. This performance reveals the bitter narrowness of Jean de Meun's portrayal, just as the scene with the book of wicked wives demonstrates the trauma, both physical and emotional, caused by misogynist texts. As I mentioned in the prologue to this part of the book, in the *Querelle de la Rose*, Christine tells a story in which a husband reads the *Roman de la Rose* to his wife and uses it as an excuse to attack her physically, comparing her to the women in the text.[44]

The *Roman de la Rose*, indeed, was a text that structured much of Christine's thought. In the *Epistre au Dieu d'Amour*, she dismisses this exceptionally influential and problematic text: 'What a long affair!' (Quel lonc procés! [390]).[45] She then became involved in a series of exchanges about the *Roman*, in which she and Jean Gerson criticised the poem, and Jean de Montreuil and Gontier Col defended de Meun and his text. In this extraordinary exchange, Christine pioneered the idea that women might actually take part in theoretical discussions about their sex. Christine praised women, and marriage, deploring de Meun's attitudes and characters such as La Vielle. The fact that she was a highly respected intellectual and writer whose own contributions to the debate were measured and reasoned did not save Christine from personal *ad feminam* abuse. While one of her opponents said she was motivated by 'presumption or arrogance,' another compared her to 'the Greek whore who dared to write against Theophrastus.'[46] Undaunted, Christine gathered and edited some of the texts in the *querelle*, curating the discussion herself. Christine's response to the *Rose* was ultimately to present herself as something unprecedented—a female clerk who could begin to build an edifice of women to oppose the relentless misogyny of clerkly writers.[47]

The *Roman* was such a significant text in the history of misogyny because (as Kevin Brownlee has argued) it was the privileged text in both of the major vernacular literary discourses of the later Middle Ages. The first part of the text was the key 'model courtly text,' with its focus on the desiring male and the silent female object of desire; the second part was the key 'model clerkly text,' dominated by the institutional, clerkly, satirical misogyny of Jean de Meun.[48] Thinking about these two models, it is worth noting that while the Wife of Bath's Prologue attacks and dismantles *clerical* misogyny through its focus on the writings of the church fathers, the Tale undermines the gender politics of *courtly* discourse. It does this first by demonstrating that rape is a predictable consequence of focusing on male desire and female objectification, and then by exploring a story in which a man is taught to consider female desire and a woman uses her voice to explain Christian ethics to him.

The fictional Alison and the real Christine perceived many of the same problems, but they often responded to those problems in different ways. Much of Alison's performative excess included precisely the kind of behaviour that Christine condemned; indeed, Christine recommended that wives behave in a traditionally dutiful way.[49] Their similarities, however, are striking. Both attempt to create a space in which women who have been married, who have worked for a living, who have struggled for economic stability could be heard. Not only did they assert that women could tell stories; both also made it clear that the suppression of women's voices had resulted in an appallingly biased and aggressive canon, a set of clerkly texts that had become the prompts for violence against women's bodies. The similarities between the sets of texts against which each was speaking are testaments to the uniformity of clerical misogyny in the late fourteenth and early fifteenth centuries.

Chaucer's circle intersected with Christine's in several fascinating ways. Putting them side by side does not reveal a direct relationship of source and response; rather it demonstrates how tightly knit English and French literary circles were, and that by the turn of the fifteenth century, some readers (such as Hoccleve) were certainly engaging with both authors. It is very probable that Chaucer and Christine knew of each other, at the least. Chaucer was about twenty years older than Christine and was certainly writing by the 1370s, while Christine turned to writing in the early 1390s, around the time that Chaucer was working intensively on the *Canterbury Tales* and revising the *Prologue to the Legend of Good Women*. Chaucer died as Christine was beginning a period of prolific writing. She outlived Chaucer by more than thirty years.

The strongest connection between them was provided by John Montagu, earl of Salisbury. Montagu was a member of the so-called Chaucer circle, a group of men with whom Chaucer is often associated in documents and who are likely to have been his earliest readers. This group mainly comprised chamber knights; they tended to be men with court associations who had been attached to the Black Prince's household in some way and who had interests in Wycliffite thought, in poetry, and in education.[50] Montagu and Chaucer travelled together to Montreuil in France for peace negotiations in 1377, and Montagu—like other members of the circle, including Sir John Clanvowe—was himself a poet. In the late 1390s, Christine and Montagu met in France. They admired each other's poetry, and Christine both praised his poems in her *Vision* and gave him a manuscript of her own verse. He then took her son, Jean, into the Montagu household to be educated alongside his own son, Thomas.[51] There is thus a very direct connection between Christine and her son and Chaucer's poetic circle. Given that French poets such as Deschamps knew Chaucer's poetry back in the 1380s, it is unlikely that Christine did not know of Chaucer's work, even though we have no evidence that she could read English.[52] Chaucer may have read her early works; he was an insatiable reader, consuming huge amounts of French poetry as well as Italian, Latin, and, to a lesser extent, English texts, and we know that Christine's texts made it to England. Shortly after Chaucer's death, his follower, Hoccleve, produced a translation of Christine's *Letter to the God of Love*. Hoccleve, like Montagu, had texts by both authors on his desk. Jean, meanwhile, remained in Montagu's household for a few years. Montagu's career took a dark turn when he spearheaded the Epiphany Rising against Henry IV and was executed. Christine's poems then found their way to the king, who invited her to come to the English court. Henry had also given gifts to Chaucer, who wrote him a poem after his usurpation of the throne, and Henry was closely connected to Chaucer's son. Christine did not come, but she does seem to have presented Henry with a manuscript.[53] Fascinatingly, Chaucer's granddaughter Alice married Thomas Montagu, childhood companion of Christine's son, as her second husband, and (as we have seen) she owned at least one of Christine's books—the *Book of the City of Ladies*.

Christine's poetic identity was bound up with her gender. She wrote explicitly about the problematic nature of the male canon and about the need for women to write in order to try to redress the balance. While there have always been female writers, the post-plague period provided a particularly fertile environment for female talent to flourish. The second half of the fourteenth century saw an unprecedented rise of vernacular writing across Europe, which helped women because they were far more likely to be literate in their mother tongues than they were in Latin. In England, our first named female author writing in English was Julian of Norwich, who was indeed writing at precisely this historical moment—she was an exact contemporary of Chaucer's and probably began writing in the 1370s. The upsurge in interest in vernacular mysticism and in Lollardy, with its focus on women's ability to preach, also helped women to get their voices heard. And other European male authors as well as Chaucer were interested in the idea of women telling stories—seven out of Boccaccio's ten tale-tellers in the *Decameron* are women.

Christine wrote that a widow had to metamorphose into a man in order to protect herself and pursue her own advantage.[54] In some texts she voiced a male perspective, but she was assiduous in naming herself and discussing autobiographical experiences in her writings. Yet we frequently see scribes actually turning her into a man and eliding female authority from her texts. Readers found it hard to believe that a woman could have written the *Le Livre des faits d'armes* (*Feats of Arms and of Chivalry*), although Christine herself had written in other texts about how important it was for well-born women to understand military matters, as they might well find themselves having to muster troops and defend their manor, for instance.[55] At the end of Christine's life too, Joan of Arc was to vindicate the belief that women could be involved in military matters—and Joan formed the subject of Christine's last text. But in several manuscripts of *Le Livre des faits d'armes*, masculine pronouns replaced feminine ones, and the invocation to Minerva was removed. The first French printed edition also followed these versions.[56] In the English tradition, the attack on her authorship was widespread and consistent. Although Christine was the most widely read female writer in fifteenth-century England, with her texts circulating in manuscript and print, when her texts were translated into English, their authorship was almost always reassigned to male clerks, whom Christine had allegedly patronised, or to male translators.[57] For instance, Stephen Scrope translated Christine's *L'epistre d'Othea* as *The Book of Knyghthode* in the middle of the fifteenth century, presenting it to his stepfather, Sir John Fastolf. He claimed, in the preface, that the text had been 'compiled & grounded by the famous doctors of the most excellent in clerge the nobly Uniuersite off Paris' and that they had done this 'at the instaunce & praer off a full wyse gentylwoman of Fraunce called Dame Cristine.'[58] Christine is thus rebranded as a respected patron but *authorship* is assigned to educated, male clergy. Similarly, in his *Boke of Noblesse*, a text heavily dependent on Christine's *Le Livre des faits d'armes*, William Worcester asserted not only that Christine 'employed many clerks in the University of Paris, and made them compile many virtuous books,' but even that she 'was born, died, and lived in a religious house in Poissy near Paris.'[59] In fact, Christine only retreated to a religious house for the very last years of her life, but here Worcester removes her from the world and from her active life as someone who knew politicians, kings, and courtiers; was a wife and mother; and earned money to provide for a family. This cloistering of Christine is fascinatingly similar to Pepwell's enclosing of Margery Kempe as an anchoress. Christine de Pizan, the pioneering authoress who explicitly wrote about the lack of female authors, the defence of married women, and the importance of women entering the canon, was, within a few years of her death, transformed into a nun whose persistent connections with writing could be explained by her patronage of clerkly men—the only acceptable storytellers in literary tradition.

Looking at the experiences of Heloise, Kempe, and Christine reveals that although medieval women did tell their stories, the discouragement, disapproval, and outright antagonism that they faced was not only real but extended from the medieval period to the modern day. When Alison complained about the painting of lions and the difficulty of getting her voice heard, she was identifying a problem at the heart of late-medieval culture, a problem that still resonates in today's very different world.

CHAPTER 5

The Wandering Woman

Woman is sedentary, Man hunts, journeys.

—ROLAND BARTHES, *A LOVER'S*
DISCOURSE, FRAGMENTS

One of the most extravagant details about the Wife of Bath, in her General Prologue portrait, is her travel history:

> And thries hadde she been at Jerusalem;
> She hadde passed many a straunge strem;
> At Rome she hadde been, and at Boloigne,
> In Galice at Seint-Jame, and at Coloigne.
> She koude muchel of wandrynge by the weye (463–467)

Now on a relatively local pilgrimage to Canterbury, in the past she has been three times to Jerusalem, as well as visiting Rome, Boulogne, Santiago de Compostela, and Cologne. Like everything else about Alison, the extent of her travels seems excessive and opulent, but it is not incredible: in the fifteenth century William Wey, an English traveller and cleric, went twice to Jerusalem, taking in Rome on the first of those trips, and he also journeyed to Santiago, recording his experiences in itineraries.[1] But a woman engaging in many pilgrimages attracted a particular kind of attention—Alison's extensive travelling is a metaphor for her adventurous and unconventional attitudes more generally. When Chaucer tells us that she knew a great deal 'of wandrynge by the weye,' he suggests that her wandering is not only literal: she deviates from the expected paths; she won't do what men want her to do. The word 'wander' suggests errancy, and harks back to Augustine's depiction of people on earth as 'peregrini' (wanderers), straying away from God, who need to focus on the kingdom of heaven, not the distractions of the journey.[2] This unease around the idea of the wanderer was intensified in the rhetoric surrounding female travellers.

Indeed, there was a long tradition of regarding with suspicion women who did not stay at home. The key source for the idea of the wandering woman is Proverbs 7, which describes the errant harlot as 'talkative and wandering [vaga], not bearing to be quiet, not able to abide still at home' (10–11). In later medieval texts, the wandering woman is specifically depicted as a pilgrim, someone who (in Lydgate's words) seeks many pilgrimages 'To kys no shrynes, but lusty yong images.'[3] By the later Middle Ages, pilgrimage was a hugely popular activity across Europe, and large numbers of women did travel to shrines, both local and more distant. While going on pilgrimage was arduous, expensive, and sometimes dangerous, it also presented opportunities that were hard to find at home. There is a good example of this in the late-medieval poem, 'The Good Wyfe Wold a Pylgremage,' in which a mother who is about to set off on 'pylgremage unto þe holly londe' (1) gives advice to her daughter on how to behave. She exhorts her daughter: 'When I am out of þe toun, loke that þou be wyse, / And rene þou not fro hous to house lyke an Antyny gryce' (7–8).[4] A 'gryce' is a piglet, and an 'Antyny' or 'Tantony' pig is the smallest pig of the litter. In this couplet, she juxtaposes two different modes of female behaviour: she herself can travel thousands of miles, leave her home, journey right across Europe and over to the Holy Land—but her daughter, staying in her community, should not even go from house to house. That kind of local wandering is compared to the behaviour of an uncontained little piglet—but the speaker sees no contradiction in advising her daughter to stay within very narrow confines while she herself traverses the globe. Pilgrimage, as (in theory at least) religiously motivated teleological travel, offered a way of expanding women's horizons.

Male pilgrims did not always welcome this. In a fifteenth-century account of his pilgrimage to Jerusalem, Brother Felix Fabri comments with admiration on the bravery of the old pilgrim women whom he met in Venice, while pointing out that the younger male pilgrims despised them:

> certain women well-stricken in years, wealthy matrons, six in number, were there together with us, desiring to cross the sea to the holy places. I was astonished at the courage of these old women, who through old age were scarcely able to support their own weight, yet forgot their own frailty, and through love for the Holy Land joined themselves to young knights and underwent the labours of strong men. The proud nobles, however, were not pleased at this, and thought that they would not embark in the ship in which these ladies were to go, considering it a disgrace that they should go to receive the honour of knighthood in company with old women.

These aristocratic male pilgrims try to persuade all the other travellers to refuse to go in the same ship as the old women, but others oppose them, so that ultimately the aggressive men depart, and the women travel on in the same company as Fabri. He later tells us that on the ships, women pilgrims do not come to the common table, but eat and sleep in their berths, separated from the men who can move more freely about the ship. Later in his book, Fabri compares their admirable behaviour with the actions of a female pilgrim of whom he disapproves— on the grounds that she is curious, noisy, and, most inappropriately, 'ran hither and thither incessantly' and was 'restless.'[5]

The later Middle Ages saw a dramatic expansion in pilgrimage. The ninth and tenth centuries were characterised by instability all over Europe, as groups including Vikings, Arabs, and Magyars mounted raids across the continent. At the end of the tenth century, as the Byzantine emperor extended his lands, reconquering cities including Antioch, it became easier for Europeans to travel to Jerusalem. Throughout the eleventh century, pilgrimage increased in popularity: hospices were constructed along the Camino de Santiago, for instance, and pressure built for a crusade-pilgrimage to the Holy Land. No clear distinction was made between crusade and pilgrimage at this time—both were seen as religiously motivated travel.[6] The conquest of Jerusalem in 1099 led to greatly increased traffic to the places of Christ's life and death—and the twelfth century also saw the rise of the important English pilgrimage to Canterbury, following Becket's death in 1170. The other major English pilgrimage, to Walsingham, which found its origins in the eleventh-century visions of a woman, Richeldis de Faverches, grew in importance in subsequent years.[7] The twelfth century was also the century of affect, a time in which Christians were increasingly interested in responding to God with emotion, in focusing on the suffering body of Christ and trying to imagine and relive his agonies.[8] While this was not a wholly new way to respond to Christ, interest in affect greatly expanded in the later Middle Ages. Pilgrims to the Holy Land followed in Christ's footsteps, attempting to imitate and repeat his life journey. The fall of Jerusalem to Saladin in 1187 did not end the pilgrimage trade, nor did the fall of Acre in 1291. Increasingly, pilgrims travelled to the Holy Land by ship from Venice, via Crete, Rhodes, Cyprus, and Jaffa.[9] Venetian merchants offered complete package tours, organising food and board, tolls and taxes, local Muslim guides to escort the visitors from Jaffa to Jerusalem and on further expeditions, and local transport such as donkeys and packhorses.[10] It became a slick industry. European pilgrimages also continued to grow in popularity, particularly boosted by 'Jubilee' years, when the Pope declared extra indulgences for those who made their pilgrimage. In 1300, for example, pilgrims to Rome could obtain a plenary indulgence if they made thirty visits to each basilica (if they were Italian) or fifteen visits to each basilica (if they were foreigners), each visit to be made on separate days.[11] Such requirements maximised the length of time that pilgrims spent in the city, and therefore greatly benefitted a whole range of local people, particularly those in the accommodation, food, and souvenir industries. In the later Middle Ages, many guides for pilgrims and accounts of journeys, in both prose and poetry, were produced, which give us a wealth of information about such matters as what to take on the boat to Jerusalem (mattresses, warm clothes, wine, extra food, spices, writing materials, and games such as cards, dice, or chess) or where it is and is not safe to drink river water in northern Spain.[12]

Women were as interested in pilgrimage as men were. In general, women were more likely to go to local shrines than to be able to travel far afield to distant centres of pilgrimage. Some historians have argued that the majority of travellers going to local shrines were women and the poor, while the majority of those visiting distant shrines were men and members of the upper classes.[13] It also seems that some shrines overall had more female visitors, as there are more recorded miracles and cures for women, rather than men at shrines including Saint Frideswide's (Oxford) and Godric of Finchale's shrine in County Durham.[14] Medieval records provide many examples of women giving donations and bequests to shrines, and of women undertaking pilgrimage to ask for healing for themselves or for their children. A stained glass window in York Minster, known as the Pilgrimage Window, features both a male and a female pilgrim (see fig. 2).[15] The woman, in the bottom right-hand corner, is dressed as a pilgrim, with a staff and scrip, accompanied by a squire on horseback holding a pilgrim's hat. As she is one of the donors of the window, this is clearly a wealthy female pilgrim. Although a range of women did travel, the majority of pilgrims going on lengthy journeys were relatively affluent—women such as 'Ida lady of Nevill of Essex,' who went to Rome in 1350 with twenty servants and twenty horses.[16] Similarly, Henry IV granted a licence in 1403 to Agnes Bardolf, lady of Wormegay, widow of Thomas Mortimer: 'to go on pilgrimage to the cities of Rome and Cologne and other foreign parts from any port of the realm with twelve men and twelve horses in her company and her goods and harness, and to pay 300 l. for her expenses to merchants of Genoa or other persons in the realm, who will pay to her letters of exchange to their fellows in foreign parts.'[17] Important here is the licence to take money abroad, and the fact that she is going to visit a number of different pilgrimage sites. Some women took multiple trips: Saint Bridget (Birgitta) of Sweden, for instance, went to Assisi and Trondheim in 1338; to Compostela in 1341, via Cologne, Aachen, and Tarascon; to Rome in 1349; to Jerusalem in 1372; and to other pilgrimage sites including Bari and Monte Gargano.[18] For women such as Birgitta and Margery Kempe, pilgrimage involved intense mystical experiences and visions and was a generative and transformational part of their religious lives and identities. Other women combined their pilgrimages with commercial activities: for instance, Agnes Proude, alias Tudor, who did business at the curia in Viterbo while also making pilgrimages to Cologne and Rome.[19] Those women who did undertake the most far-flung journeys were specifically catered for: in Jerusalem, for example, there were hospices set up for female travellers, including one on Mount Sion, founded in 1353 by Sofia de Arcangelis and attached to the Franciscan hospice there.[20]

The soundtrack in the background of women's interest in pilgrimage and travel was an insistent misogyny. Back in the eighth century, Saint Boniface, the English missionary and archbishop of Mainz, asked Cuthbert, the archbishop of Canterbury to 'forbid matrons and veiled women to make these frequent journeys back and forth to Rome. A great part of them perish and few keep their virtue. There are very few towns in Lombardy or Frankland or Gaul where there is not a courtesan or a harlot of English stock. It is a scandal and a disgrace to your whole church.'[21] Female pilgrims are obsessively connected with sexual impropriety; Boniface claims that some of these women travel frequently to Rome, engaging in sexual depravity, while others remain in European towns as prostitutes. This idea of pilgrimage as a cover for sexual excess became commonplace. The English translation of the *Book of the Knight of La Tour Landry*, for instance, criticises women 'that gone on pilgrimage to a place for foule plesaunce more thane devoccion'[22] and Christine de Pizan warns that some women go on pilgrimage 'to play about or kick up [their] heels.'[23] A particularly striking example of the idea of the sexualised female pilgrim can be found in a pilgrim badge from the Netherlands dating from the later fourteenth or early fifteenth century (see fig. 3).[24] This badge depicts the pilgrim as a walking vulva, clearly depicted, and dressed in pilgrims' garb—wearing a floppy pilgrim hat and carrying a staff and a rosary. The woman is reduced only to her genitals; the purpose of pilgrimage is purely sexual. While there are other bawdy pilgrim badges—including one in which a woman pushes a wheelbarrow full of penises, and another in which three penises carry a litter on which reigns a crowned vulva—this one is especially striking as the sexual organ is itself turned into a pilgrim. The existence of this bizarre badge exemplifies Morrison's argument that the 'sexual woman pilgrim is symbolically central to the imagination of post-plague England.'[25]

The idea of the female pilgrim as camouflaged vulva lies behind the depiction of the much-travelled and sexually active Alison, but as ever, Chaucer's portrait is complex. Antifeminists want to see Alison, and women in general, in this way, and Alison at times performs this role, even suggesting that she has come on the Canterbury pilgrimage to look for a husband when she exclaims, 'Welcome the sixte!' (45). But, just as the places to which she has been reflect the actual pilgrim sites of the day, so a note of realism, rather than stereotype, is injected into her pilgrimage history when her travels simply become part of the fabric of her life. She tells us that her fourth husband died, 'whan I cam fro Jerusalem' (495). There is no implication that she was unfaithful or lecherous on the pilgrimage. While the reference in the General Prologue to three visits to the Holy Land is excessive and reminiscent of contemporary satire, within her own prologue, the detail is embedded into everyday life. Fifty lines later, Alison refers to pilgrimage not as a devotional exercise, but not as a sexual adventure either. It is a social activity for her. She tells her audience that she often walked 'fro hous to hous'—like the temptress of Proverbs—and that she did so not to commit adultery but 'to here sondry talys' (547), just as the whole Canterbury group are listening to tales on their pilgrimage journey. Alison goes on to describe her leisure activities, which include attending vigils and processions, listening to sermons, going on pilgrimages, watching miracle plays, and witnessing weddings (555–558). All of these are religious activities, but are also social occasions—for Alison, they are opportunities to dress up in her 'gaye scarlet' clothes (559). But on the longer Canterbury pilgrimage, she eschews her costumes of elaborate headdresses and scarlet hose; with an eye to the practical difficulties of the road she wears a large pilgrim's hat and a wimple, to protect her head from the dust and sun, and a foot-mantle (a kind of petticoat tied up to protect a rider's clothes) (General Prologue, 470–472). Far from being dressed as a temptress, focused on sexual conquests, she is dressed for the difficulties of travel, as befits a seasoned pilgrim.[26]

Indeed, medieval women, like medieval men, went on pilgrimage for a wide range of reasons, but for all female pilgrims, these journeys offered opportunities and experiences quite different from quotidian life at home. Medieval women travellers, as well as stories about medieval women travellers, were varied and certainly did not all follow the tired stereotypes of the wandering harlot/pilgrim-hatted vulva. Margaret of Beverley is a fascinating example of an adventurous, virtuous, and tough medieval travelling woman. Her story is told in a Latin verse text, allegedly written by her brother, although her experiences are recounted in the first person.[27] It is quite possible that they shared authorship, although it is also clear that the story is not all factually true—it is hagiographic and uses some well-worn tropes. According to the poem, Margaret's parents travelled from Yorkshire to Jerusalem while her mother was pregnant, so Margaret was herself born in Jerusalem around 1155. She then returned there in 1187, a crucial year in the history of Jerusalem: she tells us, 'Jerusalem capta dolore gemo' (I lament miserably the capture of Jerusalem [370]). There, she was caught up in Saladin's siege of the city and fought his army, wearing a cooking pot ('lebes' [371]) on her head as a helmet. Stuck in the wrong part of the city when a treaty was made, Margaret was able to pay a ransom to free herself and joined a group of others similarly 'redemptorum' (of the redeemed). Captured again, Margaret endured a series of trials—she was tortured and made to do hard labour—'lapides lego, congero ligna' (I picked up stones, I collected wood [372]). Describing those long days, Margaret says, 'Fervida longa dies, rara brevisque quies' (The long days were hot, and rest was rare and brief [372]). Ultimately, a benevolent man paid a ransom for the group on the day of the Feast of the Virgin. After this, Margaret wandered, alone, with only her Psalter to console her; she had little to eat and endured great privations. A Turk stole the Psalter, but then repented and returned it. On reaching Antioch, Margaret was falsely accused of theft and sentenced to death, but on invoking Mary, she was freed. She went back to Jerusalem, and then was able to return to Europe, continuing on pilgrimage to Compostela and Rome. In France, she was reunited with Thomas of Froidmont, her younger brother, a monk who had spent time in the household of Thomas Becket. She herself became a nun at Montreuil.

There is no reason to doubt that Margaret existed and travelled in the Holy Land and on extensive pilgrimages, though details such as fighting with a cooking pot on her head, or wandering in a wilderness with only a loaf of bread to sustain her for several days, are almost certainly fictional flourishes. If the story were entirely fictional, it would still tell us that an adventurous and virtuous travelling woman was imaginable and admirable in this era. And some of the details of her extraordinary story chime with the experiences of other medieval women. For instance, although it might seem surprising that her mother, after conception, set off from England to the Holy Land, women certainly did go on pilgrimage when pregnant. The English Hospice at Rome specifically mention in their Schedule that 'mulieres pregnantes recipiuntur donec purificentur' (pregnant women are received until purification).[28] Raymond de Puy, the Second Master of the Hospital of Saint John in Jerusalem, wrote directions about what to do with pregnant pilgrims and with babies born on pilgrimage.[29]

In the fourteenth century, Isolda Parewastel's experiences provide interesting comparisons with Margaret's most hair-raising experiences. In 1366, Isolda submitted a papal petition to Urban V, asking for a licence to found a chapel. She says, in this petition, that she visited the Holy Land for three years, during which time she was tortured and beaten, and finally escaped from the Saracens. Isolda had been caught up in the conflicts of 1365—conflicts, incidentally, about which Chaucer was well informed. That year saw the notorious battle of Alexandria, at which Chaucer's Knight allegedly fought, and which became something of a byword for atrocities.[30] The sultan launched reprisals against Christians, including pilgrims at Jerusalem; the Franciscan church at Mount Sion was destroyed; the monks there were tortured and, in some cases, killed; and the Church of the Holy Sepulchre was closed and threatened with destruction. According to her petition, Isolda was 'nuda pro Christi nomine in eculeo capite subuerso suspense durissima verbera sustinuit, et semiuiua relicta manus sarracenorum miraculose euasit' (stripped in the name of Christ, she was hung on the rack head to the ground and sustained very hard beatings, and then, being left half alive, she miraculously escaped from the hands of the Saracens).[31] Given the context of this story in a papal petition, it is implausible that this is a complete fantasy, and the timing of her visit—at the time of the reprisals for Alexandria—adds further weight to the story. She may well have stayed at the hospice for women set up by Sofia de Arcangelis, and thus have been caught up in the attacks on the Franciscans.[32] Medieval Englishwomen did experience serious danger on their journeys, and underwent dramatic and sometimes traumatic encounters on their pilgrimage-crusades. Isolda, like Margaret of Beverley, turns to the most iconic female saint, the Virgin Mary, to explain her eventual escape from her captors, asking permission from the pope to build a chapel 'ad honorem et laudem gloriose beate marie uirginis' (for the honour and renown of the glorious holy virgin Mary).

The most famous English medieval travelling woman was Margery Kempe who, like Alison of Bath and Margaret of Beverley, travelled to the three great pilgrimage sites of Jerusalem, Rome, and Santiago. She claims to have done so at the specific command of Christ (bk. I, chap. 15). Margery Kempe had an intense burst of travelling during her early forties, though she travelled, both around England and abroad, on many other occasions in her life. Her pilgrimage frenzy started in 1413, around her fortieth birthday, when she set off across Europe, wintered in Venice, and in spring 1414 sailed to the Holy Land. Later that year, she returned via Assisi and Rome, where she remained for about six months, going home after Easter 1415. Two years later, she made a more contained trip to Spain: Kempe set sail from Bristol to Santiago in early July, returning the following month. Uniquely, she left us her *Book*, which contains detailed accounts of both her practical and her devotional experiences while on these pilgrimages.[33]

Like Margaret of Beverley and Isolda Parewastel, Margery Kempe was travelling without a husband or other protector, and without a large retinue of servants. Ida, lady of Neville, with her twenty servants, and Agnes Bardolf, with her twelve, were cushioned from many of the practical difficulties of travel that women travelling with less luxury had to navigate. Kempe was extremely anxious about her personal safety. In sharp contrast to antifeminist allegations that women pilgrims were seeking sex, they were in fact at risk of rape, and Kempe repeatedly expresses her terror that this might happen to her. While in Constance, she prays, exhorting Christ to 'kepe wel my chastite that I vowyd to the, and late me nevyr be defowlyd, for yyf I be, Lord, I make myn avow I wyl nevyr come in Inglonde whil I leve' (bk. I, chap. 27). This fear of rape was a constant pressure on Kempe while travelling (and indeed at other times too): later in life, travelling to Aachen she is mocked with 'lewyd wordys,' by priests, and has 'drede for hir chastite.' She asks the woman in charge of the inn to let her sleep with other women in the room, but nonetheless 'durst sche not slepyn for dred of defilyng' (bk. II, chap. 6). She also fears robbery and violence—when considering leaving Rome to start the journey home, 'it was telde hem that ther wer many thevys be the wey which wolde spoyl hem of her goodys and peraventur slen hem' (bk. I, chap. 42). Kempe also recounts smaller incidents, such as the time that a priest from within her company stole her sheet on the ship from Venice to Jerusalem, swearing that it was his (bk. I, chap. 28).

The majority of Kempe's problems do, in fact, come from within the groups with which she travels. It was not sensible to travel alone, so a pilgrim setting out unaccompanied, or with only one or two servants or companions, would join a bigger company—just as we see happening at the Tabard Inn in the General Prologue of the *Canterbury Tales*, when the Chaucer figure joins a group of strangers for a pilgrimage. When Kempe sets out for Jerusalem, she joins a group at Yarmouth to take a ship to the Netherlands, but the group very soon becomes frustrated with her habits, and bullies her. By her account, the 'cumpany' is particularly annoyed by her vegetarianism, and because 'sche wepyd so mech and spak alwey of the lofe [love] and goodness of owyr Lord' (bk. I, chap. 26). Even her own maid gangs up with them, and they try to push her out of their group altogether—eventually allowing her to travel on with them, but dressing her as a fool in a short gown and making her sit away from them, at the lowest seat on the table. Indeed, for much of the pilgrimage, she describes the tensions with these fellow pilgrims, who do reject her at Constance but allow her back into their group in Bologna (on the condition that she will not talk any more about the Gospel, but 'schal sytten style and makyn mery, as we don, bothin at mete and at soper' (bk. I, chap. 27). It is clear that Kempe's own views about pilgrimage are quite different from the views of her companions, who are more focused on relaxing and making merry. When she breaks the agreement, and does start talking about the Bible, they refuse to eat with her any more, and make her eat alone in her chamber for six weeks. After the pilgrimage to the Holy Land, and their return to Venice, her group abandons her again (bk. I, chap. 30).

On the many occasions when Kempe is abandoned by her company, she has real difficulties: she cannot safely travel on alone, so she needs to find a respectable and willing protector. In Constance, that role is taken by an old man from Devonshire, William Weaver, although she is very frightened of travelling without a large company (bk. I, chap. 27). Later, when she needs to travel from Venice to Rome, she is accompanied by Richard of Ireland, a 'broke-bakkyd' man, whose help had been foretold to her before she left England. He is reluctant to take on this role—explicitly saying that when she was travelling with a large group, they had weapons to defend her ('bowys and arwys'), but if she is with him, they will both be in danger of robbery, and she will be at risk of rape (bk. I, chap. 30). In the Holy Land, Kempe juxtaposes the behaviour of her English fellowship with the behaviour of Saracen strangers. Her own group refuses to help her to climb a hill near Jericho, the site of Jesus's temptation. But then a Muslim passing by agrees to help her, just as a little later, the Muslims in general 'mad mych of hir and conveyd hir and leddyn hir abowtyn in the cuntre wher sche wold gon.' Kempe even says that 'sche fond alle pepyl good onto hir and gentyl, saf only hir owyn cuntremen' (bk. I, chap. 30).

The difficulties of travel for a woman at this time are made very clear in Kempe's *Book*, but for her, they are worth enduring for the intense religious experiences that she undergoes. But for other women, travel offered more practical opportunities— opportunities to change one's life and career. The story of Kempe's pilgrimage to the Holy Land and Rome is also the story of what happened to her maid, who appears periodically in the narrative.[34] This character is a fascinating example of the social possibilities that service could open up for a bright (if, in this case, possibly unscrupulous) woman at this time.[35] In chapter 26 of book I, Kempe tells us that she was travelling with her own female servant, and that this maid betrayed her. When she is embroiled in conflicts with the fellowship of pilgrims, 'summe of the company on whech sche trostyd best, and hir owyn mayden also, seyden sche schuld no lengar gon in her felaschep, and thei seyden thei woldyn han awey hyr mayden fro hir that sche schuld no strumpet be in hyr company.' According to this account, her maid has joined forces with the others against Margery—and this is painted as the ultimate betrayal, as both those whom she most trusts, and her 'owyn' maiden turn against her. Partly, this contributes to Kempe's portrayal of herself as Christ-like, betrayed by her own follower.[36] The specific reasons that the company gives for encouraging her maid to leave her are interestingly gender-specific—despite Kempe's deep concern with chastity, her oddness is enough for the company to throw sexual accusations at her, saying that the maid may end up a 'strumpet' in her company. Or perhaps the implication is that they are acknowledging that women travelling without the protection of men will be vulnerable to sexual attack.

The betrayal of the maid, and her choosing to attach herself to new friends and employers is further emphasised in the next chapter. Kempe tells us that the other pilgrims stole her money and 'thei wythheldyn also hir mayden and wolde not letyn hir gon with hir maystres, notwythstondyng sche had behestyd [promised] hir maystres and sekyrd hir that sche schylde not forsake hir for no nede.' Here, Kempe makes clear that the maiden has broken her promise, and implicates the whole group in refusing to allow justice to take place. At home, Kempe might have had more redress; on pilgrimage, people are freer to choose their own paths. At the end of chapter 27, when Kempe has been consigned to solitary meals in her chamber, she returns to the subject of her maid, reiterating that 'hir mayden let hir alone and mad the cumpanyes mete and wesch her clothis, and to hir maystres, whom sche had behestyd servyse, sche wolde no dele attende.' Again, the betrayal of her promise—her behest—is stressed, as is Margery's isolation. At this point it might be hard to see exactly what the maid has gained—she is still doing the same kind of work, after all. But perhaps she is being paid more; perhaps she wants to make sure she can stay in the safety of the group and not be turned out with Margery to fend for themselves; perhaps she, like the rest of the fellowship, simply does not like Margery's talking about God, or her habits.

When we next meet her, it is clear that this servant girl has made some shrewd choices. In Rome, when Margery finally gets access to the English Hospice of Saint Thomas, she finds that her maid has moved up in the world—her travels have allowed her to gain new and lucrative employment. Kempe tells us:

> Than fond sche ther hir that was hir mayden beforetyme, and wyth right schulde a be so stylle, dwelling in the Hospital in meche *welth and prosperyte,* for sche was *kepar of her wyn.* And this creatur went sumtyme to hir for cawse of mekenes and preyd hir of mete and drynke, and the mayden yaf hir with good wyl, and sumtyme a grote therto. Than sche compleyned to hir mayden, and seyd that sche thowt gret swem [felt great sorrow] of her departing, and what slawndir and evyl wordys men seyd of hir for thei wer asundyr, but *wold sche nevyr the rather be ageyn with hir* (bk. I, chap. 39, emphasis mine).

Kempe recounts here that she found her erstwhile servant in a much more elevated and responsible position. She is now the cellarer of the large and important English Hospice, in charge of the wine. The former maid dispenses food and drink to Margery, and indeed is now doing so well that she even gives charity to her former mistress ('sumtyme a grote therto'). Margery complains about her leaving, but the maid will not consider returning to her service. This servant has managed completely to reverse their positions during the course of the pilgrimage, so that she is now the one in control, even in a position of patronage to someone who had earlier been her employer.

Working at the English Hospice would be a very desirable and responsible job. The English community in Rome, fronted by John and Alice Shepherd, bought the property that became the hospice in 1362.[37] Other nations too had bases in Rome that catered particularly for their own groups, though the English Hospice did also cater for the Irish, Welsh, and Scots. As time went on, the English hospital not only provided accommodation and care for those who needed it, but also lent money, looked after the property of some members, and received post for travellers and expatriates. Early on in its history, many Englishmen and women contributed to its costs—these included the great London merchant John Philipot (who was later to marry Margaret Stodeye) and his wife Jane, and Sir John Hawkwood, the most notorious and successful English mercenary, with whom Chaucer negotiated in Lombardy in 1378. Soon, the hospice became known as a 'good cause' and received many donations from England, in return for indulgences. Englishmen and -women living in Rome also bequeathed it further property: one example is Elena Clerk, who left the hospice a house in Pizzomerle in 1390, with the proviso that Agnes Taylor could stay in it for her lifetime, and that Cecilia Howden could also live there if Agnes agreed. Elena also left the hospice her three best beds, three quilts, three pairs of sheets, and a great copper kettle. By 1406, the hospice owned twenty houses and two separate shops.[38] A later inventory (1501) suggests that in usual times, about sixty people could stay there, but many more could be squeezed in at particularly busy times of year.[39] This hospice, then, was big business, and Margery's maid must have had her wits about her to have secured a job there with significant responsibility. Travelling could offer women the opportunity to reinvent themselves.

As the experiences of the maid show, travellers tended to stick with people from their own nation. The maid, along with Margery, initially travelled in a group from her own country, and in Rome she got a job at the English Hospice, working for and with (mainly) English people. Guidebooks for pilgrims sometimes make painfully clear the prejudices of the authors. The fascinating twelfth-century *Pilgrim's Guide to Santiago de Compostela*, for instance, spends some time describing the 'characteristics of the lands and people on his road.'[40] The description of the Navarrese is particularly intemperate, beginning with the assessment that they 'are repulsively dressed, and they eat and drink repulsively.' The author goes on to whip himself up into a frenzy of disgust, informing his readers that:

> This is a barbarous race unlike all other races in customs and in character, full of malice, swarthy in colour, evil of face, depraved, perverse, perfidious, empty of faith and corrupt, libidinous, drunken, experienced in all violence, ferocious and wild, dishonest and reprobate, impious and harsh, cruel and contentious, unversed in anything good, well-trained in all vices and iniquities, like the Geats and Saracens in malice.

He goes on to make claims about their sexual proclivities, claiming that Navarrese men perform cunnilingus on women, and also on mules, termed 'libidinous kisses to the vulva of woman and mule.' This, perhaps, is the direst of warnings: get involved with a man from Navarre on your travels, and you might end up experiencing oral sex—depicted as a vice equivalent to bestiality. The author implies, however, that English travellers might not need to travel so far to find such practices, as the Navarrese, are 'commonly said to be descended from the race of the Scots because they are similar to them in customs and appearance.'[41]

Other texts, however, do suggest a desire to engage with people beyond one's own travelling group while on a journey. The *Manières de Langages* texts are conversational manuals, designed to help English people with their spoken French. These could be useful for travels within England as well as on the Continent, as many people within England (both English and visitors) knew French, and it was widely spoken across many countries.[42] Some of the role-play scenes are set on the road, including one in an inn, at bedtime. This scene helps a traveller to discuss their bedbug problem with other travellers: 'He! Les puces me mordent fort et me font grant mal et damage car je m'ay gratee le dos si fort que le sang se coule et pour ce je commence a ester roignous, et tout le corps me mange tres malement' (Aagh! The fleas bite me hard and cause me great pain and harm because I scratched my back so hard that the blood's running and on account of this I'm getting all scabby and my entire body is being eaten very painfully).[43] The *Manières* texts assume that a traveller would want to be able to discuss what is happening to them, using a different language to make sure they were understood—there is an assumption of the importance of communicating beyond one's native language while travelling. One role-play even deals with how to try to find a pilgrimage companion: 'He! Mon amy, il me faut aler on pelerinage pour sercher saint Thomas de Canterbers. Vuillez vous aler avecque moi?' (Hello! My friend, I need to go on a pilgrimage to seek Saint Thomas of Canterbury. Would you like to go with me?). It also offers a neat way politely to decline such an invitation, with the interlocutor inviting his fellow traveller to look at his leg, which is so 'enfleez' (inflamed) that he has great 'cremeur qu'il devendra un mormal' (fear that it will become gangrenous).[44]

Margery Kempe several times mentions language difficulties and her desire to communicate with foreign acquaintances— and indeed she is consistently complimentary about those that she meets from other countries, including the Muslims in the Holy Land, as noted above. She gives a very recognisable picture of the attempt to communicate without a common language when she and Margarete Florentyn could not 'wel understand other but be syngnys er tokenys and in fewe comown wordys.' They then manage to communicate in a hybrid language, when Margarete asks her 'Margerya in poverte?' with Margery replying 'Ya, grawnt poverte, Madam' (bk. I, chap. 38). Margery's experience is that her fellow English travellers reject her, but strangers welcome her and try to help her in all the places to which she makes her pilgrimage. She herself, however, is the object of xenophobic stereotyping on her journey to Aachen, when a group of German priests abuse her, using the common slur against English people that they had tails, and addressing her as 'Englisch sterte [tail]' (bk. II, chap. 6).[45]

In many pilgrim accounts, however, travellers minimise their contact with those outside their national group, performing their pilgrimage, staying in the hospice and area associated with their country, and buying souvenirs to take home with them. The *Pilgrim's Guide to Santiago de Compostela*, written by a French author, discusses which door of the church French people usually enter at Santiago de Compostela and describes the money changers, hotel keepers, and merchants that abound on the 'Street of the French.' Hieronymus Munzer, writing in the fifteenth century, said that in Santiago, the citizens were 'fat as pigs and slothful at that, for they have no need to cultivate the soil when they can live off the pilgrims instead.'[46] The author of the *Pilgrim's Guide* tells his pilgrim readers that in the parvis, on the north side of the church, travellers can buy a range of things useful to pilgrims including 'wine flasks, sandals, deerskin scripts, pouches, straps, belts and all sorts of medicinal herbs and other spices,' as well as, most importantly, the scallop shells, which are still a widely recognised sign of the pilgrimage to Santiago.[47] As Laura Hodges speculates, contemporary readers of the General Prologue might well have imagined that the Wife of Bath, the only member of the company to wear a traditional pilgrim's hat, would have followed 'the customary practice of displaying her pilgrim badges from Jerusalem, Rome,

Bouloyne, Galicia, and Cologne on the crown of this hat.'[48] Medieval pilgrims wanted to display their track record and their cosmopolitan experiences, but did not always want to enter into meaningful encounters with other cultures and places, often preferring to stay in their psychological comfort zone.

⚜

In the fifteenth century, an anonymous author imagined what might have happened when Chaucer's pilgrims reached Canterbury. This text—known as the 'Canterbury Interlude'— appears in the Alnwick manuscript of the *Canterbury Tales*, in which the tales are arranged as a two-way journey, with the 'Interlude' and a non-Chaucerian Tale interpolated in the middle.[49] This fascinating piece of fan fiction describes the pilgrims arriving at the Chequer of the Hoop in Canterbury—a real inn built for the pilgrim trade in the 1390s, located on the west corner of Mercery Lane and the High Street. The Pardoner flirts with and tries to make sexual assignations with Kit the tapster (barmaid-prostitute); the pilgrims in general sort out their lodging, and then go to the cathedral, where they admire the stained glass, make offerings, pray, kiss relics, and buy souvenirs. The poet writes that 'signes there they bought / For men of contre shuld know whom they had soughte' (171–172), making explicit their self-aggrandizing motivation. After dinner back at the Chequer of the Hoop, the Knight and others go to look at the walls and fortifications of Canterbury, while the clerics go out drinking. With the exception of the Pardoner, who is pursuing Kit the tapster, every one of the pilgrims goes to explore Canterbury, save only the Prioress and the Wife of Bath.

Alison does not go out 'wandering by the way' in this text. Instead, we are told that 'The Wyff of Bath was so wery, she had no will to walk' (281). Rather than setting off on adventures, she asks the Prioress to come to the garden with her to see the herbs, and then to sit in the parlour with the host's wife, to drink wine peacefully. Their soothing environment in the herb garden is described to us: 'And al the aleyes feir i-pared, i-rayled and i-maked / The sauge and the isope i-fretted and i-staked' (And all the pathways beautifully trimmed, fenced, and crafted / The sage and the hyssop enclosed and staked). The setting for the female pilgrims is insistently described—with five verbs in two lines—as hemmed in. The garden is trimmed, fenced, crafted, enclosed, staked, and by implication the Wife of Bath too is semi-imprisoned, imagined in a traditionally female space (the enclosed garden), safely framed and put in her place.[50] In a stark contrast both to Chaucer's depiction of the curious, adventur-ous Alison and to the historical reality of what female travellers could accomplish and experience, this fifteenth-century reader hastily pushed Alison back into enclosed domestic space, where many thought that women should stay. The second half of this book will trace more of Alison's afterlives, exploring what hap-pened to her when she escaped from Chaucer's control.

PART II

Alison's Afterlife, 1400–2021

'Now Merrier and Extra Mature'

As soon as Alison started to make her way in the world, she caused a stir. Never far from the spotlight, she has had an unbroken afterlife from the late fourteenth century to the present day, constantly being reinterpreted, reshaped, and reimagined. Some responses openly mention the Wife of Bath; others do not acknowledge their debt. Some reinventions are in texts that have become canonical and in traditional forms such as poem, play, or novel; others are more obscure and experimental: we find Alison in film and on the radio, in dialect, in dub poetry, and on posters. These days, we can find her in wildly unexpected places, such as cheese shops: versions of the Wyfe of Bath cheese include the New Wyfe of Bath, 'Now Merrier and Extra Mature!'[1] Another favourite of mine is the Wife of Bath soap, marketed with the slogan, 'The soap that women most desire!'[2]

As soon as Alison appeared in Chaucer's writings, readers immediately and consistently responded to her with more passion, emotion, love, horror, outrage, and adoration than they did to any other of Chaucer's characters—or perhaps to any other literary character at all. People noticed her, and she provoked reactions. As I commented in the introduction, rather depressingly it is not the case that responses to Alison have become steadily less misogynistic across time. Some of the most aggressive readings of Alison have come in the twentieth century, as readers increasingly focused on her body and her sexual desires (rather than, for instance, her powers of rhetoric and persuasion, which were of great concern to fifteenth-century scribes). Many responses are complex: James Joyce's engagement with Alison is a brilliant example of a reworking of the Wife of Bath that, on the one hand, simplifies her in a rather regressive way, reducing her to a more generic type while, on the other, it develops what Chaucer was doing to produce an even bolder idea of the place of the female voice.

In this second half of this biography, I trace what happened to the Wife of Bath after Chaucer's death, from fifteenth-century scribes' anxious commentaries to Zadie Smith's 2021 play. I will be exploring sources ranging from Shakespeare's plays to Pasolini's film, from Voltaire's retelling of her tale to a visual image of her in communist Poland. On the way we will see printers imprisoned for printing ballads about her, stage spectaculars based on her tale performed all over Europe, and plays written about her in eighteenth-century London, twentieth-century America, and twenty-first century Brazil. Some responses are closely based on her prologue and/or tale, such as Vera Chapman's 1978 novel, *The Wife of Bath*. Others have a more glancing relationship to Chaucer's text: Shakespeare's plays refract the Wife of Bath rather than directly reprising her; Voltaire reads her through Dryden's lens.

The Wife of Bath, indeed, infuses textual culture in myriad ways: some direct (such as plays, ballads, and novels that have the Wife of Bath in their titles), some oblique. An example of this more oblique use of Alison is Margaret Atwood's *The Hand-*

maid's Tale (1985). Atwood consciously evokes Chaucer in the title, and states in her introduction to the 2017 edition that she named the novel 'partly in honor of Chaucer's *Canterbury Tales*.'[3] The epilogue, titled 'Historical Notes,' explicitly references Chaucer's *Tales*. Indeed, in these 'notes,' Professor Pieixoto discusses the Middle English pun on 'taill'—it means both 'tale' and 'female genitalia,' and it links the female body and the process of narration.[4] This pun is heavily foregrounded in the Shipman's Tale (the tale initially intended for the Wife of Bath). Here, in the 'Historical Notes,' a (fictional) male academic jokes about the pun, and discusses his own and his colleague's editorial and controlling role in bringing the text— which was found on cassette tapes—to light. While the Wife of Bath is a female character invented by a male author, and is herself profoundly interested in the cultural dominance of male authoritative texts, *The Handmaid's Tale* is by a female author and is told by a female character—but her oral account has been transcribed and edited by a patronising male character. Both texts, then, foreground some of the complexities around authorship and gender. More generally, the nature of *The Handmaid's Tale*—told by a secular woman about patriarchal oppression and the controlling of female bodies, voices, and experiences—can easily be read as a response of a kind to the Wife of Bath, though it is clearly not a direct reworking, and Alison herself is never mentioned.

My intention in this book is not to list and discuss every single retelling of or significant response to the Wife of Bath; rather, in this half of the book, I trace patterns and trends in how writers—and sometimes other artists and filmmakers—have been inspired by Alison. The next five chapters move roughly through time but sometimes circle and overlap each other. In chapter 6, I focus on attempts to silence Alison and the impossibility of doing so, looking mainly at scribal commentary in fifteenth-century manuscripts and at sixteenth- and seventeenth-century ballads, with some references to later authors such as John Gay. Chapter 7 is principally concerned with Shakespeare's complicated responses to the Wife of Bath, although I also include some discussion of other early-modern writers and of a much later artist. I then move on in chapter 8 to consider Alison's adventures abroad, looking at plays, tales, and films from the eighteenth century to the 1970s, mainly in Europe and North America. The penultimate chapter explores prose and partly prose versions of this performative character, including in Joyce's *Ulysses* and Caroline Bergvall's experimental *Alisoun Sings*. My final chapter looks at the way that, in the twenty-first century, many women of colour—including Patience Agbabi, Jean Binta Breeze, and Zadie Smith—have reclaimed Alison's voice in postcolonial contexts. The story of Alison in the world has many twists and turns; it crosses continents as well as centuries, languages as well as gender, popular as well as high culture. Her story is still very much alive and dynamic today.

When Alison first emerged onto the literary scene, Julie Walters's version of the Wife of Bath as an ageing soap opera star, or Patience Agbabi's Nigerian Wife of Bafa, or Zadie Smith's Alvita would have been truly unimaginable. But Chaucer's early readers were themselves actively and creatively responding to Alison—sometimes with dismay and disapproval. We will start the story of Alison's afterlife in the manuscripts of the fifteenth century, where some scribes were profoundly concerned about what readers might make of Chaucer's extraordinary literary experiment.

CHAPTER 6

Silencing Alison

Yt is ordered touching a Disorderly ballad of the wife of Bathe
printed by Edward Aldee and William White and Edward
White that all the same ballades shall be brought in and burnt

—*THE REGISTER OF THE COMPANY OF STATIONERS
OF LONDON, 25 JUNE 1600*

Early in her textual life, Alison got out of her own text. Medieval
readers were used to book-jumping by certain kinds of characters: mythic characters such as Gawain and Arthur, classical figures such as Helen and Dido, protagonists from folktales and
quasi-hagiographies such as Constance and Griselda, and the
plain-speaking moral figure of Piers Plowman.[1] These characters
were not seen as 'owned' by a particular author, and versions of
them proliferated. But it was far from usual for a figure clearly
invented by one author to escape its own text. Indeed, Chaucer
himself allows Alison to escape from the *Canterbury Tales* and
jump into another one of his poems—*Lenvoy de Bukton*—while
none of his other characters are given this kind of adventure. As
other authors started to respond to the *Canterbury Tales*, they

experimented with Chaucer's characters in various ways, but no
character received the attention that Alison warranted, from
poets, scribes, commentators, dramatists, and ballad writers
alike. In the fifteenth century, almost every major poet adapted
her in some way: Hoccleve (c. 1421), Lydgate (c. 1420s), Dunbar
(late 15th cent.), and Skelton (late 15th or very early 16th cent.)
all engage with her.[2] Similarly, in the sixteenth and early seventeenth centuries, we see Alison's influence in texts by Spenser,
Shakespeare, Greene, and Fletcher, and by the turn of the following century, Pope, Gay, and Dryden were all writing versions
of her or her tale.[3]

While readers were fascinated by the Wife of Bath and
wanted to amplify her voice and her body, many also demonstrated intense unease about that voice and body, and a desire
to silence her. In the decades and centuries after Alison's birth,
we see scribes trying to argue with her in order to drown out
her voice; printers imprisoned for publishing texts about her;
and plays and ballads written and obsessively re-written to present acceptable versions of this unruly character. Part of the
discomfort coalescing around Alison came from the fact that
she is so very adaptable, independent, and appealing—she is a
character with whom readers identify. Hostile readers worry
that other readers (particularly women) might believe her vision of the world and might try to copy her behaviour. The idea
that readers might be seduced by literary characters and might
try to imitate them—forgetting their fictionality—has a long
and dense history. A key medieval example is that of Paolo and
Francesca, the adulterous lovers whom Dante meets in Canto
V of the *Inferno*. Reading was their undoing: they read the story
of Lancelot and his illicit love for the married Guinevere; reading about their kisses led Paolo and Francesca to kiss, to aban-
don their reading, and to embark on their doomed affair. This

famous episode is parodied by Jankyn and Alison's scene of reading, in which the couple's reading is abruptly ended not by passion but by violence, as Alison attacks the book that teaches men to hate women, not to love them.[4]

Historically, women, as well as heretics and non-Christian readers, were stigmatised as literal readers in western Europe.[5] Seen as unable to distinguish layers of meaning or to interpret adequately, they were criticised for their simplistic understanding of texts. Alison plays with this idea when she tells us that she prefers the text to the gloss, and associates men's glossing and interpretative activities with their sexual acts ('Men may devyne and glosen, up and doun [...] / That gentil text kan I wel understonde' [26–29]; 'so wel koude he me glose, / Whan that he wolde han my *bele chose*' [509–510]).[6] The idea that women readers may be especially prone simply to copy what characters in texts do is invoked at the end of the Clerk's Tale, when the Clerk specifically (and ironically) mentions the Wife of Bath and his love for her—'for the Wyves love of Bathe' (Clerk's Tale, 1170). He encourages 'noble wyves,' to remember her example and govern their menfolk, attacking their husbands with the arrows of their 'crabbed eloquence' (1183, 1203). The Host buys into exactly the same idea about women readers, though from a different perspective, when he replies that he wishes that his wife had heard the story of Griselda (1212b–1212d)—implying that she would then copy Griselda's subservience.

In recent years, the idea that women can be dangerously influenced by texts and will naively copy the actions of female characters that they admire has not gone away. After the huge success of the film *Thelma and Louise*, critics fretted that women who watched the film would identify with the characters so much that they would want to imitate them by enacting violence against men. John Leo wrote a review of the film titled

'Toxic Feminism' (1991) in which he argued that 'it is very difficult for moviegoers, particularly women, to bail out emotionally and distance themselves' from the film. *Thelma and Louise*, he argues, is not art but 'cynical propaganda,' designed to whip up a female violence that he likens to fascism.[7] I have detoured onto this example to emphasise that the idea of women being seduced by a text or artwork into bad behaviour against men has had a long life. Some readers saw the Wife of Bath as similarly problematic, as a bad influence whose ideas needed to be countered and neutralised. Many of those participating in textual culture in the decades and centuries following Chaucer's death wanted to contain and to silence Alison of Bath—while others rejoiced in her endless multiplication.

From the fifteenth century, scribes who wrote comments and glosses on manuscripts of the *Canterbury Tales* provide fascinating evidence of how some of Chaucer's early readers responded to the Wife of Bath. Of the eighty-three extant manuscripts of the *Tales* dating from before 1500, twelve have no glosses.[8] The others vary hugely in terms of the amount and type of glossing or scribal commentary written in the margins of the text. Looking across the manuscript tradition, it is clear that the Wife of Bath's Prologue attracted particular attention from scribes. Indeed, critics note that not only is her prologue 'one of the most heavily and frequently glossed parts of the Tales,' but that her words 'provoked unusually intense responses from readers.'[9] Even in the cases where the scribal commentary is relatively benign—as is the case in the authoritative Ellesmere manuscript, for instance—the volume of glossing sets up a clear counter-voice in the text.[10] In comparison with the tales around it, the density of commentary on the Wife of Bath's Prologue is striking. Furthermore, the glosses are written in script as large as the text itself, inscribed into generous margins, and using the more authoritative Latin language, in contrast to Alison's English (see fig. 4). Even though the Ellesmere glossator is essentially backing Alison up by including partial quotations, a reader is given the impression that she—unlike the other tellers that surround her—needs the validation of male, Latinate, textual authority.

In other manuscripts, scribes can be bluntly disapproving of Alison. In Cambridge University Library Dd 4.24, next to Alison's playful comment that 'half so boldely kan ther no man / Swere and lyen, as a woman kan,' the scribe has solemnly and humourlessly noted simply, 'Verum est' or 'It is true.' He also adds the bare comment, 'Nota'—take note—next to other lines that he presumably thinks are particularly true in what they reveal about women. These include further tongue-in-cheek comments from Alison such as 'Forbede us thing, and that desiren we' (519) and also words directly from Jankyn's misogynistic tirades, including '[he who] suffreth hys wyf to go seken halwes [i.e., go on pilgrimage], / Is worthy to been hanged on the galwes' (657–658) and '[it is better] hye in the roof abyde, / Than with an angry wyf doun in the hous; / They been so wikked and contrarious' (778–780). He also adds a self-serving 'Nota' next to Alison's quotation of a proverb, 'Whoso that nyl be war by othere men, / By hym shyul othere men corrected be' (Whoever will not take note of other men / Will himself become an example for others to learn from [178–180]), implying that (male) readers should take note of the lessons of the prologue (that he is himself pointing out to them) and avoid becoming examples in the mould of Alison's husbands.

While there are sets of glosses that recur across groups of manuscripts, some witnesses reveal specific attitudes to and concerns about Alison. London British Library Additional 5140 and London British Library Egerton 2864 are derived from a common, now-lost source and share over fifty nontraditional glosses to the Wife of Bath's Prologue.[11] (For simplicity, I follow other critics in calling the writer of these glosses the Egerton glossator.) Exploring these glosses gives a fascinating insight into one way of reading the Wife of Bath's Prologue—a way of reading that the author of the glosses was trying to encourage in future readers of the manuscript. As Susan Schibanoff puts it, the Egerton glossator bursts with 'outrage and indignation over the Wife's Prologue' and tries 'to shout the Wife down' in order to 'excoriate Alison's immorality and vice.'[12]

Many scribes largely confine themselves to quoting direct sources, or highlighting parts of the text that they think are important. The Egerton glossator, however, throws himself wholeheartedly into the business of argument and attack, often departing from these norms and citing biblical texts that have no direct relation to Alison's words. For instance, Alison tells us how much she used to 'chide' (419) her husbands, saying that 'I wolde nat spare hem at hir owene bord' (I wouldn't leave them alone even at their own table) / For, by my trouthe, I quitte hem word for word' (421–422). Next to these lines, the Egerton scribe has added a very long marginal note:

> Qui profert contumeliam insipiens est et parabole Salamonis et postea Melius est sedere in Angulo domatis quam cum muliere litigiosa et in domo communi Et postea melius est habitare in terra deserta quam cum muliere rixosa et Iracunda et alibi Ascensus arenosus in pedibus veteran sic mulier lignata homini quieto Ecclesiastica et alibi linguam autem mulierum nullus hominum domari potest Jacobi Apostoli. (fig. 5)

This extensive, even excessive, angry note splices together several different Biblical quotations: 'He that uttereth reproach is foolish' (Proverbs 10:18); 'It is better to sit in a corner of the housetop than with a brawling woman, and in a common house' (Proverbs 21:9); 'It is better to dwell in a wilderness than with a quarrelsome and passionate woman' (Proverbs 21:19); 'As the climbing of a sandy way is to the feet of the aged, so is a wife full of tongue to a quiet man' (Ecclesiasticus 25:27); 'But the tongue of a woman no man can tame' (James 3:8). It is clear that the scribe is vigorously engaging with the text, determined to attack the Wife of Bath's character and opinions, and to offer an extensive array of biblical sources to support his own misogynistic views. He encourages readers to see Alison as a negative example and to condemn not only what she says but the fact that she says it at all—his own riposte focuses on the horrors of a woman who speaks. She is 'brawling' and 'quarrelsome'; for a woman to have a tongue is unbearable. He is determined to counter her over and over again, citing many different parts of the Bible here. Intriguingly, he also utterly misquotes and misrepresents the Bible to make it fit his own agenda. The last part of the comment comes from James 3:8 and properly reads: 'linguam autem nullus hominum domare potest' (But the tongue no man can tame). The context is a discussion of the importance of self-control, and turning away from cursing, envy, and contention. It is not about women, or the relations between the sexes, at all. The Egerton scribe, however, has silently inserted 'mulierum' (woman) into the verse, transforming its meaning into an attack on women's speech (the tongue of a woman). This writer himself thus enacts the way that male writers twisted and even falsified the Bible to back up their own arguments—while, with breathtaking hypocrisy, this scribe criticises Alison's speech as inappropriate, and implies that she needs to be educated by his superior Bible knowledge.

A strikingly obsessive desire to pile up examples and to counter what Alison is saying is typical of this reader's response to the text. Over and over again, rather than pointing a reader to sources, or expanding on what Alison is saying, the Egerton glossator takes up a stance contrary to Alison's and works to show the reader why she is wrong and immoral—a very odd attitude for a scribe to take. For instance, Alison describes how her husband, Jankyn, lectured her with misogynistic proverbs and anecdotes, commenting that 'Ne I wolde nat of hym corrected be. / I hate hym that my vices telleth me, / And so doo mo, God woot, of us than I' (661–663). In other words, she could not stand her husband's criticisms, and she, like many people, does not like to be told of her faults. The scribe responds to this with outrage, penning a long note alongside. The note includes nine separate biblical quotations, all from Proverbs, as he multiplies examples of why Alison is wrong to reject reproof and correction. He sees his role not as literary but as *moral*—he himself is taking on the role of correcting Alison, and of making sure that readers see that they should not admire her or be on her side. He is so anxious about this that he feels he needs an extraordinary number of examples to shore up his own position. Furthermore, his examples are telling. The first one reads: 'Disciplinam autem domini fili mi ne abicias' which comes directly from Proverbs 3:11 (with the addition of the 'autem,' 'but'). The verse means, 'My son, reject not the correction of the Lord.' It is thus clearly inappropriate to what Alison is saying; she is explicitly talking about her husband's criticisms of her, while this verse is about God correcting humans. The glossator is comparing Jankyn—by any standards a paranoid, aggressive domestic abuser—with God, suggesting that a husband automatically has a divine status.[13] The fact that the scribe is himself trying to correct Alison aligns him with Jankyn and, by his own logic, with God. He has set up an asymmetrical textual power dynamic, in which he, Alison's husband, and God are on one side, and her unruly, sinful voice is isolated on the other. His desire to correct her, indeed, seems to be a driving force of his programme of glossing.

There are many examples throughout the manuscript of this scribe's outrage about Alison's character and words, and his determination to wrest the text, and readers' interpretation of the text, into a different direction. His desire to show his superior understanding and to remove authority from Alison sometimes leads him into contradictory positions. For instance, early in her prologue, Alison declares that 'God bad us for to wexe and multiplye' (28). Many manuscripts feature a gloss next to this line, which tends simply to read 'Crescite et multiplicamini'— 'Increase and multiply' from Genesis 1:28. The Egerton glossator, however, cannot rest with this, but includes one of his mega-notes, citing four different verses from the Bible across ten lines of densely written commentary, paralleling seven lines of the Wife of Bath's text (see fig. 6). Rather comically, the length of the note means that the scribe starts it next to an earlier point in the Wife's text, so that (in MS Additional 5140), his dense glossing appears directly across from her wry comment that 'Men' like to 'glosen, up and doun,' (26) as he demonstrates precisely the desire (to take over the text) that she is mocking. Even more striking, in my view, is the scribe's final quotation here, 'Siquidem et due vxores david captiue ducte fuerat Achinoen israelites et abigail uxor nabal Carmeli'[14] (For the two wives also of David were taken captives, Achinoam, the Jezrahelitess, and Abigail, the wife of Nabal of Carmel). This seems largely irrelevant, until we follow Alison's speech over the page, and see that in the next couple of lines, she says that God 'of no nombre mencion made he, / Of bigamy, or of octogamye' (32–33). The Egerton scribe is surely responding to this—in effect saying that in fact God does talk about bigamy. His (presumably unintended) implication, then, is that bigamy is perfectly acceptable, as David had two wives—though Alison was not talking about bigamy in that sense at all; rather she was referring to marrying a second time after widowhood. In his desire to show that his biblical knowledge exceeds Alison's, and that we should attend to him rather than to her, the scribe has ended up suggesting something wholly against Christian teaching, and seeming to adhere to the kind of literal reading of the Bible traditionally associated with women and unbelievers. I think that his motivation in choosing to accumulate so many quotations in support of his arguments is also to silence her voice by the sheer weight of his Latinate authority—and whether or not he intends this, the heavily glossed text would have this effect on many readers. These are not helpful source reminders (as we often see attached to the Parson's Tale, for example); the glosses here represent a battle with female speech.

The glossator criticises Alison's violence against Jankyn but makes no comment about Jankyn's attack on her. He luxuriates in the excessive demonstration of his own knowledge (even though that knowledge is often flawed, and misquotations are frequent). At one—and only one—moment he does make a positive comment about women—but he does this purely to prove Alison wrong and thus to demonstrate his own authority over and superiority to her. When she says 'For trusteth wel, it is an impossible / That any clerk wol speke good of wyves' (688–689), he triumphantly annotates with 'Mulierum fortem quis Inueniet' (Who shall find a valiant woman?) from Proverbs 31:10. Of course, if one did not know the context, it could easily sound as if no one, in fact, could find a valiant woman. However, assuming that most readers would know the biblical context, this is in fact the beginning of a long description of an admirable, moral, wise, hard-working woman. In the context of this manuscript, however, Alison's point is entirely proved: this particular clerk has said no good of women and has devoted his glossing to humourless and outraged attacks on Alison. This one positive comment is made in order to condemn this particular woman further and to assert that he, the male clerk, knows better than she does.[15] While he tries, through his reading of the prologue, to remove authority from her voice, to condemn her as a character, and to elevate his own views by silencing Alison, the overall effect is to demonstrate just how uncomfortable she makes him. And it is noticeable that some of her most important comments are unanswerable—not only by him but by any other scribe. Not a single manuscript includes a comment next to her assertion that the canon would look different if women had had the opportunity to write stories (693–694). Even in the most hostile manuscripts, Alison's voice, and her assertions about male attempts to silence women, can be heard loud and clear.

At the same time as scribes were engaging with Alison on the manuscript page, poets were also giving her cameo roles in their own texts throughout the later-medieval and early-modern period. What we see here is amplification, not silencing—a fascination with the Wife of Bath that far exceeds readers' interest in other Chaucerian characters. A typical example is Skelton, who describes the *Canterbury Tales* in his poem, 'Phyllyp Sparowe.' He writes:

Of the Tales of Canterbury
Some sad stories, some merry
As Palamon and Arcet,
Duke Theseus, and Partelet,
And the wife of Bath,

That worketh much scath
When her tale is told
Among housewives bold.
How she controlled
Her husbands as she would,
And them to despite
In the homeliest wise,
Bring other wives in thought
Their husbands to set a nought. (614–627)

He here devotes a total of four lines to the *Canterbury Tales* as a whole, summing the collection up as partly 'sad,' and partly 'merry,' and making reference to the characters within the Knight's Tale and the Nun's Priest's Tale. He then moves on to the Wife of Bath—who fills ten lines on her own, those lines all being devoted to her prologue, not her tale. Skelton also specifically says here that her motive is to tempt other women to act like she does and control their husbands.

From bit parts in other poets'—and other characters'—texts, it was a small step for Alison to take centre stage in her own new texts. The most avidly read and long lasting of these was a ballad, usually titled *The Wanton Wife of Bath*, and it was this ballad that those in authority tried to silence. In this manifestation, Alison's own book was burnt, and her facilitators even ended up in prison.

The Wanton Wife of Bath was written sometime before 1600; it was rewritten around 1700 and remained popular throughout the eighteenth and nineteenth centuries, and it survives in fifty-four separate ballad printings as well as in anthologies.[16] In both 1600 and 1632 it caused great controversy. On the earlier date, 25 June 1600, the printers, Edward Aldee and William White, were each fined five shillings; the seller, Edward White, was fined ten; and it was decreed that all copies must be burnt. The explanation was simply that it is a 'disorderly' ballad, and that the printers are being fined for 'disorders in printinge' and the seller for 'his offence and Disorder in sellinge.'[17] There is a threat of prison, but the record states that their imprisonment is 'respited till another tyme.' On 24 June 1632, however, another printer, Henry Goskin, was summoned to appear before the Court of High Commission because he had printed the ballad, and he was sent to Bridewell prison. At this point, the ballad was criticised because in it 'the histories of the bible are scurrilously abused.'[18] So what was it about this ballad that caused such alarm, to the extent of book burnings and imprisonment? Why did those in authority want to silence Alison again?[19]

The ballad comprises a story about what happens to Alison after her death, combining aspects of her prologue and tale with an entry-to-heaven story. Told in four-line verses, rhymed ABCB, of alternating lengths (8 syllables, 6 syllables), and traditionally sung to a well-known tune known as 'Flying Fame' or 'Chevy Chase,' this was a popular, performance-based song. It describes how Alison lives in pleasure, dies, and gets to heaven's gate, which is barred to her. A series of biblical figures comes, one by one, to tell her that she is not welcome, and she refutes each of them, drawing attention to their own sins, so that they retreat. Adam arrives first, and she informs him that he is 'the cause of all our woe' (19). Next is Jacob, whom she accuses of being a 'false deceiver' (27) who tricked his father and brother; third is Lot, whom she dismisses as 'a drunken ass' (35) who slept with his own daughters. And so it proceeds—through Judith, David, Solomon, Jonas, Thomas, Mary Magdalen, Paul, and Peter. None of them are a match for her. Finally, Christ arrives, and she asks him for mercy. He counters that she has refused it, but she asserts that she will come back to his flock.

Christ tells her that she knew his laws but chose to disobey. Alison agrees that this is true but says that, nonetheless, the father forgave the prodigal. Christ then forgives her and lets her in, saying that because of her 'repenting cry' (138) he won't deny her. While the text places her in heaven, the London authorities of 1600 consigned her to the pyre.

As this summary demonstrates, this Wife of Bath, like Chaucer's, consistently opposes biblical authority figures, pointing out their sins and refusing to accept their judgements of her, speaking in an irreverent way but also, essentially, making undeniable, factually true comments about their own behaviour. Why was this so very troubling in 1600? The word 'disorderly' does not necessarily tell us much—it technically means that the ballad was published without a licence from the Stationers' Company.[20] However, in other contexts at this time the word 'disorderly' means 'violating moral order' or 'riotous' and is connected to morally sinful behaviour.[21] Such connotations may well have echoed in the minds of readers and publishers, given the challenges to authority within the ballad itself.

A new, longer version of the ballad, written around 1700 and with a Scottish provenance, gives clues as to why some readers were offended by the earlier version. The new version claims to have excised 'what was Papal or Heretical in the former' ballad.[22] This new version is often termed simply *The Wife of Beith*, and sometimes changes the key adjective—'wanton'—to 'worthy.' It is clearly advocating a Protestant understanding of redemption, in its focus on faith and grace—rather than confession and forgiveness of sins. Thus Peter tells the Wife, 'If ye had faith ye could win in,' adding, 'Faith is the feet wherewith ye come,' and 'Strongly believe or you're undone' (478, 480, 484). The Wife adheres to this lesson, saying to Christ, 'But oh! Thy mercies still do last / To save the soul that trusts in thee' and adding, 'At footstool of thy grace I'll lie' (623–624, 634). Christ confirms that, 'Thy faith, poor soul, hath saved thee' (638). There is nothing like this in the earlier version. This Wife of Bath, produced in Scotland, gives a very different message from the *Wanton Wife* of a hundred years or more earlier. At this moment, it is clear that the revisers wanted to silence the older version of the Wife of Bath and replace her with a cleaned-up version—one who was safely enfolded in reformed religion.

That is not to say, however, that it was Protestant concerns that motivated those who banned the ballad in 1600 and 1632. One critic does suggest that early seventeenth-century readers were offended by the Catholic theology of the *Wanton Wife*, arguing that she gets off too easily, by a straightforward and formulaic confession, but there is little evidence that this is what disturbed readers in the first half of the seventeenth century.[23] If we work backwards, in 1632 we do have a comment about the content of the *Wanton Wife*—that it 'scurrilously abused' the Bible. While this *could* indicate outraged Protestant sensibility, it does not clearly suggest that the text was seen as pro-Catholic or as anti-Protestant. The comment sounds generally like the kind of attack that fifteenth-century scribes had been making: Alison takes bits of the Bible and applies them out of context, or partially, so that she twists biblical truths. The ballad, after all, goes through the failings and sins of some of the most admired and important biblical figures, without discussing their lives and virtues more holistically. Moreover, the ballad depicts this ordinary woman successfully arguing with biblical authorities and sending them packing. This, along with the fact that it was printed without licence, seems to give enough cause for the Court of High Commission to see this ballad as an offensive attack upon authority, a text that sided with rebels—and did so at a time of general unease, in the decade in which Charles I attempted to rule without Parliament. The Wife of Bath, in 1632, is a subversive figure who lacks respect for authority.

The precise historical moment of the earlier attack on the ballad is even more intriguing. The atmosphere in London in the summer of 1600 was febrile, burning with suspicion, fear of rebellion, and anxiety about the power of texts to sway public opinion.[24] June 1600 was the month in which Robert Devereux, earl of Essex, appeared before a special hearing at York House, accused of treason.[25] Accusations against him included going against Elizabeth's orders in Ireland, making truces against her will, and knighting many men on his own authority—behaviour that seemed to challenge or even usurp the authority of his sovereign. The order to burn *The Wanton Wife of Bath* came just twenty days after the hearing at York House. Literary and historical texts about the medieval period were particular objects of suspicion to Essex's accusers.[26] For instance, in 1599, Sir John Hayward had published 'The First Part of the Life and Reign of King Henry the IIII.' He had included in it a speech in which the archbishop of Canterbury argued that there might be circumstances that justified loyal men taking action against a bad king. Hayward had included a dedication to the earl of Essex, which lauded him with the words, 'great thou art in hope, greater in the expectation of future time.'[27] The following year, the Attorney General, Coke, claimed that the author was 'intending the application of it to this time.'[28] This anxiety about a version of the history of 1399–1400—the months in which Henry Bolingbroke returned to England, defeated Richard II, took the throne, and ultimately murdered his cousin—is reminiscent of the anxiety surrounding a more famous version of this episode of history. Shakespeare's *Richard II* has long been associated with the earl of Essex. Most importantly, his supporters watched Shakespeare's play on 7 February 1601, on the eve of their rebellion, and ordering this play to be performed was specifically termed treason at the trial of Sir Gelly Meyrick, one of Essex's key allies.[29]

This was the context in which the Stationers ordered that the ballad about the Wife of Bath should be burnt. I think it highly unlikely that it was *written* 'about' contemporary politics, but it is very possible that it could be *read* in such a way. *The Wanton Wife of Bath* depicts someone speaking boldly to authority, rebelling against her superiors, perhaps even speaking truth to power. Furthermore, her rebelliousness and plainspeaking are ultimately not punished but rewarded. The authority figure (Christ) forgives her, shows her mercy, and welcomes her. It is a text that counsels against punishment and revenge and promotes reconciliation and acceptance. This certainly resonates with the situation for Essex in the summer of 1600, when he was desperately hoping that Elizabeth would forgive him for his actions in Ireland and welcome him back to court. Elizabeth famously (if perhaps apocryphally) said, 'I am Richard II. Know ye not that?'[30] Perhaps in the case of the *Wanton Wife*, she was Christ, and Robert Devereux, soldier and favourite, the gilded earl of Essex, could equally appropriately have said, 'I am the Wife of Bath. Know ye not *that*?'—hard though it might be to imagine the debonair earl in Alison's dress. Hilariously, printers tended to reuse woodcuts fairly freely, and a version of the ballad printed in 1660 features Alison looking suspiciously like Elizabeth herself (see fig. 7).

The rewriting of the ballad circa 1700 removed some of its oppositional, subversive tendencies, both by swapping Alison's 'wanton'-ness for 'worthy'-ness and, more significantly, by making her religiosity fit with contemporary Scottish Protestantism. This was not the only occasion in which a Wife of Bath text was rewritten and reshaped in an attempt to make her less un-ruly and more conformist. John Gay's play, *The Wife of Bath*, went through a comparable process. It premiered at Drury Lane in 1713 but was only staged twice (12 May and 15 May), although Gay was paid well for the copyright (£25). Gay returned to the play almost two decades later, and it was staged again in 1730. Again, it had little dramatic success—there were three performances—but Gay did very well out of the copyright sale (£75). The rewritten play is a much toned-down version of the earlier play. In the words of a critic, it was, 'prettified, cleaned up, made right for polite society.'[31] The popular music was re-moved from the play, and the farcical elements were greatly muted, so that the play became a more sober, less exuberant, less performative affair. The character of Chaucer, who, in the first version, directed the action, disguised himself as an astrolo-ger, and planned to marry Lady Myrtilla to save her from be-coming a nun, is removed altogether and becomes 'Sir Harry Gauntlet.' The removal of Chaucer is really puzzling—perhaps Gay is putting clear water between his source text and himself, making it plain that this is a Wife of Bath for the eighteenth century, not the fourteenth. He also humiliates the Wife of Bath in the later version. In 1713, in the last scene of the play when all the couples are uniting, Alison suggests to the Franklin that they should get together, asking him to give her his hand, and saying that the world could not find 'another such like Couple,' and that they represent an 'Italian Autumn that even excells the Spring' (act V, p. 63). Other characters enter at this point, and the Franklin does not reply, so we assume that they have indeed joined hands, literally and metaphorically.[32] In the 1730 version, their final encounter mirrors an earlier moment in the 1713 play. Alison woos the renamed Franklin, 'Plowdon,' suggesting that they should 'divert [them]selves' for a 'frolick,' and advising him to:

'Revenge yourself by your own marriage.' His reply is unequivocal: Plowdon ripostes that if he did that, the revenge would 'light upon my own head too,' sourly adding, 'I wish women would be less impertinent' (V.vii, p. 78).[33] Alison is comprehensively rejected, and soon afterwards, she points out to everyone that she alone is single: 'Every body provided but me!' (V.ix, p. 79). Gay has cut her out of the 'happy ending' of comedy, marking her as the character that does not deserve to be part of the string of couples with which such plays traditionally conclude.

Comparably, a later play about the Wife of Bath was also rewritten with the goal of putting Alison in her place. Percy MacKaye's early-twentieth-century play started off with the title *The Wife of Bath*. However, when funders and actors expressed disquiet about a woman's role dominating the piece, MacKaye agreed to rewrite and even retitle his play, reducing Alison's role and rebranding the play as *The Canterbury Pilgrims* (1903).[34] Right across time, we see authors not only writing Wife of Bath texts but anxiously returning to them in the wake of audience responses, usually in order to diminish, punish, or limit Alison in some way.[35]

John Dryden was explicit about the fact that there were aspects of the Wife of Bath that were simply not appropriate for his audience and had to be ignored. Those aspects were, in fact, everything about her as a character, leaving only her tale. In 1700, Dryden published his famous *Fables, Ancient and Modern*, comprising translations of texts by Boccaccio, Chaucer, Homer, and Ovid. In the 'Preface,' he says: 'If I had desir'd more to please than to instruct, the Reve, the Miller, the Shipman, the Merchant, the Sumner, and above all, the Wife of Bath, in the Prologue to her Tale, would have procur'd me as many Friends and Readers, as there are Beaux and Ladies of Pleasure in the Town.' However, he goes on to say that he does not wish to 'offend against Good Manners' and that if any 'Profaneness' has 'crept into' his poems, he disowns it entirely (in true Chaucerian fashion, as Chaucer is notorious for his disavowals of responsibility). Having stated here that he in some ways wanted to translate the Wife of Bath's Prologue but decided not to do so, he still cannot leave her alone. A couple of pages later, he again turns to the issue of not translating the prologue, writing that, 'I translated Chaucer first, and amongst the rest, pitch'd on the Wife of Bath's Tale, not daring, as I have said, to adventure on her Prologue, because tis too licentious.'[36] The Wife of Bath's Prologue becomes a presence behind the *Fables*—as the text he wanted to translate but did not dare to attempt, the text that could not be spoken although he knew his audience would love to hear her voice.

Alexander Pope, however, did translate the Wife of Bath's Prologue, which was published in 1713, and it also appeared in *The Canterbury Tales of Chaucer, Modernis'd by several Hands* (1741). Later in the eighteenth century, Joseph Warton rebuked Pope for attempting the Wife of Bath, writing that

> The Wife of Bath is the other piece of Chaucer which Pope selected to imitate. One cannot but wonder at his choice, which, perhaps, nothing but his youth could excuse. Dryden, who is known not to be nicely scrupulous, informs us, that he would not versify it on account of its indecency. Pope, however, has omitted or softened the grosser and more offensive passages.[37]

Pope's version is about half the length of the original. He has chosen to cut, for instance, the section about what genitals are for (115–137), the funny comment that if there were no sex, no virginity could be grown (71–72), Alison's declaration that she has the 'best quoniam' (608), her reference to her 'chambre of Venus' (618), and the comment that she has the mark of Mars in a 'privee place' (620). He has also removed her statement that she has sex evening and morning with her husbands (152) and that her husbands were her slaves (155). While he has tried to make medieval legal norms seem less shocking by making her marry first at age fifteen rather than twelve (Pope, 7), he has also made her personally more sinful, by saying that she 'pawn'd [her] honour' (Pope, 293) to Jankyn while still married (in Chaucer's version she merely has ambiguous 'daliance' [565] with him). He has also toned down the economic storyline by saying that her first three husbands merely gave her presents, rather than signing over land to her (Pope, 64). The depiction of misogyny is made less compelling as the interruptions of the Pardoner and the Friar are removed completely, so we no longer see the performance of male clerics' discomfort with female speech. This is a less interesting, less socially situated Wife of Bath—and, most noticeably, a character whose speech is far less sexually explicit and daring.

Dryden's motivation in suppressing the Wife of Bath's personal voice and story, he says, is that it is 'too licentious,' and this is clearly a driving force behind Pope's translation choices too. This is a different motivation from the Egerton glossator, who found her too aggressive and disrespectful; from the censors of the ballad in 1600 and 1632, who found her too rebellious; or from the Scottish rewriters who found her too Catholic. Dryden is more fascinated by the Wife of Bath's Prologue than by any of the other rejected texts, as we can see by his returning to it in his 'Preface,' but he sees it as broadly similar to five of the tales—four of which are sexually explicit and deal with adultery (Reeve, Miller, Shipman, and Merchant), and one of which includes a detailed discussion of the science of farting (Summoner). For Dryden, it seems that it is Alison's discussion of the body and sex that is particularly problematic, more so than her attacks on church fathers and Biblical interpretation. The Chaucer that Dryden wanted to promote can be ascertained from the tales that he did include in his *Fables*: the Knight's Tale, the Wife of Bath's Tale, and the Nun's Priest's Tale, as well as an apocryphal work, *The Flower and the Leaf*. The first two are romances that end in marriage and the continuation of a stable patriarchy, in sharp contrast to the fabliaux that depict the downfall of patriarchs in a world upside down. The Nun's Priest's Tale also ultimately depicts the restoration of order, the patriarch, and the status quo after invasion and chaos, while *The Flower and the Leaf* promotes courtly entertainments and the value of virginity. It is somewhat comic that Dryden chose a text not by Chaucer at all as an ideal representative of Chaucer's writings. In contrast, the Wife of Bath's Prologue threatens to destabilise this carefully curated image of what the 'father of English Literature' was doing in the *Canterbury Tales*.

Across the very different texts and writers that I've been looking at in this chapter, one constant is a resurfacing concern about the Wife of Bath as a disruptive and challenging figure. Whether readers and writers are more worried about her as a sexual, political, or religious rebel, those who wish to silence her are all motivated by seeing Alison as a threat to established authority and order. But we also keep seeing Alison's return. She spawned far more commentary and many more new texts—ballads, plays, poems—than any other Canterbury pilgrim. When authors were uneasy about her, they still could not leave her alone—hence the obsessive scribal annotations and continual rewritings of texts about the Wife. If an author such as Dryden chose not to write about her prologue, he still felt he had to draw our attention repeatedly to that very absence. The Wife of Bath was decidedly *not* silenced, but male readers' insistent attempts at suppressing her voice tell their own story about just how fascinating, disturbing, and threatening they found her.

CHAPTER 7

When Shakespeare
Met Alison

I have heard of the Wife of Bath, I think in Shakespeare.

—JONATHAN SWIFT, LETTER TO JOHN GAY,
20 NOVEMBER 1729

William Shakespeare was a great Chaucerian.[1] Indeed, Chaucer was a towering figure for Elizabethan and Jacobean poets and playwrights, and his influence is evident in the work of almost every significant author from these decades, including Spenser, Peele, Day, Sidney, Lyly, Marlowe, Marston, Jonson, Dekker, Greene, Chapman, Middleton, Beaumont, and Fletcher.[2] While antiquarians and scholars were fascinated by his work, it was also popularised in ballads, as we have seen, as well as in plays and poems.[3] In 1532, William Thynne published a complete *Workes of Geffrey Chaucer*. This was the first time that a vernacular author was honoured with a grand collected-works edition, and over the following seventy years, five more of these authoritative folio editions were published (Thynne 1542, 1550; Stow

1561; Speght 1598, 1602), and they came to be accompanied by formal textual apparatus—biographical sketches, family trees, and summaries.[4] Chaucer was made particularly palatable to his readers by his repackaging as a proto-Protestant, explicitly characterised as such by Foxe, who calls him a 'right Wicklevian' in his *Acts and Monuments* (1570).[5] This new image of Chaucer was enabled by the capacious editing of Thynne and his successors, who included Wycliffite texts that were definitely not by Chaucer—*Jack Upland* and *The Plowman's Tale*—in Chaucer's *Works*. This was a Chaucer who shared the Protestant, reformist values of the Elizabethan state. He remained protean in other ways: while Spenser focused more on the 'romance' Chaucer, Greene imagined an earthy, fabliau Chaucer competing with a more serious Gower. Plays were written based on individual Chaucerian texts, and the concept of the *Canterbury Tales* as a whole inspired texts such as *The Cobbler of Canterbury*, a collection of tales told by pilgrims travelling by boat from London to Kent.[6]

Chaucer meant many things to his Elizabethan and Jacobean successors. He was a poet of romance and moral seriousness; he was a philosopher and astronomer; he was bawdy and rude; he was an inadequate versifier; he was the father of their literature.[7] The Wife of Bath looms large in these decades not only in the wildly popular ballad but in, for instance, Fletcher's play *Women Pleas'd*, which is based on her tale, or in Braithwait's *Commentary*, the first piece of 'criticism' written on vernacular poetry in English, which analyses the Miller and the Wife of Bath.[8] One of the interesting aspects of the Wife of Bath is the fact that her prologue and tale juxtapose different aspects of Chaucer's concerns. Both prologue and tale, though particularly the tale, are ethical and serious, with the tale emphasising the importance of education, reform, and Christian *gentillesse*. Yet the prologue is also notably scandalous, dotted with sexually explicit language and outrageous ideas. Here we have both the bawdy, irreverent Chaucer and the serious, religious Chaucer bound up together.

Shakespeare's contemporary, Robert Greene, who memorably dismissed his fellow playwright as an 'upstart crowe,' had a particularly interesting relationship with Chaucer, setting him up both as literary patriarch and as a bit vulgar and inconsequential. In both of his 'Chaucerian' texts, Greene circles around the Wife of Bath. Greene was almost certainly the author of *The Cobbler of Canterbury*, a text that he ostentatiously disavows in his *Vision*.[9] In the *Cobbler*, six passengers on a barge from Billingsgate to Gravesend tell stories. One of them is an 'old wife.' Indeed, it is clear that having an old wife telling a tale was the defining aspect of the *Canterbury Tales* for Greene, who writes: 'We have imitated ould Father Chaucer having in our little Barge, as he had in his travel sundry tales and amongst the rest, the old wives tale.'[10] The old wife herself is a combination of the Wife of Bath and a viscerally described loathly lady figure. In Greene's *Vision*, Chaucer himself features as a character. Chaucer and Gower appear to Greene as patriarchs representing two different forms of literature—essentially Chaucer speaks for comedy, Gower for seriousness. In the end, Gower wins but is then himself trumped by Solomon. During the debate, Chaucer and Gower each tell a tale, in an imitation of the contest of the *Canterbury Tales* itself, and the text as a whole is underpinned by careful responses to their writings.[11] The tale that Chaucer tells is influenced by a number of sources—most obviously both Chaucer's Reeve's Tale and the Gentleman's Tale from the *Cobbler of Canterbury*. It also has affinities with the Wife of Bath's Prologue and Tale: he describes a working woman who still goes wandering about after her marriage, despite the jealousy of her husband, who worries about neighbours resorting to his house to see her; women also scheme and gossip together to put husbands in their place. There are nods in the story to several of Chaucer's fabliaux, but the audacious wandering woman is more like Alison than she is like Chaucer's fabliaux heroines, who tend to stay at home. Greene's two texts illustrate something of the hold that Chaucer had over writers' imaginations at this time as an author who could not be ignored, and who had to be somehow rewritten, mastered, or improved upon.[12]

Chaucer is foregrounded in the prologue to Shakespeare and Fletcher's *Two Noble Kinsmen*. After somewhat comically comparing plays to virginity, the playwrights say of this play that

> It has a noble breeder and a pure,
> A learned, and a poet never went
> More famous yet 'twixt Po and silver Trent.
> Chaucer (of all admir'd) the story gives;
> There constant to eternity it lives.
> If we let fall the nobleness of this
> And the first sound this child hear be a hiss,
> How will it shake the bones of that good man,
> And make him cry from under ground, 'O, fan
> From me the witless chaff of such a writer
> That blasts my bays and my fam'd works makes lighter
> Than Robin Hood!' This is the fear we bring;
> For to say truth, it were an endless thing,
> And too ambitious, to aspire to him,
> Weak as we are, and almost breathless swim
> In this deep water. (10–25)

There are many fascinating aspects about the ways in which Shakespeare and Fletcher position both themselves and Chaucer here: the image of them flailing in the water as they attempt

to follow the master sets up a profoundly authoritative prede-
cessor, a serious poet, 'of all admir'd,' untouchable by others.
The language used to describe him also reveals the playwrights'
detailed knowledge of the Chaucerian oeuvre: this prologue is
heavily indebted to a Chaucerian prologue, the Clerk's, in
which the river Po is also invoked, along with an authoritative,
but dead and buried source—in that case, Petrarch (29, 48). As
Petrarch was to Chaucer, so Chaucer is to Shakespeare and
Fletcher—and in both cases the veneration is laced with liberal
reminders that their ancestor is deceased and, by implication,
decaying, potentially irrelevant, now replaced by fresh voices
and able only to haunt the new text by his underground rattling.
The contemporary authors, in other words, are staking their
claim to create a new, living piece of art while acknowledging a
profound debt.[13] In *The Two Noble Kinsmen*, Chaucer is presented as a figure well known to the writers and their audience,
and peerless amongst vernacular poets. Finally, Shakespeare
and Fletcher nod to the sometimes downmarket reputation of
medieval vernacular literature, clearly separating Chaucer's poetry from popular romances, bawdy stories, and oral ballads,
here captured by the catch-all term 'Robin Hood.'

It is rare for Shakespeare to foreground Chaucer so
ostentatiously—and indeed these lines may owe more to
Fletcher than to Shakespeare—but his careful reading of a wide
range of Chaucer's writings is evident in many of his plays.
Some plays owe an obvious debt to Chaucer: *Troilus and Cressida* to *Troilus and Criseyde* and *A Midsummer Night's Dream* and
Two Noble Kinsmen to the Knight's Tale are the clearest examples. For instance, both the *Dream* and the Knight's Tale use the
wedding of Theseus and Hippolyta as a frame for a story set in
Athens and its nearby woods where rival lovers fight over a
woman. Specific verbal echoes include the name 'Philostrate,'

references to Diana's altar in the context of the heroine's reluctance to marry, and some phrases such as 'do observance to a morn of May' (*Dream*, I.i.166) and 'doen his observaunce to Maie' (Knight's Tale, 1500). Critics have traced dozens of direct allusions to and quotations from Chaucer's texts in almost every single Shakespeare play.[14] But we might also think about Shakespeare's response to Chaucer as something more profound than remembering particular lines or downloading plots. As Maguire and Smith write, 'the most significant source may be the most thoroughly assimilated, most subliminally absorbed—and therefore the most invisible.'[15] Similarly, Cooper argues that Shakespeare produces 'a reconceptualization of Chaucer so radical as scarcely to be recognisable.'[16] Elsewhere, Cooper writes that Chaucer gave Shakespeare 'high-octane fuel for his imagination.'[17] Analysing the *Dream*, she moves beyond the clear indebtedness to the Knight's Tale, suggesting that it is also a radical transposition of the *Canterbury Tales* itself, restaging the *Tales'* interest in social range and a clash of styles and cultures, while also using texts as varied as the *Legend of Good Women* and the Tale of Sir Thopas.[18]

Yet Shakespeare's indebtedness to Chaucer and the depth of his reading of and interest in Chaucer's works has been consistently underplayed, often by critics more interested in classical or European sources than English ones. It is surprising, for instance, that in a discussion of the relevance of the *Cobbler of Canterbury* to the *Merry Wives of Windsor*, a recent book tells readers that the *Cobbler* is a response to *Tarleton's News* and to Italian novellas such as the *Decameron*, while making only one very brief parenthetical mention of another tale collection source, this one explicitly staged on the way to Canterbury and directly mentioned in the *Cobbler*.[19] Shakespeare is clearly separated here from his English medieval antecedents. Similarly, another article about *Merry Wives*, titled 'What Do Women Want?' focuses on Freud's famous interest in that question, with no reference at all to the fact that this question drives the whole narrative of the Wife of Bath's Tale—even though there is no doubt that Shakespeare knew the Wife of Bath's Tale well.[20]

Indeed, the Wife of Bath influenced Shakespeare deeply, as the rest of this chapter will discuss. First of all, and of least importance, we can see this at the level of direct allusion. In *Richard II*, Bolingbroke's reference to fire and the Caucasus clearly recalls the Wife of Bath's use of an image of fire and the Caucasus in her tale.[21] The 'meanings' of the metaphors are completely different, so it seems to me to indicate how steeped Shakespeare was in Chaucer—that he remembers, or almost 'misremembers,' Chaucer's words as part of his own lexicon.[22] In *All's Well That Ends Well*, the King gives a speech that strongly recalls the loathly lady's speech in the Wife of Bath's Tale: both emphasise the importance of not despising low birth, and that deeds rather than ancestry convey honour.[23] Interestingly, these two moments, in two quite different plays, recall the same speech from the Wife of Bath's Tale, the crucial moment at which the loathly lady teaches the rapist knight about ethics, prejudice, and virtue.

However, the Wife of Bath had a much more profound effect on Shakespeare than these specific moments alone suggest. When Shakespeare met Alison, two things happened. She influenced how he thought about what a literary character can be and can do—emerging, transformed and transgendered, as John Falstaff. And she inspired his only England-set and only middle-class play, a play about empowered women, transformation, educating knights, and ethical female behaviour: *The Merry Wives of Windsor*.

FIGURE 1. The Wife of Bath in the Ellesmere Chaucer manuscript, c. 1400

FIGURE 2. The Pilgrimage Window, York Minster, early 14th century

FIGURE 3. Vulva pilgrim brooch, Netherlands, late 14th or early 15th century

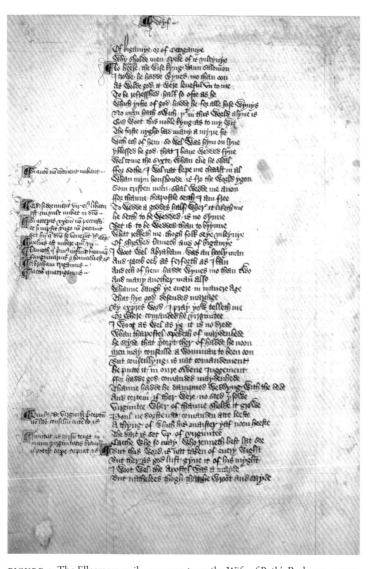

FIGURE 4. The Ellesmere scribe comments on the Wife of Bath's Prologue, c. 1400

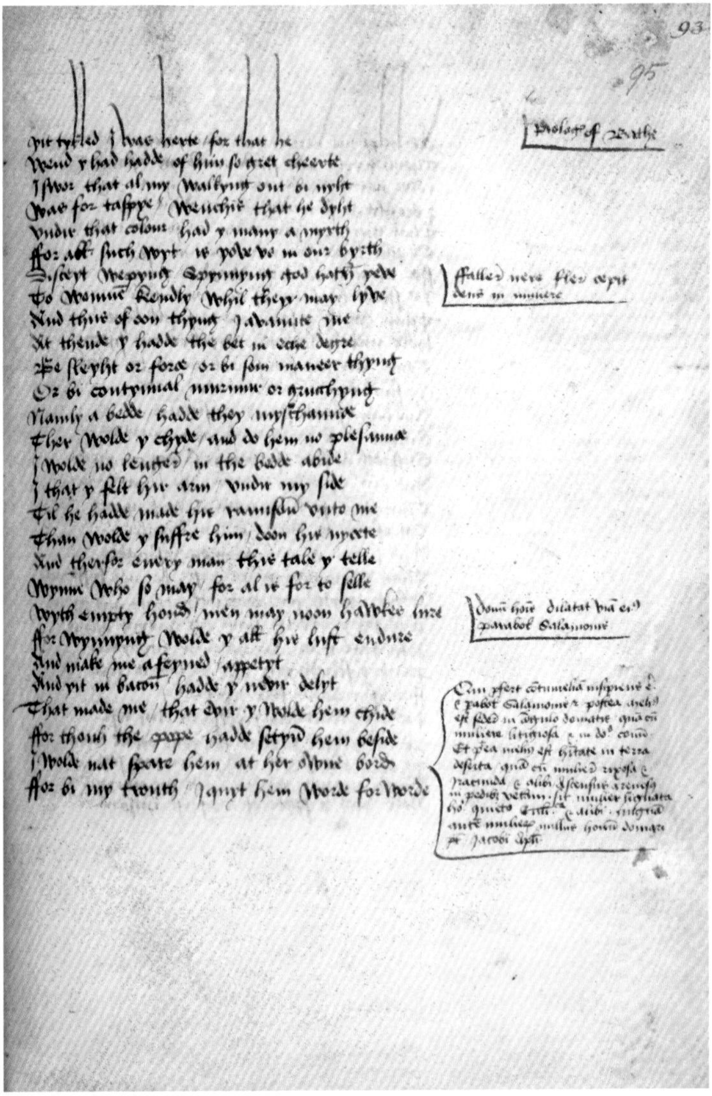
Yit tykled I his herte for that he
Wend y had hadde of him so gret cheerte
I swor that al my walkyng out bi nyght
Was for tasspye wenches that he dyght
Vndir that colour had y many a myrth
For al such wyt is yove vs in our byrth
Deseyt wepyng spynnyng god hath yeve
To wymmen kendly whil they may lyve
And thus of oon thyng I avaunte me
At thende y hadde the bet in eche degre
Be sleyght or force or bi som maner thyng
Or bi contynual murmur or grucchyng
Namly a bedde hadde they myschaunce
Ther wolde y chyde and do hem no plesaunce
I wolde no lenger in the bedde abide
If that y felt his arm vndir my side
Til he hadde made his raunsoun vnto me
Than wolde y suffre him doon his nycete
And therfor every man this tale y telle
Wynne who so may for al is for to selle
With empty hond men may noon hawkes lure
For wynnyng wolde y al his lust endure
And make me a feyned appetyt
And yit in bacon hadde y nevir delyt
That made me that evir y wolde hem chide
For though the pope hadde setyn hem beside
I wolde nat spare hem at her owne bord
For bi my trouth I quyt hem word for worde

Prolog of Bathe

FIGURE 5. The Egerton scribe comments on the Wife of Bath's Prologue, late 15th century

FIGURE 6. The Egerton scribe comments on the Wife of Bath's Prologue, late 15th century

FIGURE 7. Frontispiece of *The Wanton Wife of Bath*, c. 1660

FIGURE 8. Henry Fuseli,
the bedroom scene from the
Wife of Bath's Tale, c. 1812

FIGURE 9. Henry Fuseli, Falstaff in the laundry basket, c. 1792

THE WIFE OF BATH'S TALE.

In days of old, when Arthur fill'd the throne,
Whose acts and fame to foreign lands were blown,
The king of elfs and little fairy queen
Gamboll'd on heaths, and danc'd on ev'ry green;
And, where the jolly troop had led the round,
The grass unbidden rose, and mark'd the ground:
Nor darkling did they dance, the silver light
Of Phœbe serv'd to guide their steps aright,
And, with their tripping pleas'd, prolong'd the night.

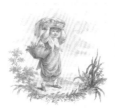

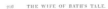

FIGURE 10. Lady Diana Beauclerk, illustration of the victim, from John Dryden, *The Wife of Bath Her Tale*, 1797

216 THE WIFE OF BATH'S TALE.

And so may all our lives like theirs be led;
Heav'n send the maids young husbands, fresh in bed:
May widows wed as often as they can,
And ever for the better change their man;
And some devouring plague pursue their lives,
Who will not well be govern'd by their wives.

FIGURE 11. Lady Diana Beauclerk, illustration of the bed scene, from John Dryden, *The Wife of Bath Her Tale*, 1797

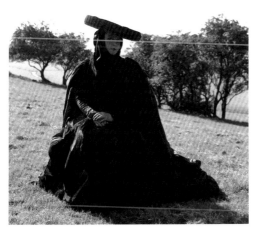

FIGURE 12. Laura Betti playing the Wife of Bath in Pier Paolo Pasolini, *I Racconti di Canterbury*, Produzioni Europee Associate (PEA)/Les Productions Artistes Associés, 1972

FIGURE 13. Jan Sawka, poster advertising *The Canterbury Tales/Opowieści Kanterberyjskie*, Poland, 1976

FIGURE 14. Marc Brenner, photograph of Clare Perkins playing the title role in Zadie Smith, *The Wife of Willesden*, Kiln Theatre, 2021

As the Wife of Bath is to Chaucer, so Falstaff is to Shakespeare. Both Chaucer and Shakespeare invented one character who was different from their other characters. In each case, the character jumps across multiple texts and genres (The Wife of Bath's Prologue and Tale, the Clerk's Tale, the Merchant's Tale, *Lenvoy de Bukton*; *Henry IV Parts 1 and 2*, *Henry V*, *The Merry Wives of Windsor*), as if they cannot be contained. Alison and Falstaff are both wordsmiths and world creators; they are funny; they are physically vital celebrators of the body and its appetites; they challenge authority. Both quote, misquote, and reinterpret the Bible comically and insistently as part of their crafting of arguments and construction of their own worldviews. And both characters speak extensively, even immoderately, taking over texts, attracting all attention to themselves. Crucially, both characters are fully aware of their own sinfulness and acknowledge it. This self-awareness disarms many readers while antagonising others, and contributes to the readerly appreciation of them as startling literary characters. They know themselves, and we (or many of us) want to know them too. They do divide critics, with 'moralizing critics' responding to both characters with horror and disgust;[24] indeed, Roberts aptly comments that Falstaff functions as a kind of Rorschach test for readers.[25] They both spark obsessions in readers—as they did in their authors, who could not leave them alone. Alison and Falstaff can both be seen as representatives of life, of vitality. Middle-aged characters well past their physical best, they both refuse to slow down. Moreover, neither really dies in their texts—and both take part in resurrection scenes.

Correlation is not causation, of course, and many of the similarities between Alison and Falstaff could, on their own, merely seem to be coincidence. But when we put it all together, the case is compelling. Harold Bloom asserts that 'Falstaff involves Shakespeare in only one authentic literary debt,' seeing the connection between Falstaff and Alison as 'tenuous but vibrant.'[26] It is important to remember that—as I've been discussing—we are certain that Shakespeare was an attentive reader of the *Canterbury Tales* and knew the Wife of Bath's Prologue and Tale well. This is a case, I think, of a source that Shakespeare had so 'thoroughly assimilated' that the source itself becomes almost invisible, a hidden foundation without which the text could not stand up in the same way. Readers have always seen Alison and Falstaff's profound similarities and have responded to them in similar ways. Indeed, both characters went on to live long afterlives in texts penned by others. We might compare the texts considered in this book (such as *The Wanton Wife of Bath*, John Gay's *Wife of Bath*, and Jean Binta Breeze's *The Wife of Bath in Brixton Market*) with texts including William Kenrick's *Falstaff's Wedding*, Verdi's opera, *Falstaff*, and Robert Nye's *Falstaff: A Novel*.

Henry IV Parts 1 and 2 have been renamed by some critics as the Falstaffiad because Falstaff takes over those plays so comprehensively.[27] He dominates the plays by virtue of the amount and power of his speech. Falstaff speaks at length and compellingly, just as Alison's prologue dwarfs any other prologue in the *Canterbury Tales*. Both characters demand our attention by their determination to be heard and by their verbal abilities—their wit, their facility with complex sentences and ideas, their skill with imagery and wordplay. They create a bond with their listeners through confession. Falstaff tells us, for instance, that he, 'swore little, dic'd not above once in a quarter—of an hour, paid money that I borrow'd—three or four times, liv'd well and in good compass, and now I live out of all order, out of all compass' (1 *Henry IV*, III.iii.15–20). The Wife of Bath stages her

whole prologue as a self-revelatory confession, packed with
comments such as, 'What sholde I taken keep hem for to plese /
But it were for my profit and myn ese?' (213–214) and 'Oh
Lord! The peyne I dide hem and the wo, / Ful giltelees, by
Goddes sweete pyne!' (384–385). They both show us that they
know their own faults, and even tell us that they are liars. Falstaff, for instance, pretends to have killed Hotspur. He finds his
body, and tells us, 'I'll swear I kill'd him,' adding, 'Nothing con-
futes me but eyes, and nobody sees me' (*1 Henry IV*, V.iv.125–
127). Alison is similarly open with her audience about her men-
dacity, detailing how she told Jankyn that she had dreamed
of him and a bloody bed, and adding to us that 'al was fals;
I dremed of it right naught' (582). She uses the same phrase,
'al was fals' (382) to describe how she lied to her first three
husbands too, pretending that they had abused her when they
were drunk. Their deceit and acknowledgement of that deceit
to themselves and to their audiences makes many readers and
listeners feel complicit, even sympathetic. They are pleased
with themselves, and their delighted solipsism draws many
readers into their worlds.

They also hold our attention and interest by the power of
their speech; they are notable for both their rhetorical skill and
their careful deployment of tropes such as anaphora, isocolon
(repeating clauses or sentences of equal length), and questions.[28] The way that they structure their sentences and convey
their personalities is strikingly effective. For instance, Alison
reprimands the Pardoner like this:

And whan that I have toold thee forth my tale
Of tribulacion in marriage,
Of which I am expert in al myn age—
This is to seyn, myself have been the whippe—

Than maystow chese wheither thou wolt sippe
Of thilke tonne that I shal abroche [barrel that I shall
   open]. (172–177)

This long sentence begins with three subordinate clauses
(whan that . . . ; Of which . . . ; This is to seyn . . .) before Alison reaches the delayed main clause—'Than maystow chese. . . .'
These qualifying clauses increase the readers' sense of anticipation while also demonstrating Alison's absolute control over her
material and over her interlocutor. They also contribute to our
sense of Alison as an exuberant speaker, whose ideas expand,
digress, and spill over. In miniature, this structure represents her
refusal to be contained, to get to the point and then recede. Her
language is also appealing: she continues the metaphor of listening as drinking that she had started in her previous sentence,
while also introducing a metaphor for herself, describing herself
as a 'whippe.' Her diction and versification are also notable, especially her aurally striking juxtaposition of a line made up entirely of ten monosyllabic words with a line containing only four
words, one of which has five syllables, another three: 'And whan
that I have toold thee forth my tale / Of tribulacion in mariage.'
Throughout the sentence, her sense of self comes across in her
insistence on the first person—'whan that I have toold'; 'I am
expert'; 'I shal abroche.' In that final phrase, she insists on her
control of the future, although at this point it cannot be certain—
but she stakes her claim to imagine and to determine what will
happen. She creates a world through her speech.

    Falstaff's brilliance at world crafting also dominates his
speech. Here is an example:

I know not: here he is, and here I yield him, and I beseech
your Grace let it be book'd with the rest of this day's deeds,
or by the Lord, I will have it in a particular ballad else, with

mine own picture on the top on't (Coleville kissing my foot), to the which course if I be enforc'd, if you do not all show like gilt twopences to me, and I in the clear sky of fame o'ershine you as much as the full moon doth the cinders of the element (which show like pins' heads to her), believe not the word of the noble. (2 *Henry IV*, IV.iii.45–54)

Again we see the desire to extend a sentence for as long as possible to hold the attention of the listeners—the same refusal to be contained that Alison demonstrates. This is all one sentence, packed with multiple clauses and an excess of detail. Falstaff is here asserting his right to have the world as he wishes: he constructs an exaggerated future in which he will appear in a commemorative ballad, adding in details ('Coleville kissing my foot'), and appealing to his audience with elevated imagery, comparing himself to the full moon; his companions to little stars, themselves like pinheads. The layers of comparison again demonstrate his desire to keep control of the narrative, to keep talking. His repeated use of the first person, and his insistence on the force of his own actions—'I yield him,' 'I beseech,' 'I will'—reveals his determination to dominate the discussion. Furthermore, while Alison was speaking to, and contradicting, a male cleric, Falstaff is asserting himself to a royal prince: both claim their rights to make a space in the world for themselves in the face of opposing authorities.

Challenging authority and authoritative ideas is central to the identity of both Alison and Falstaff. (This is hardly unusual in literary characters, particularly 'carnival' types, but it is nonetheless important to note.) Perhaps Falstaff's most famous speech is his assault on the idea of honour. It concludes:

What is honor? A word. What is in that word honor? What is that honor? Air. A trim reckoning! Who hath it? He that

died a' Wednesday. Doth he feel it? No. Doth he hear it? No.
'Tis insensible, then. Yea, to the dead. But will['t] not live
with the living? No. Why? Detraction will not suffer it.
Therefore I'll none of it, honor is a mere scutcheon. And so
ends my catechism. (*1 Henry IV*, V.i.133–141)

This attack on ideas and assertion of pragmatism in the service
of life is central to Alison's character too. One good example is
her attack on the excessive emphasis placed on virginity by
church fathers, as she demands, for instance, 'Virginitee, thanne
wherof sholde it growe?'; 'where comanded he virginitee'; and
'to what conclusion / Were members maad of generacion, / And
of so parfit wys a [wright] ywroght?' (72, 62, 115–117). As these
examples show, both characters are particularly fond of rhetorical questions, winning us over by the seeming inevitability of
their conclusions.

Their challenges to authority are especially showcased in the
way that both Falstaff and Alison use the Bible—one of the
most characteristic aspects of their speech. Falstaff has been
termed 'Shakespeare's most scripturally aware character,' with
one critic commenting that 'No character alludes to the Bible
more self-consciously, more frequently, or with more boldly
revisionary misapplication.'[29] This could also serve as a description of Alison, whose hilariously skewed interpretation of the
Bible, especially of Paul, is notorious. Both characters even use
the same Pauline phrase to justify their own bad behaviour. The
verse is 1 Corinthians 17:20: in the Vulgate, 'unusquisque in qua
vocatione vocatus est in ea permaneat.' The Wycliffite Bible
(c. 1380s) translated this as 'Ech man in what clepyng he is
clepid, in that dwelle he,' and the Wife of Bath's version is, 'In
swich estaat as God hath cleped us / I wol persevere' (147–148).
The Geneva Bible's (1560) translation reads, 'Let every man

abide in the same vocation wherein he was called,' and is echoed by Falstaff's 'Why, Hal, 'tis my vocation, Hal, 'tis no sin for a man to labor in his vocation.' Alison is talking about having plenty of (marital) sex; Falstaff about thieving; in both cases they are comically pretending to think that God has called them to these roles, in a knowing misuse of Paul's words. Both consistently demonstrate a general lack of respect for the Bible and an insistence on using it for their own ends.

As well as being excessively wordy, both Falstaff and Alison are excessively bodily, strong physical presences, whose bodies are extreme—and this larger-than-life quality is the heart of the vitality that so many readers have recognised in both of them. Alison continually emphasises her sexuality—'I hadde the best *quoniam*' (608)—as well as her appetite for 'sweete wyn' (459). Falstaff's body is the first thing we learn about him, as Hal describes him as 'so fat-witted with drinking of old sack, and unbuttoning thee after supper' (*1 Henry IV*, I.ii.2–3), and his fatness comes to define him: 'did you not tell me this fat man was dead?' (*1 Henry IV*, V.iv.132), and 'he has put all my substance into that fat belly of his' (*2 Henry IV*, II.i.74–75). The fact that they are both driven by appetites is part of the depiction of both characters as representatives of life itself.[30] Alison is determined to maintain an active sexual life regardless of age and decay— early in her prologue she tells us that she is looking for a sixth husband (45), and later, after acknowledging that age has taken her beauty (475), she nonetheless insists that she will keep embracing life, 'yet to be right myrie wol I fonde' (479). Falstaff's reluctance to think about his own mortality is crystallised when he tells Doll, 'do not speak like a death's-head, do not bid me remember mine end' (*2 Henry IV*, II.iv.234–5). They both push back death, and this is brilliantly illustrated by the fact that each of them enacts a resurrection scene.

Alison's comes at the end of her prologue, when she pretends to be dead, lying on the floor 'as I were deed' (796). Her husband is horrified, and she pretends to be uttering her dying words, saying she will kiss him before she dies. He approaches to beg forgiveness, at which point she hits him hard on the face in a vivid return to life. Falstaff's resurrection scene also comes at the end of the first part of his text, in the penultimate scene of *1 Henry IV*. Falstaff, like Alison, feigns death, and Hal laments his passing, bidding him 'Poor Jack, farewell' (V.iv.103). After Hal leaves the stage, the directions tell us that Falstaff rises up and tells us that he 'counterfeit[ed]' dying' (117). The fact that both characters stage their own resurrection within their own texts also acts as a kind of prescient precursor to their resurrections across time. Both have been brought back to life over and over again: it is wonderfully appropriate that this capacity for reinvention is embedded even within their original incarnations.

While Alison never dies, we are told in *Henry V* that Falstaff *has* died. But this is immediately qualified by Mistress Quickly's assertion that he is 'in Arthur's bosom'—a comic mistake for Abraham's bosom, but also a reminder of the stories of Arthur's immortality as a spirit of past Britishness, the once and future king abiding in Avalon. The existence of an alternative timeline for Falstaff in *The Merry Wives of Windsor* also qualifies the idea of his death. Nonetheless, the arc of the Henry plays, with Henry's coming to power, his rejection of Falstaff, and Falstaff's fall from grace and death, suggests that Shakespeare took a bleaker view than Chaucer of the inevitable triumph of orthodox political power structures.

When Falstoff is introduced to us in *1 Henry IV*, there are interesting indications that Shakespeare had Chaucer on his mind. These plays are set in medieval times and include characters that Chaucer knew personally (such as Henry himself).

Falstaff is based on real medieval people, Sir John Oldcastle and the historical Fastolf. Shakespeare moves between tavern and court in this play in a way quite different from his previous history plays, but quite similar to the movement from Tabard to tales, proto-realism to romance, that we see in the first fragment of the *Canterbury Tales* in particular. Like the *Canterbury Tales*, *1 Henry IV* emphasises the idea of carnival and, just as Harry Bailly the innkeeper takes on the role of Lord of Misrule or tavern king in the *Canterbury Tales*, so Falstaff plays the part of the king in the tavern, when he and Hal role-play. Very early in the play, Poins tells his companions that 'there are pilgrims going to Canterbury with rich offerings, and traders riding to London with fat purses' (I.ii.125–127), in a deliberate nod to the medieval setting of the play, a nod that might encourage the audience to think about a well-known poem on the subject of pilgrims on their way to Canterbury.

Chaucer is thus a haunting presence behind *Henry IV Parts 1 and 2*, and the Wife of Bath specifically has a strong claim to be a major inspiration behind Falstaff. Falstaff has other inspirations too—such as the 'miles gloriosus' or 'swaggering soldier' figure, who has his ultimate origin in Aristophanes, filtered through Plautus, and resurfacing in a number of sixteenth-century plays. As Anne Barton argues, Mathew Merygreeke, in Nicholas Udall's *Rafe Royster Doyster* (1552), combines this type with vices from morality drama, for instance.[31] This character type is a self-serving older man, an appetite-based deceiver, who has no time for ideals—a character very like Chaucer's Pandarus. Specific aspects of Falstaff, such as his rejection of warrior values and his relationship with Hal, owe a major debt to this character type. Yet there are many aspects of Falstaff that Shakespeare did not take from these characters and that he instead found in the Wife of Bath. In

particular, his profound confessional self-awareness and understanding of temporality, his appealing and persistent vitality, his use of the Bible, and his extreme verbal dexterity all link
him to Alison. Ultimately, Harold Bloom was right to term
Falstaff the Wife of Bath's 'only child.'[32]

Even more important than Shakespeare's use of the Wife of
Bath to create his own favourite character, however, is his use
of the Wife of Bath's Prologue and Tale to create one of his least-
loved plays. The *Merry Wives* was not always an unloved play;
quite the contrary. It was one of Shakespeare's most popular
plays until well into the eighteenth century. In the first critical
essay ever published on Shakespeare, Margaret Cavendish particularly praised his female characters, picking eight to
discuss—four of whom are from the *Merry Wives*. The play was
produced more than two hundred times in the first half of the
eighteenth century, and in 'The Companion to the Playhouse'
(1764), David Erkine Baker said that there was no other text, 'in
which so extensive a Group of perfect and highly finished Characters are set forth.'[33] It declined in popularity in the nineteenth
and twentieth centuries: as Phyllis Rackin points out, it is a
fascinating comment on twentieth-century taste that this comedy about virtuous female power and ability lost favour while
the disturbing *Taming of the Shrew*, which highlights (perhaps
approvingly) the abuse of women grew to be more liked than
ever before.[34]

Imagine a text. It is about middle-aged, economically competent married women who bond with each other to trick men,
punish male cruelty, and mock male jealousy, while themselves
maintaining their marriage vows. The text goes on to deal with
the issue of educating men to think better of women and, specifically, to teach a knight that women are not necessarily sexu-

ally available to him. It is a text that sets women against knights, and shows women winning. There is a scene in the woods dominated by a woman who is both a fairy queen and an ordinary, ageing woman (she transforms), with fairies accompanying her. One of the final morals of the text is that women can be trusted and, further, that they can be trusted with power over men.

Which text was I describing? Everything about that description fits both The Wife of Bath's Prologue and Tale and *The Merry Wives of Windsor*. These are texts that are linked together by tie upon tie. Again, while one or two of these connections might seem coincidental, there are so many similarities that it is very hard to believe that Shakespeare's reading of the Wife of Bath did not influence the construction of his play.

The Merry Wives of Windsor is unique in Shakespeare's corpus in being set in contemporary England.[35] Only the brief 'frame' story of *The Taming of the Shrew* is comparable. *The Merry Wives* explicitly interrogates Englishness and the English past. Falstaff is himself a figure from the early fifteenth century, and he compares himself to the medieval Robin Hood, calling his followers 'Scarlet' and 'John' (I.i.158). The title of the play itself gestures towards nostalgia—but a disturbing, even treasonous nostalgia. In the later sixteenth century, the phrase 'merry world' was associated with Catholic recusants. Between 1568 and 1601, nine people were indicted for seditious talk, including making reference to the 'merry world,' before the Reformation.[36] The play invokes a wide range of folk customs: from the legend of Herne the Hunter to the dance around the Fairy Queen in the woods to the aggressive carnival traditions of skimmington and charivari—in which a man is dressed as a woman and ducked in water.[37] This is a play that foregrounds the ongoing survival of older traditions, texts, and ideas in the Elizabethan world.

Mistress Ford and Mistress Page reflect and refract many aspects of the Wife of Bath's texts. Highly unusually for a Shakespeare play, these women are middle-class, middle-aged heroines. When Mistress Page receives Falstaff's love letter, she herself tells us that she has passed the 'holiday-time' of her beauty. She then reads out to us his hilariously unflattering proposal: 'You are not young, no more am I; go to then, there's sympathy. You are merry, so am I; ha ha! Then there's more sympathy. You love sack, and so do I; would you desire better sympathy?' (II.i.2–10). In other words, he courts her for her middle age, her 'merry' behaviour, and her enjoyment of alcohol. These aspects of the two women, along with their solidly middle-class credentials as the wives of provincial burgesses, are clearly reminiscent of the Wife of Bath. Indeed, Mistress Ford is even named Alice. The women set out to teach Falstaff that 'Wives may be merry and yet honest too' (IV.ii.105)–essentially that women can be talkative, outgoing, and risqué in their conversation without losing their virtue. This compares really interestingly with Alison of Bath's character as a flamboyant woman who is not adulterous or promiscuous outside marriage—the key change from antecedents such as La Vielle. An image used by Mistress Ford in this same scene also evokes the language of the Wife of Bath. Mistress Ford says that they should give hope to Falstaff, until 'the wicked fire of lust have melted him in his own grease' (67–68).[38] In the Wife of Bath's Prologue, Alison says that she flirted with others to annoy her husband, so that 'in his owene grece I made hym frye / For angre, and for verray jalousye' (487–488). The idea of frying or melting in one's own grease is used occasionally in other texts, but usually in the context of someone who is actually burning to death. The only other example that I have found of this image being used metaphorically is in a minor Lydgate poem, clearly influenced by the

Wife of Bath.[39] Here, both Alison's husband and Falstaff are imagined stewing in their own grease and being punished by their own immoderate feelings (lust/anger) which have been stoked by the deliberate actions of the women.

The plot of *The Merry Wives of Windsor* centres on the need for women to educate men about women. Ford is taught that he should not be jealous of his wife but rather should allow her autonomy ('wife, henceforth do what thou wilt' [IV.iv.6–7]). Falstaff, a knight, is taught that he should not assume that women are sexually available to him and that he has been brought low by women's intelligence ('I do begin to perceive that I am made an ass' [V.v.119]). There are clear parallels here with Chaucer's text: Jankyn is taught to stop trying to control his wife and to allow her power in their marriage ('He yaf me al the bridel in myn hond' [813]); the rapist knight is punished for his assumption that he can forcibly have sex with women, taught to think about what women desire, and gives power up to them, recognising his wife's superior wisdom ('I put me in youre wise governance' [1231]). The foci on educating men, allowing women to control their own bodies and marriages, and demonstrating women's cleverness in shaping constructive punishments are fascinating parallels across Chaucer's and Shakespeare's texts.

Shakespeare turns Chaucer's mysterious faerie scene in the forest into high farce. In the Wife of Bath's Tale, the questing knight rides through a forest and sees a large group of ladies dancing. When he gets close, they vanish, leaving only a woman who now appears to be old and ugly. She ultimately proves to be authoritative (saving his life and teaching him ethics), magical in her ability to metamorphose, and beautiful. In *The Merry Wives of Windsor*, there is no magic in the scene, but there is transformation. Mistress Quickly, an older woman, dresses up as a fairy queen to hold court in the woods, accompanied by revelling fairies (children dressed up). In the Wife of Bath's Tale, the forest is the place where the rapist-knight begins his transformation, meeting the woman who will give him the answer to the question of what women want, teach him about female desire, and ultimately marry him and educate him about *gentillesse*. In the *Merry Wives*, the woodland scene is the point at which Falstaff is comprehensively shown the error of his ways—though here it is done through humiliation, in a strange and extraordinary enactment of scapegoating.[40]

Shakespeare's response to the Wife of Bath involves transformation in gendered ways too. The Wife of Bath herself was, of course, invented and written by a man, and in early readings of the text she was almost certainly performed by a man (Chaucer reading his text aloud to friends and acquaintances), adding to the perceived comedy of the character. In Shakespeare's plays, all female characters were acted by males.[41] Chaucer and Shakespeare both lived in cultures in which women were routinely acted by men, in which drag was a standard part of performance. While Shakespeare frequently wrote plays in which female characters dress up as men (e.g., Rosalind or Viola), the *Merry Wives* is the only Shakespeare play in which an adult man dresses as a woman (and it also features two boys dressed up as Anne Page in V.v). In act IV, scene ii, Falstaff dresses up as the 'witch of Brainford'—and, because he is in that garb, is targeted by Ford, who knows he can attack and beat this old woman with impunity, accusing 'her' of fortune-telling, making charms, and doing other secret things when men are not present (174–178).[42] Earlier in the play, Falstaff is also treated like a woman: he hides in the laundry basket, under dirty clothes including female underwear, and ends up being thrown into the Thames and ducked under (III. iii; III.v).

This imitates the punishments traditionally given to sexually promiscuous women.[43] Conversely, Mistress Ford also imagines herself changing sex and becoming a knight. When she receives Falstaff's protestations of love she tells Mistress Page that she 'could be knighted,' meaning both that she could have sex with a knight and that she could become a knight. Mistress Page pretends only to understand the second meaning and calls her 'Sir Alice Ford' (II.i.50–51). A reader of Chaucer might well think about Alison's portrait in the General Prologue: Chaucer makes her knight-like in his description of her sharp spurs, and her hat that looks like a shield (470–473). Her tale also places the knight in the position of a woman, when he loses control of his own sexual destiny and begs the loathly lady to 'lat my body go' (1061). Much more broadly, both Chaucer's and Shakespeare's texts engage in gender play in their carnival insistence on the idea of women on top, of women taking men's roles and controlling events.

In responding to the Wife of Bath, Shakespeare divided her up—splitting her across Falstaff and the merry wives. The wives have greater affinity with the more respectable 'tale' that Alison goes on to tell—they are virtuous, ethical, older women educating a knight. They do take on aspects of the Wife of Bath herself as well—for instance, in Mistress Ford's obtaining power over her own jealous husband, or in the depiction of the women's alliance with each other. But much of the Wife of Bath as a character, as demonstrated in her prologue, is filtered into Falstaff. Her intense self-awareness and self-delight, her fascination with using language to re-imagine the world, and her powerful attack on biblical and textual authority are all elements that Falstaff, rather than the wives, inherits. The disturbing complexity of Alison is given to a male character, so that the radicalism of what Chaucer was doing is diluted.

Nonetheless, the *Merry Wives* is a worthy successor to the Wife of Bath's Prologue and Tale. Both Chaucer and Shakespeare were familiar with the idea of carnival: a time when the world is turned upside down. Boy bishops might replace real bishops; women might beat men; the body might triumph over the spirit; festive comedy might dominate over serious morality. When carnival is over, established hierarchy is supposed to return—and there is much critical debate about whether carnival operates as a safety valve, or has the capacity to be genuinely transformative and anarchic.[44] In the history plays, if Falstaff represents carnival, then carnival is put firmly back in its place when Hal repudiates him at the end of *Henry IV Part 2* and when Falstaff dies, offstage, in *Henry V*. But in the *Merry Wives of Windsor*, the resolution is quite different. Falstaff is brought down, to be sure, but he is re-assimilated; and female power, the other incarnation of carnival in the play, is not put back in its place. On the contrary, the play ends with Mistress Ford still in charge of her marriage, just as the Wife of Bath's Prologue ends with Alison in triumphant control of hers. What Shakespeare took from the Wife of Bath, and restaged in the *Merry Wives*, is the radical idea that women can be trustworthy, virtuous, and in charge.

As a postscript to this chapter, I want to foreground a double image, painted by Henry Fuseli in the late eighteenth century. The painting, now owned by the National Trust and on show at Petworth House, West Sussex, is a scene from the Wife of Bath's Tale, showing the moment when the rapist knight pulls back the curtain, looks into the enclosed bed, and sees that his wife is beautiful (see fig. 8).[45] The painting depicts her naked, with light falling on her body as she reaches towards him. The part of this painting that makes it particularly interesting to me, however, is concealed. On the back of the canvas, hidden beneath a layer of orange paint and discovered during restoration in 1957, is a painting of Falstaff being hidden in the laundry basket from *The Merry Wives of Windsor*. The women are clearly visible, but Falstaff himself was either unfinished, or has been scratched out or damaged.[46] A finished version of the scene, in the Kunsthaus, Zurich, makes Fuseli's interpretation of the scene clearer (see fig. 9).[47] The women are covering him with heavy, curtain-like fabric, while a man, presumably Ford, peers through the doorway. Fuseli literally painted these scenes on opposite sides of a canvas: one showing a man being hidden from, the other a woman being revealed to, the male gaze. Both are scenes of transformation: a man is made to disappear, hidden beneath female clothing; an old woman metamorphoses into a young object of desire. Fuseli's transformation of his canvas from a Shakespearean picture to a Chaucerian one enacts the dynamism of art itself—and inverts the process by which Chaucerian texts were hidden beneath Shakespearean ones. Behind one image, we find another, just as the Wife of Bath continued to transform cultural understandings both of literary character and of women's ethical power in the world.

CHAPTER 8

Alison Abroad

I must confess that it was only on account of what you had
said that I ever cared for the prologue to the tale of the wife of
Bath and the tale itself. I have always regarded them with
extreme disfavour, knowing that, as a matter of fact, among
the men I knew, of every ten who had read them nine had
done so for improper reasons; but after reading what you said
I took them up and read them from a changed point of view,
and am now a convert to your ideas.

—THEODORE ROOSEVELT, LETTER TO
THOMAS LOUNSBURY, 1892[1]

In the eighteenth century, Alison started to travel widely and to
emerge in new incarnations in various languages and countries.
She was taken up by an extraordinary variety of thinkers—
ranging from the eighteenth-century French philosopher Voltaire to the twentieth-century Italian Marxist filmmaker and
poet Pier Paolo Pasolini. Alison reached her adaptors in different
forms: while Voltaire read Dryden's version, Pasolini read an Italian translation.[2] And while Voltaire therefore knew only the tale,

which he adapted into a *conte* or story, *Ce qui plaît aux dames* (1763), Pasolini was only interested in the prologue, which became part of his film, *I racconti di Canterbury* (1972).[3] These are just two examples of continental responses to the Wife of Bath, who ended up having a successful life in a stage spectacular, *La fée Urgèle* (1765), performed across Europe, in Paris, Geneva, Brussels, Amsterdam, The Hague, Copenhagen, Vienna, Moscow, and all over Germany.[4] Meanwhile, she also travelled to America from the seventeenth-century onwards and spawned plays, operas, and performances there across the centuries.[5] One of the most striking examples is the 1917 production of an opera based on Percy MacKaye's 1903 play, *The Canterbury Pilgrims*, with the Wife of Bath as the main character. The opera was staged in New York by the Metropolitan Opera, with a mainly German cast. Partway through the fifth performance, news arrived that the president had asked Congress to declare war on Germany. The audience sang the national anthem (twice) and when the Wife of Bath, played by a German singer, came on stage, she promptly fainted. The singer, Margarethe Arndt-Ober, was no longer seen as America's friend and was soon summarily dismissed from her job, as German opera and German opera singers were sidelined. She sued for breach of contract but was effectively forced out of the country and went back to her native land.[6] But Alison herself was not returned to England by any of her adoptive countries; rather, she continued to have polyglot afterlives around the world—many of which utterly distorted the life that she had in Chaucer's texts.

Voltaire wrote his version of the Wife of Bath's Tale late in 1763.[7] He was sixty-nine years old and residing mainly at his estate at Ferney. Since the previous year, he had been particularly taken up with a monstrous miscarriage of justice enacted against a Huguenot man, who had been wrongfully convicted

and executed. Voltaire's pamphlet on the case, which emphasised the problems of France's secret judicial system, had reached
Madame de Pompadour and Prime Minister Choiseul. He followed this up with his *Treatise on Tolerance*, printed in 1763,
which foregrounded the corruption, intolerance, and fanaticism
of the French Catholic church.[8] In the midst of this serious cam-
paigning, Voltaire also returned to poetry and wrote a series of
contes, or fairy stories, that winter. *Ce qui plaît aux dames* was the
first of seven tales that he wrote and then published under a
pseudonym the following year.[9] Chaucer's writings had been
enjoying a mini-vogue in France in the middle years of the eighteenth century. Part of his Pardoner's Prologue had been translated into French directly from Middle English in 1755, and in
1756 Dryden's version of the Knight's Tale was condensed and
translated. But it was Dryden's Wife of Bath that really took off:
it was translated in 1757 and again in 1764.[10] Voltaire seems to
have written his version in November 1763. Reading Dryden's
English would certainly have posed no problems for Voltaire: he
had lived in England from 1726–1728, where he knew Pope,
Swift, Congreve, Gay, and Cibber, went to the theatre a great
deal, and attained fluency in the language.[11]

Voltaire wrote to the Marquise du Deffard that he hoped his
story 'could pass a quarter of an hour of time when the winter
evenings are long' (pourrait faire passer un quart d'heure de
temps attendu . . . que le soirees d'hiver sont longues).[12] He
opens the story by setting the audience in winter, exhorting his
'friends' (amis) that as 'winter's eve draws in again' (l'hiver al-
longe la soirée), they should 'Listen' (écoutez) and enjoy a 'post-
prandial' (après souper) tale (4–6).[13] He imagines the story as
something to entertain, to pass the time after dinner amongst a
listening group of people, perhaps in a salon. In the tale, he imagines a mythical past for France. The king is not Arthur, but

Dagobert, a Merovingian monarch who ruled from 603 to 639. Guinevere is replaced by Berthe, who was the mother of Charlemagne. At the end of the story, he tells us that in the olden days, people listened to such stories 'Seated round the hearth in every castle hall' (Dans son château, prés d'un large foyer [419]) and that in those days, even the clergy could be in harmony with such entertainment, as 'The chaplain was the teller' (monsieur l'aumônier, / Qui leur faisait des contes de sorcier [420]), whereas in his times, fairies and fairytales are banished, and 'the heart grows dull in a world of grey' (Livresent nos coeurs á l'insipidité [426]). The fairytale is a gateway to a world of imagination, wit, and wonder, a reminder of a cultural world beyond the quotidian. At the same time, Voltaire also uses the tale as a way to make digs at the contemporary church, emphasising its corruption, as 'all the money seemed to end up with the Church' (L'argent n'allait qu'aux mains des gens d'église [20]). Given that Chaucer's own version opens with a joke against friars, this is in keeping with his own tone and concerns.

When we turn to the gender politics of the tale, however, Voltaire makes more radical and disturbing changes to the text that was before him. As we have already seen, Dryden refused to translate the Wife of Bath's Prologue, claiming that it was simply too 'licentious' to be acceptable.[14] His version of the Wife of Bath's Tale does clearly attach the tale to its female teller however—it is titled *The Wife of Bath Her Tale*—and it stays fairly faithful to its source. There are, however, some significant changes. Chaucer's version of the story stands out among other versions for its lack of focus on women's appearance. The Wife of Bath does not tell us anything about the rape victim's appearance, in what we might read as a refusal to suggest that her appearance has any relevance to the crime. This also shifts our perspective away from what the rapist is seeing and desiring and onto his criminal acts. Uniquely in 'loathly lady' stories, the Wife of Bath also refuses to dwell on the physical details of an ageing woman, when she comes to the arrival of the loathly lady on the scene. Other medieval versions, in contrast, tend to detail at great length the horror of female old age, delighting in every facet of her no longer youthful face and body. Dryden makes some moves to reverse Chaucer's very interesting authorial decisions. In his translation, he writes 5½ lines about the victim's appearance, telling us about her clothes, and about how she looks from both back and front, encouraging us to look through the rapist's eyes (*Fables*, 481). He maintains absolute clarity about the rape, however, writing of the knight that he: 'By Force accomplish'd his obscene Desire.' When he comes to describe the loathly lady, Dryden again pads Chaucer's text a little: 'But fowler far / Than Grandame Apes in Indian Forests are / Against a wither'd Oak she lean'd her weight' (*Fables*, 487).

Voltaire takes Dryden's tale and goes much further in his reversing of the gender politics of the original. Just as Chaucer's 'He saugh a mayde' was expanded by Dryden to focus on her attractiveness, so Voltaire takes Dryden's lines and builds on them, encouraging readers to see the girl through the eyes of his hero, John Robert (usually referred to as Robert). First, Voltaire tells us that

Il aperçut la fringante Marton,
Dont un ruban nouait la blonde tresse:
Sa taille est leste, et son petit jupon
Laisse entrevoir sa jambe blanche et fine (29–32)

He spied the blonde and frisky Marton,
Who wore a pretty ribbon in her hair;
A figure trim, a step so sprightly,
A petticoat short and a leg so sightly

In the next line, the knight draws nearer to the girl and meets her eyes. We are now told that her look 'would tempt the very saints in paradise' (tenterait les saints du paradis [34]). It is clear that Robert is being excused for what is about to happen: the girl is a temptress, no one could have resisted. Another five lines describe the flowers between her breasts, and her beautiful skin. Marton, Voltaire explains, was on her way to market to sell provisions. The story continues as Robert dismounts, 'his passions now quite stirred' (ému de convoitise [44]). Just as she tempted him, so he is passive here, stirred by outer forces that he cannot control. Now, he offers her money for sex, in case she is unwilling. What happens next is presented in a deeply disturbing and ambiguous way: Marton says no, but he pushes her so that she falls to the ground and he falls on top of her. While these lines depict a rape, Voltaire strongly implies in the subsequent lines that he does not see it as a 'real' rape. He portrays Marton calmly doing her hair, and asking for her money. As Robert's horse and money were stolen while he was raping Marton, he cannot pay her. It is this refusal to pay that makes Marton decide that this is not fair, and that sends her to the king. Here, she complains of rape, but she adds that the worse crime is that he will not pay her. Whether we are supposed to understand her wish for the money as payment for prostitution or as a kind of fine or compensation for rape, as would be familiar in many law codes, either way she is not presented as a suffering victim. This is a very different scene from Chaucer's 'By verray force, he rafte hire maydenhed'; from Dryden's 'By Force accomplish'd his obscene Desire'; or from the 1757 French translation, 'Il usa de violence pour satisfaire sa brutale passion.'[15] The implication of the scene in Voltaire's version is that pretty women are asking for it or, at the very least, they can easily be persuaded or soothed with money.

Chaucer's decision to make rape the crime in the story, and to make the knight unambiguously guilty, had clearly differentiated his version from other versions of the loathly lady tale. These radical choices had made the tale far more coherent and hard-hitting and, in particular, had emphasised the educative function of the punishment: a man who paid no attention to what women wanted had to think about female desire. Voltaire's changes dilute the force of the Wife of Bath's Tale, and alter the gender politics considerably.

Voltaire's different attitude to the gender politics of the story is also evident in his depiction of the loathly lady herself. Again, Chaucer—or the Wife of Bath—chooses not to linger over the details of the old woman's appearance, saying simply, 'A fouler wight ther may no man devyse' (999). As detailed above, Dryden very slightly expands this, adding a comparison to 'Grandame Apes in Indian forests' and an implicit connection with the 'wither'd oak' on which she leans. But Voltaire eschews this restraint, writing much more in the manner of other tellers of loathly lady stories. He gives us eight lines of detailed description of this monstrous woman, 'toothless' (édentée), 'shrunk with age' (pliée en deux), with 'wrinkled thighs' (cuisse ridée), a 'shrivelled chin' (court menton), and 'scab-lined eyes' (D'un rouge brun sa paupiére est bordée). Her ugly old age is mixed up with dirt and poverty: she is grimy and unwashed, with rags instead of clothes—and her effect is to scare this poor man with whom we are encouraged to identify: 'she frightened our brave knight' (Elle fit peur au brave chevalier) (140).[16] As the tale proceeds, Voltaire keeps reminding us of how repulsive she is, and how dreadful this is for Robert. Ultimately, although he sticks with some aspects of Chaucer/Dryden's version and does present the loathly lady as wise and entertaining, the focus of the story is not on the (misogynist) choice that is given to the knight (that his wife can be ugly and loyal or beautiful and unreliable); or on the importance of recognising *gentillesse* as a quality that can inhere in the old, poor, and ugly; or on the idea of educating a criminal so that he truly learns what he did wrong; or on the concept that a woman can be more ethical than a man, even than a knight. Rather, the focus of the story is on Robert's difficulty in getting an erection and his extraordinary resilience and virility in managing eventually to do so and to have sex with his monstrous wife.

When they first get into bed, the thought of the 'difficult duties' (devoirs rigoureux)[17] of marriage revolts him, and indeed he feels that it will be 'impossible' for him. He thinks to himself that in Rome they say that grace is sent to give desire and ability (le vouloir et le faire), but on this occasion it is lacking. A little later, he tells his wife that he wants to desire her as she desires him, but he cannot. He asks 'what can I do?' (que pourrai-je?), and she replies that he can do 'everything' (tout) and that it is easy at his age. With attention, art, and courage (des soins, de l'art et du courage), he will be able to manage. Now, motivated by his desire for 'glory' (gloire), he harnesses his 'rare valeur,' and invokes the help of heaven (ciel). Having gathered all his strength in this way, he is finally able to set to his work (mit a son devoir). Voltaire makes the scene highly comic, by writing about Robert's attempt to get an erection in heroic terms, imagining that ladies 'will celebrate this prodigy of love' (Celebreront ce prodige d'amour). In the story, it is this act, presented as exceptionally chivalrous, that fits him for his reward—the transformation not only of his wife into a beautiful woman who is in fact a fairy, but also of his environment into a sparkling palace. His erection takes over the story, which becomes a celebration of male virility, triumphing even when faced with an ageing, unattractive woman. This is a very strange transformation indeed of the Wife of Bath's tale of ethics, educative punishment, and female power.

Back in England, at the end of the same century, an aristocratic woman was crafting a response to Dryden's version of the Wife of Bath. Lady Diana Beauclerk—born Lady Diana Spencer—illustrated *The Wife of Bath Her Tale* in 1797. She was the first person to picture the rape victim—but in contrast to Voltaire's description of her sexual attractiveness, Beauclerk depicts her as a child, wrapped up in layers of clothing (see fig. 10). As Bowden writes, 'she could not appear less sexually provocative or more assiduously protected.'[18] The illustration emphasises the victim's extreme youth and innocence and therefore, by implication, the rapist's depravity, in sharp contrast to Voltaire's interpretation of the scene. Beauclerk's choice to imagine the girl as a child is disturbing in other ways, however: her depiction of the marriage bed scene shows both knight and the transformed loathly lady as children, in a bizarre and uncomfortable image (see fig. 11). The illustrations also suggest that the initial victim is the same person as the loathly lady/bride, a plot twist that also developed in the story of *La fée Urgèle*.

The transformation of the lady into a fairy—*la fée Urgèle*—was another innovation of Voltaire's. The 'real' identity of the loathly lady/beautiful young bride is treated variously in different versions of the story. The fundamental concept of the loathly lady story—the story of the monstrous woman who transforms into a beautiful, desirable girl after a hero has some kind of sexual encounter with her—can be found in myths from many different cultures. In many of these myths, the lady is a representative of the power of the land itself.[19] One example is the Irish story of the sons of Eochaid Mugmedon. The five sons—four legitimate and one illegitimate (Niall)—went hunting and were seeking water. Each in turn went to a well and found it guarded by a monstrous old woman, who said they could only have water if they kissed her. Four of the sons refused, but Niall agreed, and when he enthusiastically kissed her, she transformed into a beautiful woman. She then told him that she was the sovereignty of the country, Erin (Ireland). On his return to his brothers, they all ceded seniority to him, and he became king after his father.[20] Indeed, in many traditions, for instance in India and Cambodia, the story is framed as a myth about an immigrant warrior or prince who gains the right to rule from some kind of sexual union with a lady of the land, an earth goddess, who appears as a snake, dragon, or mermaid.[21] In these traditional myths, the loathly lady is always a supernatural force.

The medieval versions changed this. In the 'Tale of Florent' and *The Wedding of Sir Gawain and Dame Ragnall*, the loathly lady's real identity is an ordinary, mortal human. In both cases, she has been changed by dark magic wrought, significantly, by an older, evil woman. The story is no longer a primal myth but a fairytale of enchantment. Female power is no longer chthonic; rather it is a kind of malicious trickery, and the woman that the hero actually has sex with is a straightforward young, well-born, attractive virgin. The Wife of Bath, in contrast to both of these possibilities, simply offers no explanation. We are never told which identity is the 'real' one, or if the lady even has a 'real' identity. Voltaire does something new, in making the lady a named fairy—Urgèle—and thus transforming the whole story into a fairytale, in which heroine and fairy godmother figures are one.

This innovation proved extremely popular, and when the story was rewritten as a stage spectacular (with a libretto by Charles-Simon Favart and music by Egidio Duni), it was named *La fée Urgèle*. In this much-produced, frequently printed *opera comique*, further steps were taken to rehabilitate Chaucer's rapist.

La fée Urgèle opens with Marton—who is also now Urgèle—
declaring her love for Robert. She plans the whole imbroglio
herself, effectively entrapping the hero. He does not rape her,
nor is there any suggestion of such a thing—he merely kisses
her as the catalyst for the plot.[22] This was the version of the tale
that spread like wildfire across France, Germany, Russia, Den-
mark, Austria, Belgium, and Switzerland. It was no longer a
story about male criminality and the need to educate men to
think about female desire. Crucially, it had become a story in
which the audience's sympathies are squarely with the male
hero. The tale had been made safe for mass audiences, just as in
children's versions, the 'crime' tends to be described somewhat
vaguely as an 'insult.'[23]

Indeed, children's versions of the *Canterbury Tales* took off
in the nineteenth and twentieth centuries and, while the 'Wife
of Bath's Tale' was favoured, it was made less hard-hitting and
shocking by the removal of the rape. Even in versions aimed at
children, however, the knight tends to have far more culpability
than he does in *La fée Urgèle*. In the early Victorian *Tales from
Chaucer* by Charles Cowden Clarke, for instance, published in
1833, the knight sees a woman whom 'in a transport of wilful-
ness and brutality, he ill-treated' (114).[24] But in this and other
children's adaptations, the omission of the Wife of Bath as teller
changes the framing and overall effect of the story. Rather than
ending with Alison's exaggerated and exuberant demand for
mastery over her husbands, this version ends with the lady
'obeying him in all things and making his pleasure her happiness' (121). In a prefatory 'Address to My Young Readers,' Clarke
wrote that his primary aim was that his audience, 'might become
wise and good by the example of the sweet and kind creatures
described in [the Tales]' (1). Given that his selected tales include *none* of the fabliaux that dethrone patriarchal authority

(such as the Miller's, Reeve's, Cook's, Merchant's, Shipman's), and *all* of the tales in which women submit to oppressive patriarchal desires against their own wills (Knight's, Man of Law's, Clerk's), the idea of a woman making male pleasure her happiness seems to reflect Clarke's understanding of the 'wise and good' behaviour of 'sweet and kind creatures.' The Wife of Bath loses much of her bite, and all of her personality, in such truncated adaptations. Her removal from the text is so complete that the section at the end of the Clerk's Tale in which reference is made to her, and to the possibility of wifely dominance, is also cut from the text (145).

Audience sympathy was squarely directed towards the male characters and away from Alison in the early twentieth century in the United States, where, as had happened across the Continent in the eighteenth century, the Wife of Bath was put on stage. Like *La fée Urgèle*, Percy MacKaye's *Canterbury Pilgrims* became an extravagant spectacle, performed as a play, an opera, and a wildly ambitious pageant. Unlike Voltaire and his imitators, and also unlike those who adapted the tales for children, MacKaye was more interested in the Wife of Bath's Prologue than the Tale, although he does include part of the tale in his version. Throughout the play, the Wife of Bath is set up as an antagonist to the decent men of the play. They are embroiled in a conflict, a battle of wits. The story is based on Alison's desire to marry Chaucer, a fellow pilgrim. Chaucer, on the other hand, is in love with the Prioress, a sweet, innocent virgin. This participates in a long-standing critical tradition to see the two women as two poles of womanhood: Blake writes, 'The characters of Women Chaucer has divided into two classes, the Lady Prioress and the Wife of Bath. Are not these leaders of the ages of men? The lady prioress, in some ages, predominates; and in some the wife of Bath.'[25]

In MacKaye's play, the Prioress is on her way to meet her long-lost brother, who will recognise her by her 'Amor vincit omnia' brooch. This brother turns out to be the Knight. Alison tells Chaucer that she is sure that the Prioress is in fact on her way to meet a lover; Chaucer is so certain of the Prioress's virtue that he promises that, if the Prioress gives her brooch to someone other than her brother, he will marry Alison. (The plot device itself adapts the promise in The Wife of Bath's Tale, as well as the rash promise of The Franklin's Tale.) This prompts Alison to dress up as the Knight in a fascinating scene of cross-dressing, a scene that returns to the theme of 'knights versus women' that the tale itself had foregrounded, but in a very different way. Here, the Knight is the victim—kidnapped and tied up by Alison and her henchmen—and the woman is dramatically usurping his role, in a threat to patriarchy. This transvestism is part of a successful bid to convince the Prioress that Alison is the Prioress's brother, so that Alison-as-the-Knight can receive the brooch and trap Chaucer into marriage. Chaucer, however, knows that an alliance of privileged men will be able to beat any woman. In a final triumphant scene, Alison is confounded. When they arrive at Canterbury, Chaucer conspires with the most important men in the land—John of Gaunt and Richard II himself—and with the machinery of the law, represented by the Man of Law. These authoritative men happily make up laws on the spot in order to beat Alison, telling her that women are not allowed to marry a sixth time—unless they marry a miller. Alison is thus put in her place and coerced into marriage with the low-class, un-prestigious Miller, while the richer, more educated men can delight in their victory over her, a victory of the established, educated male characters over the vulgar lower classes and over sexually active women.

In the prologue to the first part of this book, I wrote about the connections between misogynist texts and lived experience, between literature and life. The promotional material for a production of MacKaye's play in Berkeley in 1917 jovially encourages the audience to treat it as a learning experience, an experience that is strictly gender-demarcated. The poster reads:

GIRLS: Are you trying to catch a Man? See how the Wife of Bath does it.
MEN: Are you Women Haters? If so, beware of Alison, she has caught forty already.[26]

What the play teaches the audience is that men need not fall victim to conniving women if they use their intelligence and social networks amongst other men. The 'girls' watching are decisively taught that successful men will always win in the end.

Both Favart and MacKaye make men the victims in their interpretations of the Wife of Bath, crafting stories in which women plan to trick men into marriage and in which women rate their own powerful sexual desires as more important than male desire. While this might seem to be a reasonable development of Alison's focus on the prime importance of female sovereignty, it is in fact a gross distortion of the ethical message of her tale and of its focus on male aggression and the violence of male sexual desire. It also distorts her prologue: Mackaye turns a fun, intelligent, pleasure-seeker who can parry words with any man into a quasi-rapist, who wants to marry Chaucer against his desire but who is ultimately not clever enough to win against him and his male allies.

Moving forward in time, Pasolini's interpretation of the Wife of Bath similarly distorts her character and values, and utterly changes the gender politics for which she stands. Like Voltaire, Pasolini is far more interested in the male erection and in male virility than he is in the abuse of women or the skewed gender power dynamics of patriarchal society.

Pier Paolo Pasolini (1922–1975) remains one of the most celebrated and notorious art-house filmmakers of the twentieth century. His film of the *Canterbury Tales*—*I racconti di Canterbury*—was the second in his 'trilogy of life' sequence, following a film based on Boccaccio's *Decameron*, and preceding one based on the *Arabian Nights*. *I racconti di Canterbury* premiered in 1972 and won the Golden Bear at the Berlin International Film Festival, although most critics' and viewers' responses have been less enthusiastic. The film does not attempt to link tellers and tales. It opens with a scene that focuses on some of the pilgrims, with the Host eventually proposing a tale-telling competition, but after this the tales are not 'told' by pilgrims; nor do the pilgrims comment or appear in links. Some of the tales are linked by the figure of Chaucer—played by Pasolini himself—trying to write the stories, and reflecting on them. The opening sequence prominently features the Wife of Bath, dressed all in luxurious red fabric, including an enormous hat, talking about herself at some length (see fig. 12). We see and hear far more of her and her prologue here than we do of any of the other characters. This scene is followed by eight separate tales: the Merchant's Tale, the Friar's Tale, the Cook's Tale, the Miller's Tale, the Wife of Bath's Prologue, the Reeve's Tale, the Pardoner's Tale, and the Summoner's Tale. The film then ends with a kind of arrival at Canterbury and with Chaucer finishing his book.

Pasolini's choice of tales, as well as his treatment and embellishment of them makes his interests clear. Those interests are dramatically skewed and unbalanced: in one critic's words, the film is 'a serious distortion of the complexity and grandeur of Chaucer's conception.'[27] In his later repudiation of the trilogy of life films, Pasolini writes about his desire, in these films, to represent bodies and the 'archaic, dark, vital violence of their sexual organs,' as the 'last bulwark of reality.'[28] His selection of tales included three about adultery (Merchant, Miller, Reeve); one about prostitution (Cook), and one about multiple marriage (Wife of Bath). While his other chosen tales are not, in the *Tales*, about sex, Pasolini alters them dramatically. The Friar's Tale now opens with graphic scenes of homosexual men being spied upon and the burning to death of a gay man. The Pardoner's Tale begins with brothel scenes featuring oral sex and flagellation. The Summoner's Tale concludes with an astonishing depiction of hell, developing a brief reference in Chaucer's text into a lengthy, zoomed-in depiction of the devil's bright red and extraordinarily capacious anus forcing out armies of friars. Across the tales, Pasolini's sympathies are with young, sexually active men. The camera repeatedly dwells on penises, flaccid when naked, erect when filmed under clothing. Bodies are easy of access, and the sex between May and Damian in the Merchant's Tale, Alison and Nicholas in the Miller's Tale, the students and the miller's wife and daughter in the Reeve's Tale, and Perkin, his friend, and the prostitute in the Cook's Tale is depicted as vital and joyous. Indeed, when Pasolini abjured the films, he lamented that television and education had 'degraded all youth and boys into being the worst type of second-rate, hard-to-please, complex-ridden, racist bourgeoisie.'[29] For Pasolini, the sub-proletariat, and especially boys and young men, should not be corrupted by bourgeois values but should retain a kind of primal vitality.[30] He was profoundly against consumerism and sexual liberation, which he saw as a false (because not complete) tolerance.[31]

This is the context in which Pasolini—whom critics have suggested had 'a misogynistic blind spot'—adapted the Wife of

Bath's Prologue.[32] The sequence opens with Alison in bed with her fourth husband, having sex with him, but eager to be gone. Her husband is clearly overexerting himself, and she leaves him in a dying state as she goes to see her friend. Together they spy on her friend's lodger through a keyhole, looking at his naked body, as the camera lingers on his genitals. As her husband dies from sex, Alison goes to a spring festival. Dressed all in red and crowned with her incredible red hat, she pulls Jankyn away from the crowd and masturbates him as he reads a book, telling him that he must marry her. In an admittedly comic scene, she attends her husband's funeral at one side of the church and then crosses to the other side to marry Jankyn. Cutting to their wedding night, Pasolini shows Jankyn as passive and uninterested in sex with Alison. Instead, he reads his book of wicked wives, and Alison attacks the book vigorously, at which point he, somewhat inadvertently, knocks her over. She dramatically feigns death, and when he bends close to her face, she viciously bites his nose.

The main message that comes out of this adaptation is that sexual activity with an older, experienced woman is a form of death. In direct opposition to the life-giving vitality of the young men's sexual experiences with other women in the film, which are accompanied with laughter, fantasy-packed dreams, and ecstasy (and also in opposition to the much-commented-on vitality of Chaucer's Alison), Pasolini's Wife of Bath is a harbinger of doom. Sex with her actually, literally, kills her fourth husband. Jankyn cannot get an erection with her—he is flaccid in the spring fair scene and unresponsive when she masturbates him; on their wedding night he is similarly not aroused. Like John Robert in Voltaire's *Ce qui plaît aux dames*, he is simply not sexually interested in this older woman who is depicted as trying to coerce him into sex. Again, as in MacKaye's text, the woman has become the rapist figure. And the idea of Alison as deathly is given a new twist in the final moments of the scene. Her violent and prolonged biting of Jankyn's nose is an obvious and recognisable symbol of castration.[33] Indeed, the fear that sex with Alison will kill a man bears similarities with the myth of the *vagina dentata* common in many cultures—the idea that women will devour and destroy men's virility.[34] This myth draws on fears similar to the fears motivating early versions of the loathly lady myth: women can look beautiful but be hiding their monstrosity; their sexuality is frightening; men have to tame and control their sexual power. Chaucer, via the Wife of Bath, was not telling those stories. He was consciously turning away from them, in his emphasis on Alison's appealing vitality and wit, in his shift to a quasi-realism rather than myth, and in his radical rewriting of the tale into a story about male criminality and female ethics. But over and over again, we see Chaucer's successors re-inscribing the story with patriarchal, misogynist myths about the horror of female sexuality.

My final example of this kind of distortion of Alison as she went on her travels comes from Poland and, like Pasolini's film, dates from the 1970s. It is an extraordinary testament to the power of the character of the Wife of Bath that she remained a crucial figure in so many cultures, and across so many centuries, political systems, and generic traditions. In 1976, the People's Republic of Poland was going through a crisis. Huge increases in state-set food prices led to protests and strikes in June, which were followed by a dramatic crackdown and the formation, in response, of the Workers' Defence Committee (later the Committee for Social Self-defence), an anti-communist group that supported workers and victims of government brutality, and was a precursor to the Solidarity movement. This same tumultuous year saw a production of the *Canterbury Tales*: the

Opowieści Kanterberyjskie premiered on 5 December at the Jan Kochanowski Theatre in Opole.[35] It was publicised with a poster designed by the dissident artist Jan Sawka (see fig. 13). He was exiled that very year and went to France and ultimately the United States; in later life he worked with, for instance, the Samuel Beckett Theatre and the Grateful Dead. In Poland he had been associated with intellectuals who opposed the communist state and supported greater freedom of expression. In art, they rejected socialist realism and the communist aesthetic orthodoxies, embracing pop art and political satire.[36]

Sawka's *Canterbury Tales* poster centres on the highly sexualised body of the Wife of Bath. Behind her is a cream sky, with a blazing red setting sun. She lies on her back, staring blankly upwards, though her face is hardly visible behind her exaggerated, pneumatic breasts. Her legs are clad in purple and orange striped stockings, attached with suspenders to a purple garment, and red shoes are just visible, while her skin is a lurid pink. Her arms and feet sink into a black morass of earth or fabric in which she seems to be rooted. Peeping up from between her breasts and legs are three tiny men, wearing hats and sunglasses and leering.[37] Her body serves as a table covered in bottles, cups, food, and a whole cooked chicken. It is a visually arresting and shocking image, and its meanings are manifold. As an advertisement for a play about a pilgrimage, it suggests that the female body is the pilgrimage route along which the tiny men can journey. They are the active agents, looking at the audience, while she lies prone, sinking into the ground, a corrupted version of an earth goddess. Her placement as a table again emphasises her passivity, and her role as something supporting male appetite—her body and sexual availability are paralleled with the meat and wine that cover her. We are certainly not encouraged to identify with the male figures, however: they are depicted as corrupt, lascivious figures, older men salivating over material pleasures of the flesh. If they are representatives of the communist political establishment, it seems that they are drawn as enjoying the luxuries of life and, specifically, the western culture that they purport to condemn. Is the Wife of Bath complicit in their corruption? She is not shown as enjoying herself in any way here; rather, she is a passive, recumbent figure. The poster also seems to bring together the Wife of Bath and the Pardoner: the three feasting figures are reminiscent of the three corrupt rioters of the Pardoner's Tale.

In Sawka's fascinating poster, then, the Wife of Bath has lost all semblance of autonomy, never mind wit, desire, and intelligence. She has become a symbol of the flesh, the appetite, and corruption. Portrayed primarily as a hyper-sexualised body, she also represents the enervating desires of declining old men. The sun is setting on their world, although they do not realise it. Yet the very style of the poster also brings the *Canterbury Tales* into the living culture of the 1970s, with its strong nod towards contemporary pop art.[38] Most interesting of all, perhaps, is that the Wife of Bath was still a powerful enough figure to take centre stage in a politicised art poster in Poland in 1976.

Alison's journeys around the world took her to all kinds of places, and enmeshed her in all kinds of politics. She never lost her ability to shock and to provoke reaction. Most often, that reaction was a desire to label her in some way, as a symbol of primal femininity or of fleshliness itself. Adaptations tended to simplify her complexity, to return to myths about gender and the earth, and to present her as conquered by men, to put her in her subordinate place. They turned away from Chaucer's interests in proto-realism and in depicting a woman who is intelligent, funny, and fully aware of the prejudices of patriarchal textual and sexual culture. Her playfulness, willingness to send herself up, and ability to hold her own in repartee all tended to vanish. Famous freethinkers such as Voltaire and Pasolini turned out not to be so freethinking when it came to women: adapting the Wife of Bath exposed their rather reactionary and conservative misogyny.

   It is a breath of fresh air, then, to see that in 2017 a Brazilian actress, Maite Proenca, herself a highly educated, well-travelled writer and feminist, commissioned and starred in a production of *A Mulher de Bath*, based on Jose Francisco Botelho's 2013 translation of the *Canterbury Tales* into Portuguese.[39] The promotional material tells us that this is a story about 'uma mulher de vasta experiência e de ardorosa oratória.'[40] Her two attributes here are her 'vast experience' and her 'ardent oratory': she is a rhetorician again, a dazzling speaker, who takes over texts and continents by the extraordinary power not of her body but of her speech. This is a much more faithful international representation of the Wife of Bath, who intimidated and frightened so many male writers and artists across time, but who, ultimately, would not be suppressed.

CHAPTER 9

Alison and the Novel

Nevertheless, she persisted.

—MITCH MCCONNELL, CONDEMNING
ELIZABETH WARREN, 2017

The Wife of Bath is a performer. Chaucer crafted a distinct voice for her, a voice that ventriloquises and demolishes the voices of her husbands and of church authority, a voice that is interrupted by and triumphs over male clerical pilgrims. The nature of medieval textual culture in the fourteenth century was such that the *Canterbury Tales* was read out to groups of people; it was designed to be performed and heard.[1] Across the centuries, as we have seen, responses to Alison have tended to be crafted in oral forms: ballads in the sixteenth and seventeenth centuries, plays from the sixteenth century up to the present day, Voltaire's *conte* in the eighteenth century, modern films and TV adaptations. In the last chapter of this book, I will be discussing twenty-first-century performance poetry and dramatic retellings of the Wife of Bath's Prologue and Tale. But in the twentieth century, Alison also metamorphosed into the traditionally silent form of the novel. Putting Alison into prose, and into a form that is usually private and silent, gives rise to particular challenges—which have been met in various creative ways. In this chapter, I will discuss one straightforward novel, one highly experimental, modernist novel, and one text that mixes prose, poetry, songs, and languages to make an entirely new form. Perhaps surprisingly, after all the knocks that she took from authors such as Voltaire and MacKaye, Alison staged a kind of comeback when she shape-shifted into prose.

This chapter of her life starts in the 1920s, when James Joyce was redefining what the novel might do. Fascinatingly, the Wife of Bath was reincarnated in Molly Bloom, one of the central characters in *Ulysses*, and one of the most famous female characters in twentieth-century literature. *Ulysses*, often considered the defining work in modernist writing, is set on one day, 16 June 1904, and follows three characters who correspond with figures from the *Odyssey*—Leopold Bloom (Odysseus), Stephen Dedalus (Telemachus), and Molly Bloom (Penelope). An extraordinarily allusive and complex novel, it is both highly structured and seemingly associative and digressive. Joyce, a passionate medievalist, transposed and transformed Chaucer in a number of ways in his novel. It is particularly significant that he responded both to the character of Alison and to the form in which she spoke. Indeed, in my view, Joyce's most profound rewriting of Chaucer came in his *structural* response to Alison's speech.

Although many might more immediately think of Joyce as a classicist, given the fact that *Ulysses* is based on a re-imagining of the episodes of the *Odyssey*, Joyce himself said that 'the medieval, in my opinion, had greater emotional fecundity than classicism.'[2] This aspect of his intellectual world has generally been underdiscussed. A recent collection, however, suggests that the fact that Joyce 'was medieval . . . is surely uncontroversial,' quoting part of *Finnegan's Wake* to describe Joyce himself: 'He's weird, I tell you, and middayevil down to his vegetable soul.'[3] In the Oxen of the Sun episode of *Ulysses*, Joyce demonstrates his mastery of English prose style right across time, as he parodies every era, beginning with Old English 'Before born babe had bliss. Within womb won he worship,' and moving through later-medieval style, 'let us speak of that fellowship that was there to the intent to be drunken as they might.'[4] He imitates a huge range of authors—including Milton, Browne, Pepys, Defoe, Sterne, Pater, Dickens, and Newman, before language collapses into a variety of dialects, slang, and doggerel. This is not a teleological progression but a brilliant depiction of the archaeology of prose style, a depiction that demonstrates Joyce's profound knowledge of the history of literature in English.[5] He also, however, had an equivocal relationship with the language, and there are parallels to be drawn between medieval Europe and twentieth-century Ireland as places in which a 'common language' struggled against a more authoritative, transnational language (vernaculars vs. Latin; Irish vs. English).[6]

Joyce's interest in the medieval went far beyond the English. He was fascinated by, and knowledgeable about, many aspects of medieval thought, philosophy, and literature, but Chaucer held a special place in his imagination. He said, 'Of all English writers Chaucer is the clearest'—though of course we should not ignore the qualifying 'English' here.[7] His friend Louis Gillet wrote that Joyce 'always had an unbounded admiration for Chaucer,' and that he thought that the General Prologue was 'a miracle of artistry.'[8] Joyce worked on 'The Good Parson of Chaucer' in Padua in 1912 and received full marks.[9] Engaging in detail with the Parson's Tale suggests a deep commitment to the *Canterbury Tales* in its overall complexity. He owned two scholarly editions of Chaucer's complete works, plus several anthologies that included excerpts from Chaucer's writings.[10] At one point, when he was in Paris without access to his own books, he found it necessary to borrow another copy of Chaucer immediately.[11] While Joyce was working hard on *Ulysses*, in 1919, he read the General Prologue out to his friend Frank Budgen.[12] In the 1930s, he expended a surprising amount of energy in trying to pressure publishers into printing a version of Chaucer's 'ABC to the Virgin'—one of Chaucer's short, probably early, poems—illustrated by elaborate initials, or 'lettrines' that he had persuaded his daughter, Lucia, to create. Encouraging Lucia (who suffered from acute mental illness) by attaching these lettrines to Chaucer's poem and getting it published became an important project for Joyce, who eventually managed to achieve publication for the edition in a 300-copy print run, accompanied by an introduction by Louis Gillet.[13] This strange episode attests to the specific importance that Chaucer had for Joyce throughout his adult life.

That importance comes out particularly clearly in his creation of Molly Bloom, whom many critics have compared to Alison of Bath.[14] Justman, for example, writes that 'Molly Bloom bears witness to the Wife of Bath as powerfully as the Wife does her own much closer original,' while Cooper calls the Wife of Bath's Prologue 'the fullest literary precursor to Molly's speech.'[15] Others point out their close similarities but think that this was not a conscious decision on Joyce's part, suggesting both that Joyce perhaps did not realise how much his reading of Chaucer shaped his work and that at least some of the similarities between the characters arose from Chaucer and Joyce's parallel situations in patriarchal, Catholic societies.[16] In Joyce's own lifetime, in comments praised by Joyce himself, his friend

Gillet wrote that perhaps Molly 'is a descendant of that laughing, lively, and buxom Wife of Bath.'[17]

The two characters and their extraordinary speeches are indeed strikingly similar. Both women speak at extreme length—one in an interior monologue (the final section of *Ulysses*, known as 'Penelope'), the other to the pilgrim company—and in the form of a confession that seems to be unfiltered. While Alison's prologue is many times longer than anyone else's, Molly's sentences immediately stand out for their unmeasured rush of language—the first sentence is 2,500 words long. Her largely unpunctuated, seemingly authentic stream of memory and opinions replicates the illusion of hearing a voice. Joyce's innovations with prose style here represent one way of dealing with the problem of trying to create a voice in a non-oral form.

Both characters tell us about their lives from the time they entered the sexual economy: we hear about Alison's marriages from the age of twelve and Molly's teenage sexual experiences with Lieutenant Mulvey. They are both conscious of themselves as ageing women—Alison is in her forties, Molly is thirty-three—and talk about their memories, especially of lovers and sexual experiences, which are described graphically. Molly's description of men in her life is far more similar to Alison's detailing of her husbands than it is to Penelope's attempts to hold off her suitors. Both Alison and Molly are sexually interested in younger men of around age twenty ('He was, I trowe, twenty wynter oold, / And I was fourty, if I shal seye sooth; / But yet I hadde alwey a coltes tooth' [600–602]; 'I wonder is he too young . . . I suppose hes 20 or more Im not too old for him' [725]). They focus on the body and on desire, and on the naturalness of that desire, claiming that having sex has an obvious rightness about it: 'to what conclusion / Were membres maad of generacion . . . ?' (why were genitals made? [115–116]); 'what else were we given all those desires for I'd like to know' (726–727).

Although neither character is wholly either an archetype or a fully realised individual, Joyce is more interested in universals than Chaucer and conceived of Molly in more mythic terms that those in which Chaucer imagined Alison. Joyce wrote of 'Penelope' that:

> It begins and ends with the female word *yes*. It turns like the huge earth ball slowly surely and evenly round and round spinning, its four cardinal points being the female breasts, arse, womb and cunt expressed by the words *because, bottom* (in all senses bottom button, bottom of the class, bottom of the sea, bottom of his heart), *woman, yes*. Though probably more obscene than any preceding episode it seems to me to be perfectly sane full amoral fertilisable untrustworthy engaging shrewd limited prudent indifferent *Weib. Ich bin der Fleisch der stets bejaht* [woman. I am the flesh that always affirms].[18]

He reiterates elsewhere the idea of Molly as essentially representing woman in general and the flesh—a very medieval way of thinking about sex, but one that Chaucer had refined, nuanced, and questioned in his creation of the Wife of Bath.[19] Chaucer's depiction of Alison, as I have been discussing throughout this book, brought together gendered stereotypes, historically specific circumstances, and a depiction of an individual, within certain constraints. A crucial aspect of Alison's character is that she explicitly foregrounds the idea of women as pure flesh, unintellectual, and unable to form arguments, and demonstrates that such an idea is born out of a profoundly biased canon and idea of authority. Indeed, we do hear in Molly's confession a faint echo of Alison's 'Who painted the lion?' when she says, while reading stories, that 'sure theres nothing for a woman in all that invention made up' (703) and even, in a comically self-referential moment, 'I don't like books with a Molly in them' (707). Joyce thus allows her to complicate his stated intention, to seem to step outside of his imagination. But we do not see in Molly anything resembling Alison's proficiency with, for instance, rhetorical technique, clerical modes of quotation, and detailed knowledge of the inadequacies of the church fathers. Critics who suggest that they are both 'the same archetypal character' or that they share the 'same primary female instincts' reveal more about themselves than they reveal about their understanding of Chaucer in particular.[20]

Joyce's sense of what he wanted his text to do, and what he wanted Molly to represent, was different in many ways to Chaucer's vision of the *Canterbury Tales* and the Wife of Bath. But Joyce was a careful reader of his sources. Umberto Eco writes that 'Joyce's concept of imitation was closer to that of the medieval, which entailed transformation rather than simple copy.'[21] In Joyce's structural transformation of the Wife of Bath's *medial* prologue into Molly's *concluding* monologue, we see a crucial response to Alison and a suggestion of her importance to Joyce. While Chaucer did not set a clear ordering of his tales, there is no doubt that the Wife of Bath came somewhere in the middle. She is not part of the first fragment—the General Prologue and four tales—nor is she part of the final four tales. The Parson's Tale is established as the last tale, the tale told with Canterbury on the horizon, the day drawing to its close, the scales of judgement in the sky. The final word is given to the cleric whom Alison seems to oppose in the endlink to the Man of Law's Tale, and a representative of the class with whom Alison is in conflict more generally. That does not necessarily give the Parson authority, but he does have the last word. In absolute contrast, Joyce gives Molly the last word, and the literal last word is 'yes,' a word that, for Joyce, represented female genitalia, while also being a word of more general affirmation and vitality. Structurally, while Penelope is important throughout the *Odyssey*, it is in the last few books that Odysseus returns to Ithaca and they are reunited—so she has more of a 'concluding' role than Alison does. But Penelope is not part of the last book (and she never reveals her interiority in the way that Alison and Molly seem to reveal theirs). The fact that Joyce lets his own relatively ordinary, sexually active, working, middle-aged woman conclude his text is a transformation of Alison that Chaucer would surely have appreciated.

Fifty years later, a female author, Vera Chapman (1898–1996), wrote a novel titled simply *The Wife of Bath*. One of the first women to matriculate at Oxford and the founder of the Tolkien Society, Chapman wrote a number of novels inspired by medieval literature.[22] Chapman's version is not formally experimental: it is a short novel that expands the Prologue and Tale, fleshing out Alison's earlier life and her experiences on the pilgrimage and giving her a happy ending with another marriage. Chapman tells us about Alison's parents and siblings, how she lost her virginity, her working life, her encounters with men of other religions in Palestine and in North Africa, and her children.[23] On the way, Chapman makes changes to Alison that make her more conventional, and less interesting, as she strives to make her more 'likeable.'

Chapman has many of the same preoccupations as earlier adaptors of the Wife of Bath, but she is noticeably more sympathetic to her than many of her predecessors were. For instance, many rewriters of the Wife of Bath foreground the Prioress as well, presenting the two women as two versions of femininity—

one promiscuous, the other chaste; one bold, the other modest; one worldly, the other cloistered. In Percy MacKaye's version, the Prioress is the object of Chaucer's affections. She is attractive and innocent, and the sexual suggestiveness of her 'Amor vincit omnia' brooch is neutralised by MacKaye's insistence that it relates to her brother. Chaucer ultimately wins her for marriage, with the fact that she is a nun simply being ignored at the end. Throughout, Alison is her antagonist. In John Gay's version, the Lady Myrtilla is the nun figure, and again Chaucer is in love with her. Her innocent femininity is set against Alison's ageing, experienced sexuality, and while the other girls are married off, Alison is left alone in the later version of the play. In stark contrast, Chapman presents the Prioress in a wholly unflattering light. Alison and the Prioress were childhood acquaintances, and the Prioress is now depicted as a selfish and malicious woman who taunts Alison and torments the younger nuns who travel with her. The Prioress also voices the misogyny of the Wife of Bath's Prologue, citing the wedding of Cana to tell Alison that she should only have married once. She is a bitter and unpleasant character, in comparison with whom Alison is far more appealing.

Similarly, Chapman changes Alison's relationship with Chaucer. While MacKaye imagined Alison trying to entrap Chaucer, making them antagonists, Chapman portrays them as allies. Although they kiss once, neither desires the other—they are depicted as friends, with Chaucer listening with fascination to Alison's confession of her past life. MacKaye and Gay both present her as rather desperately husband-hunting on the Canterbury pilgrimage. In Gay's play she at first possibly manages to snare the Franklin, but this is changed in the later version, as discussed earlier, when she ends up alone. In MacKaye's play, she is forced into marriage with the Miller through the legal trickery of the men. But in Chapman's novel, Alison is not desperate, and even turns down the Knight's proposal. Ultimately, Alison and the Franklin are happily united in marriage, with Chaucer giving her away. Indeed, it turns out that she lost her virginity to the Franklin many decades earlier, but they had been separated through an unfortunate set of circumstances— he had been called suddenly to his father's deathbed and had no way of contacting her.

Over and over again we see Chapman presenting Alison in a more flattering light than many other adaptors. In an extraordinary episode in Morocco, Alison heroically saves a group of nuns from rape, by offering herself to the Bey, the leader of the Moors, instead. In Palestine, she demonstrates her open-minded nature by falling in love with a Muslim. Back near Canterbury, it is concern for the Squire, who does not wish his father to marry again, that makes her reject the Knight. She also rejects the Squire himself, knowing that he is too young and that a relationship would be inappropriate. We are also encouraged to sympathise with her as she is twice nearly the victim of rape, both in her youth and on the Canterbury pilgrimage. On the first occasion, a friar attacks her; on the second it is the Summoner. Each time she, an archetypal damsel in distress, is rescued by a man—the Franklin and then the Knight. These episodes also allow Alison's tale to permeate her own life. Her tale begins with a girl raped outside in the countryside; similarly, the attacks on Alison both happen outside in the woods. At the centre of the Wife of Bath's Tale we see a strange, faerie scene, in which mysterious dancers in the woods suddenly vanish. Chapman transposes this scene into the Canterbury pilgrimage. Chaucer and Alison together see the dancers in the woods, and Chaucer knows that this foreshadows a change in

Alison's own life (which turns out to be her reuniting with Gilbert, the Franklin).

Another significant change to Alison's life is that Chapman explicitly makes her a mother, of five sons, one of whom dies in infancy. The first is conceived out of wedlock, to Gilbert, after whom he is named, but she passes him off as her first husband's. The other four are born to her third husband. Chaucer never says that the Wife of Bath is childless. We do not know anything about the children, or lack of children, of most of the male pilgrims, and this causes no assumptions or speculation one way or the other. It could be that whether or not she has children is simply not relevant to the aspects of her life that she wants to talk about in her prologue. The fact that she tells us so much about her personal life without mentioning children does, however, make it more likely that we are supposed to see her as childless. There is even a phrase in the General Prologue description of her that may imply her familiarity with contraception and abortion. The narrator tells us that she knows well the 'remedies of love' (General Prologue, 475). While this may refer to Ovid's Remedia Amoris, or to ways of finding love, or to aphrodisiacs, love potions, or cures for lovesickness, it could also refer to contraception and abortion, as the Middle English Dictionary suggests.[24] Birth control certainly existed in many forms in this era, and it would fit in with the general picture of Alison for her to be in control of her fertility.[25] Setting aside these debates, it is clear that Chaucer does not actively present her as a mother. But for Chapman, her motherhood is important: in later life Alison lives with her son and daughter-in-law, and just as Chapman encourages sympathy for her by repeatedly placing her in the damsel-in-distress role in which she is rescued by a heroic man, the author also makes her a softer, less threatening character by turning her into an affectionate mother. Women are 'supposed' to be fertile, to be maternal, to love their children. Furthermore, she is given a stereotypically happy-ever-after ending with her first and true love, returning with him to a life of secure domesticity. Throughout the novel, then, Chapman wants readers to like Alison and works hard to make her likeable, but she does this by making her less idiosyncratic, more akin to familiar heroines. Across the novel as a whole, Alison loses her verbal brilliance, her wit, her complexity, as she is reshaped into a rather conventional form.

In a very recent iteration of Alison, her form is anything but familiar. Caroline Bergvall's *Alisoun Sings* (2019) is not exactly a novel—it is mainly prose, and set into chapters, but also includes sections in poetry and song.[26] It is the third in a trilogy of works that all blend medieval and contemporary sources and languages. Part Middle English, part a variety of modern Englishes, sometimes formal, sometimes colloquial, sometimes ventriloquizing pop lyrics, *Alisoun Sings* is a startling and idiosyncratic text. The playful innovations of this work engage with the problem of muting an oral text by emphasising the spoken voice. In the preface, Bergvall writes about the process of creating the text as an experience in which the Wife of Bath spoke through her. She writes about spending years listening for her voice, which can be heard 'wherever the veils of time draw thin' (vii). Later in the book, she depicts Alisoun and the author (herself) fighting with each other (58), and at another point depicts their relationship as tense, partly because of the difficulty of re-imagining Alisoun's spoken voice: 'Looking for relevant ways to reinvest your iconic figure's speaking habits as the impressively loudmouthed past-future era maximalist female that you are has been a pretty taxing task for the troubled foibled comlicated 21st century writer fighta that I be' (49).

As Bergvall makes explicitly clear here, she is concerned with foregrounding the relevance of Alisoun to twenty-first-century politics and problems, and with mixing different times and stages in language. In 'Stitch' (69–87), for instance, she runs an extraordinary gamut through Alisoun's work in the cloth trade and how it relates to trade with Ghent and Flanders, the development of buttons, sumptuary laws, and the birth of fashion in the fourteenth century; to textile factories, the environmental damage wreaked by modes of cotton production, craftivism, Gandhi, and the use of certain items of clothing or colours for protest by women in Israel, Argentina, the former Yugoslavia, the United Kingdom, the United States, Catalonia, Uganda, and Russia. Or, to take an example of how Bergvall deals with one word of Alisoun's description, she analyses 'gat-toothed' (General Prologue, 468; Wife of Bath's Prologue, 603) in an associative and deeply creative way (97–101). Starting with the description itself, she takes the idea of the 'gap' in the teeth to talk about the gender gap, gaps in the Carolingian (punning on Caroline) script, the etymology of 'gap' through Old Frisian, Old Saxon, and Low German, making connections with Sanskrit and Greek, moving on to Mary Douglas's key work *Purity and Danger*, with its focus on anthropological ideas about the proper functions of gaps and orifices, and ending with a horrifying story of gang rape and the violence enacted on women, which leads us to the damage wrought on Alisoun's ear, implicitly returning us to the General Prologue reference to her deafness. Bergvall tells us: 'I see gaps everywhere! Xlaims Alisoun enchanted' (99).

Bergvall is steeped in medieval and modern culture. Women such as Beyoncé, Gina Miller, Mary Beard, Judith Butler, Audre Lorde, Diane Abbott, and Arundhati Roy all feature in Alisoun's speech.[27] But medieval examples are also prominent. For instance, she retells a story from the preface to Caxton's *Eneydos*

(29–30). The fact of her quoting this story demonstrates her interest in medieval writing, but the story itself is also significant: it is a famous story about language change, and individuals within England not understanding each other because they use different words for the same thing (eyren and egges). Bergvall is concerned with the otherness of older language forms, and with performing those forms. Alisoun often talks about language saying, for instance, 'Ive gotta traders grammar, lovers declension, indeedy me loins may stoppe blede, will get to that, but ma lovejuice is out of this worlde, has just begun aflowe the banks and whan I speech like this ma thoughts & aventures, tis like I am ysitting the lap of Sherazade & she axe for it 2 be longe 2 be loude, thats my whole megafony!' (5). Medieval—or faux-medieval—forms such as 'y' at the beginning of a verb, or final 'e's, and medieval spellings such as 'whan' or 'aventures' are juxtaposed with informal, modern words such as 'lovejuice,' or 'megafony,' and texting language such as '2' for 'to.' The whole effect is not mimicry or re-enactment; it is obviously performative and excessive, declaring and luxuriating in its artifice. This form of writing itself enacts the question that animates and drives the whole text—how can the past best speak to and in the present?

This question is, in a way, answered in the last sentence of the book, when Alisoun declares that she is 'not bygone just bigonne' (120). In other words, she is not finished with or left behind in the past; she is just beginning. The punning language play, and the use of older spelling and forms to declare immediate relevance itself insists on the applicability of the history of language and literature to the modern words that we use and stories that we tell. Alison has been changed by Bergvall, but not out of all recognition. She brings Chaucer and the medieval into her new incarnation.

This text is about the importance of metamorphosis—of form, of time, of bodies, and of gender. Bergvall is interested in queer and trans bodies—in 'Alisouns of all genderings' (52)—and in making those bodies part of Alisoun's conversation. She mentions contemporary trans women such as Chelsea Manning (43), and writes about her own queer relationship (53–54). The story of John/Eleanor Rykener, a medieval trans woman, is also told (11–12). Rykener lived in the late fourteenth century, and her story survives in court documents. She was tried as a man who had had sex 'as a woman' under the direction of a bawd, mainly with clerics. It is unclear from the documents what was 'really' happening: if this was a transgender woman or a transvestite man, for instance, and if the clients knew exactly what was going on or not.[28] But it is a case that demonstrates the complexity of sex and gender in the Middle Ages; as Bergvall writes, 'Many such stories abounden of sexual richesse & its problems wit the lawe. Many with more dire consequences' (12).

Bergvall does not shy away from writing about dire consequences. Her text is full of stories of the oppression of female and queer bodies across time, of sometimes graphic descriptions of sexual violence, of references to climate change, and of descriptions of political oppression and injustice. However, it is ultimately a profoundly affirmative text that asserts the ongoing importance of the past and specifically of this unique, pioneering female character and what she stands for. Earlier in this chapter, I mentioned Molly Bloom's final 'yes,' and the fact that this female affirmation is the last word of Joyce's masterpiece. 'Yes,' is a crucial word in *Alisoun Sings* as well. At the end of the chapter 'Pilgrimming,' a poetic section of the text concludes with a six-line stanza (111). The first line reads, 'Everything in the world began with a Yes.' The next five lines repeat the same sentiment in five more languages: Greek, Arabic, German, Catalan, and

Portuguese. The languages range from national, widely spoken languages to a minority, under-threat dialect, and they use three different alphabet systems. The ideas that Alisoun seems to stand for in this text—survival, rebellion, challenging authority, especially when it comes in the form of male violence, the importance of speaking your truth, the validity of sexual desire and experience, the ongoing power of telling tales, the importance of keeping languages and stories alive—are presented as ideas that cross cultures, languages, and times.

Alisoun Sings is optimistic about the power of these messages. The book encourages, even exhorts, its readers to say yes to Alisoun in a true moment of pleasure. By writing in a hybrid form and in a hybrid language, Bergvall has created a character who, in her complexity, vitality, and commitment to protest suggests that a woman can make a difference in the world without sacrificing her enjoyment. The singer of this text is an extraordinarily weird, but wonderfully appropriate, new version of Alison of Bath.

CHAPTER 10

Black Alisons: Wives of Brixton, Bafa, and Willesden

She nah easy and she speak as she find.

—ZADIE SMITH, *THE WIFE OF WILLESDEN*

In the twenty-first century, Alison reinvented herself through new authors in postcolonial Britain. Over the last couple of decades we have seen Black female poets voicing, performing, rewriting, and rethinking Alison, from Jean 'Binta' Breeze's 'The Wife of Bath in Brixton Market,' performed in the multicultural space of an ordinary London market, to Patience Agbabi's Wife of Bafa, in which Alison becomes Mrs Alice Ebi Bafa, a cloth seller from Nigeria, to Zadie Smith's Alvita, a much-married woman living in Willesden, North London, with her roots in the West Indies. In all of these cases, Alison becomes a Black woman with a transnational identity that stretches across multiple cultures. In each version, she is written by a woman—finally, women have decisively started to claim Alison's voice after hundreds of years of male appropriations—and she is written in an oral form. All three texts can be read on the page, but can also be heard and viewed, in an apt echo of medieval reading practices. Alison has given herself a makeover in the twenty-first century and has come to new life in a number of rich postcolonial contexts, a Wife of Bath firmly born out of the contemporary moment. In the Royal Shakespeare Company's production of *The Canterbury Tales* in 2005, we also saw a Black Wife of Bath, as Alison was played by the Antiguan-British actress Claire Benedict.

Black female poets from other parts of the world have also been inspired by the *Canterbury Tales*, but less specifically by the Wife of Bath. Marilyn Nelson's *The Cachoeira Tales*, Karen King-Aribisala's *Kicking Tongues*, and Gloria Naylor's *Bailey's Café* all take the *Canterbury Tales* as a jumping-off point and use the text as a way to explore 'African diasporic identities.'[1] All three texts are structured around telling tales and around questions of identity. Nelson and King-Aribisala structure their texts through the idea of the pilgrimage-esque journey (from America to Brazil; from Lagos to Abuifa). Indeed, Nelson explicitly positions her text as 'a reverse diaspora,' 'a pilgrimage,' to somewhere 'sanctified by the Negro soul.'[2] All three writers are interested in the Wife of Bath: Jesse Bell, a character in Bailey's Café (a version of Harry Bailly's Tabard Inn), is a sexually promiscuous woman who talks about the tricks of the trade, such as feigning jealousy, and also laments the fact that she, unlike men, does not have control over texts. In *The Cachoeira Tales*, the Director—a character known, like the Canterbury pilgrims, by her occupation—has obvious affinities with the Wife of Bath. She is 'an ample sister, middle-aged' described as 'a champagne cocktail of faith and outrage / With one tooth missing from her ready smile.'[3] This is a marked reference to Alison's gap-toothed mouth. She has affinities with other pilgrims too, however. Her ascetic devotion to her art evokes the Clerk; the short tale she tells with its focus on a bare bottom emerging on a ski slope is a little reminiscent of the Miller's Tale, the denouement of which also involves a naked behind.[4] The influence of different parts of the *Tales* across the text is disparate and creative. Another moment in the text is, I think, particularly influenced by the Wife of Bath. The pilot tells a story about someone taking a Rorschach test. He ends his anecdote:

> So the shrink says, 'My goodness, Mr. Green,
> you have the filthiest mind I've ever seen!'
> the brother says, 'It's just like the white man
> to blame the Negro! Dr Smith, you can
> say what you want, but you got to admit you're
> the one that showed me all them dirty pictures!'[5]

This is the same kind of message as 'who painted the lion?' emphasising that the powerful have control over narratives, but that the object of a narrative will have a very different perspective on what has happened. The power dynamic, however, is changed from man and woman to white and Black. The Wife of Bath is a part of these Chaucer-inspired texts, but none of these poets takes the Wife of Bath as their focus, and it is also fair to say that these adaptations are not closely bound to Chaucer's text, unlike the texts that I will focus on in this chapter.

It is particularly striking that three of the most important Black British female poets of the twenty-first century have written texts that directly and explicitly rework the Wife of Bath as the centre of a new poem or play. All three create modern versions of the Wife of Bath, and retell her life—and in two cases, her tale as well—in new settings. Jean 'Binta' Breeze, who was born in Jamaica in 1957, moved to the United Kingdom in 1985, and died in 2021, was a pioneering poet, the first woman to write and perform dub poetry.[6] She published her 'Wife of Bath speaks in Brixton Market' in 2000 within a collection, *The Arrival of Brighteye and Other Poems*.[7] The title poem in the collection was commissioned by the BBC (British Broadcasting Corporation) in 1998, as part of the fifty-year anniversary celebrations of the arrival of the Windrush generation in 1948. 'The Wife of Bath Speaks in Brixton Market' is a loose translation of the first 130 lines of the Wife of Bath's Prologue into Jamaican English. A striking performance of the poem can be viewed on Youtube: Breeze performs the poem as she walks through Brixton Market, peopled with the buyers and sellers of an ordinary day, many of whom look bemused at the presence of this charismatic woman reciting poetry to camera as she moves through the space of the market.[8]

The second version of the Wife of Bath that I discuss in this chapter is Patience Agbabi's Wife of Bafa. Agbabi, born in 1965 in London to Nigerian parents, originally wrote 'The Wife of Bafa' as a stand-alone text, a version of the Wife of Bath's Prologue, in Nigerian English. She writes that, having studied Chaucer at Oxford, she 'had a lifelong ambition to reinterpret the character,' talking about Alison as 'a timeless, complex character' who is recognised everywhere that Agbabi performs. Agbabi is a performance poet, and in her discussion of the poem, she emphasises that it changes 'each time it's delivered.'[9] 'The Wife of Bafa' was published in 2000, in the collection *Transformatrix*. Agbabi then—like so many authors across time—realised that she was not done with Alison and returned to her, and to the *Canterbury Tales* as a whole. In 2014, she published *Telling Tales*, a remix of the entire text, including every single tale. 'The Wife of Bafa' is expanded in this text to include a version of the tale set in Ghana, as well as the prologue.[10]

The final text that I explore in this chapter is Zadie Smith's *The Wife of Willesden*, a hugely ambitious dramatic adaptation of the Wife of Bath's Prologue and Tale, with a version of the General Prologue and the Retraction framing it. This play was supposed to be premiered and published in 2020, when Brent, a London borough, was London's Borough of Culture. The pandemic caused a delay in both performance and publication, and it was premiered in November 2021. The Wife of Willesden is a faithful but creative version of the Wife of Bath—now Alvita—a woman from a Jamaican background who lives and loves in a multicultural and meticulously depicted local community in London. Her voice is split across multiple characters, who act out the scenes that she describes, as she tells her own story and opines about marriage and sexuality. Some of these characters are, for instance, her aunt, her niece, and her husbands, but others are the authority figures of the text—including Socrates, God, and Saint Paul. Nelson Mandela even makes an appearance. Alvita, described in the stage directions as 'a world-class raconteur,' speaks in a 'North Weezy' accent—that is, the accent of a specific area of North West London—but is a consummate performer, sometimes lapsing into 'deliberate poshness,' 'Jamaican patois,' or 'cockney.'[11] The play begins General Prologue style—in a pub, with a 'General Lock-In,' and the publican suggesting a tale-telling contest. Alvita then reprises the Wife of Bath's Prologue. It is an astute reading of the prologue, translating many ideas, idioms, and images directly, while also bringing it right up to date. Like the original, it is long and luxuriant.

Once Alvita gets on to her tale, it is flagged as 'Transferred from Arthurian Camelot to Maroontown, Jamaica' (71), and again we hear a story that is both familiar and unfamiliar. Rather than being set in a pre-Christian Arthurian Britain, it is now set in eighteenth-century Jamaica, a place where Jamaican folklore and belief in duppy (spirits/ghosts) dominate. The play was first performed at the Kiln Theatre, with the extraordinary Clare Perkins in the title role (see fig. 14). She dominated the stage, entirely in keeping with Alison's dominance of the space of storytelling in the *Canterbury Tales*, shouting down interruptions, interacting with and winning over the audience, commanding other actors to become her memories and to play out the voices in her head. The nuances of the text were also brilliantly conveyed through the staging: the moment when the rapist Maroon self-pityingly bemoans the loss of his own bodily freedom, and his rape victim silently appears and looks him in the eye, was devastating. In this play, the fourteenth-century poem enters the world of #MeToo.

Just as Breeze's text is connected to Windrush through its association with *The Arrival of Brighteye*, so Smith dedicates her play to 'the Windrush generation, with much love and respect.' The arrival in Tilbury Docks, Essex, of the ship HMT *Empire Windrush*, on 22 June 1948 came to symbolise the era of postwar mass migration to the United Kingdom by people of colour from the Caribbean, because it was the first ship to arrive after the 1948 British Nationality Act. This law gave British citizenship and right of settlement in the United Kingdom to anyone born in a British colony and prompted major demographic change in the United Kingdom, which now had a far larger non-white population than it had had previously.[12] Over the last few years, the Windrush generation has become a symbol of British institutional racism. In the wake of the 'hostile environment' government policy (2012) that moved against migrants, many members of the Windrush generation were deported, often because they lacked immigration documents. These were documents they had not needed, as they had arrived as British citizens. In many cases, elderly British people, who had come to the United Kingdom as young children, were deported to countries that they had not been to for perhaps fifty years, and where they had no family or connections. The scandal has been heavily publicised since 2017, and a dedication to the Windrush generation since that date inevitably evokes not only the experiences of arriving in the United Kingdom in the 1940s, and the lives that migrants made for themselves out of the opportunities and oppression that they faced, but also the ongoing outrages of the treatment of this generation in the last few years.[13] Indeed, *The Wife of Willesden* is insistently a text of the present moment, as well as a text of the past, a play that presents its Wife of Bath as 'a Kilburn girl at heart' but that is written entirely in Chaucer's iambic pentameter.[14]

How did the Wife of Bath get herself noticed by these three poets? Of course, they are not all doing the same thing, but they clearly share some concerns and interests. First of all, then, why use Chaucer for inspiration? All three poets focus their attention on what English and Englishness are, and on how specific locations tell the story of a changing nation. Like Chaucer, Breeze, Agbabi, and Smith's lives are all bound up in the London area. Across the centuries, Chaucer has come to be seen as the Father of English Literature, at the head of the English canon, and for some, he is the original 'dead white male,' symbolising a particular kind of authority and exclusion, and representing a literary tradition and nation that was created by men to prop up a conservative white establishment. While it is inarguable that Chaucer is indeed a dead white man, the idea that he represents conservative authority and a monocultural England is profoundly misleading. Chaucer was an experimental, even radical, poet whose poetics were driven by the idea of hearing multiple voices and perspectives, and who asserted the importance of listening to marginal voices. He was born in the ward of London that contained more immigrants than any other, and he grew up watching the ships come in, bringing spices from as far away as Indonesia.[15] He lived in a multilingual environment and travelled widely, including to Navarre, where there were significant Jewish and Muslim communities.[16] We know that he was aware of the intellectual achievements of Muslim scholars, and indeed he translated a treatise into English from Latin that was itself translated from Arabic.[17]

As historians have discussed, there have always been Black people in England. This has also been an important issue for fiction writers: Bernardine Evaristo, the first Black woman to win the Man Booker prize, wrote a novel in blank verse in 2001 (at around the same time as Breeze and Agbabi wrote their versions of Alison) that focused on the presence of Black women in Roman London.[18] *The Emperor's Babe* is centred on a Sudanese woman in London in the early third century, drawing readers' attention to England's long history of migration.[19] In Chaucer's time too, there is evidence of visitors to London from Africa, such as 'Affrikano Petro' (African Peter).[20] In the introduction to *The Wife of Willesden*, Smith mentions the 'Black Madonna' (x) in Saint Mary's Willesden, a church that also appears in her earlier novel, *NW*. The Black Madonna of Willesden was a focus for pilgrimage for hundreds of years, until it was destroyed in the Reformation. In the early sixteenth century, a reformer disparagingly described the image as 'a brunt-tailed elf,' and in 1535 it was said to be 'in colour like ebony.'[21] Images of the Black Madonna could be found all over Europe at this time. It is important for anyone who is interested in history and culture to recognise that Chaucer's world was not a monocultural, exclusively white world: it was an environment that was itself varied and deeply connected to other parts of the global system.[22]

This sense of historical diversity also extends to a consideration of the English language. Chaucer wrote in the dialect of English that became Standard English, the English that was promoted by the printing press and against which regional dialects today now define themselves, or are defined, often as having less cultural capital. But when Chaucer himself wrote, he was writing not in Standard English but in the East Midland dialect. Although this already had more prestige and currency than, say, the North-Western dialect of the Gawain-poet (because the East Midland/London dialect was the version of English used in Chancery for bureaucratic documents), it was nonetheless a changing form that lacked fixed spelling norms, for instance.[23] Chaucer himself borrowed many words from other languages, as did his contemporaries, as they tried to expand their fairly inadequate vernacular to make it a suitable vehicle for the poetry that they wished to write. Far from being the language of the colonial oppressor that it was to become, English at this point was a poor relation kind of language and had much less prestige than Latin or French—the languages of the peoples that had colonised England. So English was a language that was obviously in a state of change and development; it was flexible, it was adaptable; it was very different from the stable language of authority—Latin, the tongue that did not change (much). Crucially, poetry was also an oral form in the Middle Ages: Chaucer's poems were meant to be heard as well as read on the page, and modern performance poetry and drama have strong affinities with the medieval cultural norm of speaking poetry aloud.[24]

In asserting the multicultural nature of England, and specifically London, and in foregrounding the dynamic immediacy of contemporary dialects (Jamaican and Nigerian English), Agbabi, Breeze, and Smith are therefore drawing out aspects of Chaucer's own world, while also focusing on ways that his poetry can speak to and of new communities in our own time and place. Writing about Breeze and Agbabi, Coppola has argued that 'they recuperate and creatively manipulate most of the subversive elements *already present* in Chaucer' (emphasis mine).[25]

The changing nature of London, and current residents' investment and participation in its long history, including very recent changes, is an essential part of these poems. In choosing Brixton Market as the place in which the Wife of Bath—played by herself, a migrant Black woman—speaks, Breeze explores the history of a specific part of London, south of the river. The *Canterbury Tales* begins in Southwark, about three miles north of Brixton, and both locations are part of a South London area that has been known since the 1940s for its multicultural character. After the arrival of the Windrush, many migrants were housed initially in Clapham and went to the nearby Brixton Job Centre to find work; later, in the 1980s, it became a centre of race-related riots. In 1998, as Breeze was writing a poem to celebrate the Windrush generation, a square in Brixton was renamed Windrush Square, but Brixton also marks the English literary canon in its topography: it contains Chaucer Road, Spenser Road, Shakespeare Road, and Milton Road, all parallel to each other.[26] Southwark also has a high proportion of nonwhite residents, especially from the Nigerian community. In choosing Brixton Market as her Wife of Bath's milieu, Breeze reminds us that South London is the home of Chaucer's pilgrims *and* of one of Britain's most diverse communities, that it is a place in which journeys end as well as begin. This is where many people arrived in the 1940s and stayed, while for the Tabard group, it was the departure point for their pilgrimage.

The idea of movement comes across in Breeze's articulation of the text, as she walks through the market space, enacting the dynamic movement of the life that she describes, and the movement of poetry itself. Agbabi also emphasises movement and journeying through the London-Kentish environment, but far beyond as well. She sets her collection of tales along the traditional pilgrimage route, moving through the Old Kent Road, Shooter's Hill, Dartford (where Mrs Alice Ebi Bafa tells her tale), Stone, Gravesend, Strood, Rochester, Sittingbourne, Harbledown, and finally Canterbury. Dartford is technically in Kent, but today it is a suburb of London, located inside the M25 (London's ring road). Agbabi says that she imagines her character 'delivering her tale to a London audience' but adds that her audience is, of course, much wider than that.[27] In the imagined communication with a London audience, the Wife of Bafa immediately establishes London as a global centre, connected with many other parts of the world through figures such as herself. In her second line she tells us that she is from Nigeria, and she goes on to try to sell her wares, from Lagos, Italy, and the Netherlands. A few lines later, she is detailing her husbands—from Ghana, Sierra Leone, England, and Nigeria. While the Wife of Bath went on pilgrimage to places such as Jerusalem and returned to England to find her fourth husband had died, the Wife of Bafa comes to England and returns to Nigeria to find that her fourth husband has passed away. In other words, England is her pilgrimage destination rather than her home, a peripheral place for her.[28]

Smith is the most concerned of all of these poets with depicting a densely imagined, historically rich, multi-ethnic locale. Indeed, the idea of local identity, specifically in her own childhood home, has been a concern of Smith's throughout her career: Vaddi notes that 'To be a local in Smith's novels means to be part of a place that was co-created and whose imagination is still an unfinished project.'[29] *The Wife of Willesden* was written in response to a kind of commission (itself a rather medieval way for a text to come to fruition), as Smith describes in the introduction (ix). This area of London is Smith's childhood home: she was born there, in Willesden itself. The play is set not in Harry Bailly's South London Tabard, but in a different pub: the Colin Campbell on Kilburn High Road, run by Publican Polly. The Colin Campbell is a real pub, founded in 1898 and named after a British Army officer who had a long career, fighting in many campaigns and rising to become Commander-in-Chief of British forces in India. His name therefore has a strong colonial resonance that works interestingly alongside the diverse group that meets in the pub—a group that is telling tales for the prize of 'a full English breakfast' (7). Englishness and Britishness are expansive identities here:

> We had all types of people in that night,
> Young and old, rich and poor, black, brown and white—
> But local: students, merchants, a bailiff,
> People from church, temple, mosque, shul. (7)

It is key that 'all types' of people are 'local' here: this community has a strong identity of its own, an identity marked by the 'North Weezy' accent but an identity that also embraces and celebrates many different origin points, religions, and ethnicities. Countries such as Jamaica, Nigeria, or Bangladesh are implicitly marked as part of British identity, countries whose histories have constructed modern Britain just as much as the imagined Arthurian past of Britain itself. One character, Asma, is Muslim, and has been left by her husband because she went out without her veil (51). An evangelical Christian pastor interrupts Alvita and tries to scam money from the audience

(64, 94). The Polish bailiff (64), probably a more recent immigrant, 'belongs' as much as Alvita, who seems to be from a longer-established Jamaican migrant family, does, and both are as integral a part of Willesden as the Black Madonna herself.

This commitment to the idea that local British identities are varied and multicultural is most powerfully expressed through the English language itself. The Wife of Bath's Prologue opens:

> Experience, though noon auctoritee
> Were in this world, is right ynogh for me
> To speke of wo that is in marriage;
> For, lordynges, sith I twelve yeer was on age,
> Thonked be God that is eterne on lyve,
> Housbondes at chirche dore I have had five—
> If I so ofte myghte have ywedded bee—
> And alle were worthy men in hir degree. (1–8)

Breeze translates these lines into Jamaican English, to open her 'Wife of Bath Speaks in Brixton Market':

> My life is my own bible
> wen it come to all de woes
> in married life
> fah since I reach twelve,
> Tanks to Eternal Gawd,
> is five husband I have
>   (if dat is passible)
> but all of dem was wort something
> in dem own way (p. 62)

Breeze follows Chaucer's text fairly closely, transposing it into Jamaican idiom and at times making specific changes. The replacement of authority with the Bible remains true both to the sense of Chaucer's text and to the authority still wielded in many communities, including many Black British communities, today. The accurate rendering of Jamaican dialect emphasises the orality of the text; it replicates the spoken word within a particular community.

Agbabi's text similarly immediately comes across as a text to be performed:

> My name is Mrs Alice Ebi Bafa,
> I come from Nigeria.
> I'm very fine, isn't it?
> My nex' birthday, I'll be . . . twenty nine.
> I'm business woman.
> Would you like to buy some cloth? (p. 31)

The absence of the article in line 5 and the use of 'isn't it' in line 3 mark the text as non-standard, emphasising that this is Nigerian English. Its orality is also suggested by the question to the audience. These are spoken texts that declare the vitality of all kinds of versions of English and use postcolonial Englishes to rethink Middle English poetry.

Like Breeze, Smith opens Alvita's speech with a fairly direct transposition of Chaucer's opening:

> Let me tell you something: I do not need
> Any permission or college degrees
> To speak on how marriage is *stress*. I been
> Married five damn times since I was nineteen!
> From mi eye deh a mi knee. But I survived,
> Thank God, and I got to say, of the five,
> None of them were total wastemen. (10)

Aspects of her mode of speech such as 'five damn times,' 'I got to say,' or 'total wastemen,' are mildly colloquial; other parts, 'Let me tell you something: I do not need /Any permission or

college degrees,' are standard English; others still are ostentatiously patois, 'From mi eye deh a mi knee.' Indeed, this patois
phrase is given a footnote, just as obscure Middle English words
and phrases are glossed and given explanations in modern editions of Chaucer. Smith thus creates the impression of English
as a dense language, a language with so many layers that some
readers/listeners will always need explanations of particular ac-
cents or dialect words. Smith also uses the same poetic form as
Chaucer—the iambic pentameter, which makes Alvita's declaration of not needing a college degree seem comic. Indeed,
when she says that marriage is 'stress,' the word 'stress' is stressed
not only by italics but also by the fact that it falls on the fourth
stress of the iambic pentameter line. The stage directions have
already told us that Alvita is a 'world class raconteur' (10) and
her very first words here demonstrate to us that she indeed a
consummate performer, fully in control of an allegedly authentic performance. This also might remind us that the author is highly educated in the English poetic tradition as well
as being from a multicultural part of London—that she, like
Agbabi and Breeze, and most of us, has multiple aspects of her
identity, and affinities with many different communities and
traditions. All three poets foreground the voices of their own
communities and use dialect throughout their texts to reclaim
English poetry from an exclusive standardised tradition, suggesting a wider resonance for Chaucer's texts, and for poetry in
English itself.

So far in this chapter, I have been looking at why Chaucer
and the *Canterbury Tales* are sources of inspiration for Breeze,
Agbabi, and Smith. I want to turn now more specifically to the
Wife of Bath herself. Her attraction for these authors demonstrates the arguments that I have been making throughout this
book: Alison is unique, a literary character like no other, who

exerts a magnetic pull on readers and writers across time. Where else could authors turn if they want to find a dramatic, interesting, larger-than-life, yet accessible, female character with instant recognisability and a long literary history in English? As a figure who blurs the boundaries between extreme stereotype and mundane everywoman, and who is at once a funny performer, a defender of women's rights to speak and not to be abused, a skilled orator, a self-avowed liar, and a font of knowledge and self-knowledge, Alison is an extraordinarily rich source of inspiration. Her appeal to some Black female poets might also specifically lie in the fact that she embodies a marginalised voice that speaks back to power. The insistency of 'who painted the lion'—with its implicit emphasis on who has *not* had the opportunity to tell their own story—gains even more power in the context of Black women, doubly oppressed by misogyny and racism. In *The Wife of Willesden*, the group telling stories is characterised as

> All telling their stories. Mostly
> Men. Not because they had better stories
> But because they had no doubt that we should
> Hear them. (7)

A few lines later, we are reminded that 'The shock never ends / When women say things usually said by men' (9). When those things are said in North Weezy and Jamaican patois, the shock is even more intense.

The oppressive canon of misogyny is materialised in Jankyn's book of wicked wives. Although Breeze does not engage with the latter part of the Wife of Bath's Prologue, Agbabi and Smith both modernize this book. In the Wife of Bafa's tale, it becomes *Playboy*, a pornographic magazine that takes as its premise the idea that women's bodies are objects for the male gaze and for male pleasure, and that women are valued only for their bodies, and only when those bodies conform to particular conventions of youth, size, and beauty. For *The Wife of Willesden*, it is a collection of recent profoundly misogynist books by men: Jordan Peterson's *Twelve Rules for Life*, Warren Farrell's *The Myth of Male Power*, Neil Strauss's *The Game: Penetrating the Secret Society of Pick-Up Artists*, and Steve Moxon's *The Woman Racket*.[30] Most of these authors argue that men are in fact the disadvantaged sex in Western societies, and that patriarchy and misogyny are myths. These have been extremely successful, much-read books, just as *Playboy* is a much-'read' magazine, a disturbing reminder of how relevant the idea of a book of wicked wives still is. Dressed up in specious statistics and faux-academic reasoning, and reiterating what many readers want to believe, these books package woman-hating and woman-blaming for the twenty-first century. The importance of the book as the symbol of the oppressive authority of the ruling group is reminiscent of Homi K. Bhabha's discussion of the book as the 'insignia' of authority in colonial discourse. Bhabha discusses the repeated scene in writings of colonialism of the 'sudden, fortuitous discovery of the English book,' a myth that inscribes English writing as the marker of civility, education, knowledge, religion, and power. But, as Bhabha writes, 'the dazzling light of literature sheds only areas of darkness.'[31]

Agbabi and Smith both rewrite the Arthurian story that forms the Wife of Bath's Tale, relocating it from the English landscape to Ghana (Agbabi) and Jamaica (Smith). The significance of this change in geographical locale is that it challenges the reader/listener/audience to expand their understanding of which histories matter, or are relevant, in twenty-first-century

Britain. It is not that Arthurian myths and myths about the British landscape are no longer relevant, but that all modern Britons, regardless of their own ethnic background, should think about the fact that Jamaican history and Ghanaian history, for instance, are part of British history too.

The details of the Wife of Bafa's tale, as well as the way it is told, insistently remind us of its Ghanaian setting. The knight has become a 'big man soldier' who lives in the king's 'compound.' As he seeks the answer to the question, 'What do women like bes'?,' he comes across women 'dancing in kente cloth, / traditional dress of Ghana,' and when he delivers his answer to the queen, 'Even mosquito quiet for his reply' (34–35). Smith's much longer tale depicts eighteenth-century Jamaica in detail. The tale is specifically set in Maroon Town, Jamaica, in the time of Queen Nanny and Captain Cudjoe, real historical figures. Maroon Town was founded by runaway slaves (maroons). Queen Nanny, also known as Granny Nanny, and Nanny of the Maroons, led the Windward Maroons in the First Maroon War against the British in the early eighteenth century. According to legend, she herself was born in Ghana around 1686, and she lived until about 1755.[32] Captain Cudjoe (c. 1690s–1764) led the other major group of maroons in eighteenth-century Jamaica, known as the Leeward Maroons. The fairies of the Wife of Bath's Tale become duppy, the spirits and ghosts that dominate Caribbean folklore: 'All the island was filled up with duppy,' with specific mentions of River Mumma and Ol' Higue, described in a footnote as 'fearsome female figures from Jamaican folklore' (72). (Breeze includes a poem called 'Duppy dance' in her *Arrival of Brighteye* collection.)[33] When we reach the 'gentilesse' speech, the Wife of Bath's emphasis on the fact that high birth does not bestow morality is given a colonial context as Smith's loathly lady figure says:

If all it took to be noble was roots
In some old family plot, then these clans
From H'england with dey grand old posh names and
Sugar, they'd be good, all generations.
But *he* beat his wife. *He* ran plantation. (91)

We are reminded of the English colonialists in eighteenth-century Jamaica and the horrors of the sugar trade. In the final line quoted above, abuse of women and abuse of Black people through slavery (implicit in owning plantations) are paralleled.

The moral is also brought right up to the present day, when Alvita says that people who are called 'Rees-Mogg or what have / You' should realise that 'you can still be a chav / In your soul' (92). The reference is to Jacob Rees-Mogg, currently an MP on the right of the Conservative party, known for his inherited wealth, his extreme positions about issues such as Europe and same-sex marriage, and his old-fashioned, highly stylized persona. A 'chav' is a pejorative term for a low-class, badly dressed, vulgar person, often used in the United Kingdom as a derogatory term for poor people in general. Throughout the text, Smith brings the story right up to the present day, with references to, for instance, the 'Time's Up' movement, flexing (i.e., boasting), twerking, and owning one's privilege (75, 51, 26, 25).

The Wife of Willesden's Prologue and Tale remain extremely close to Chaucer's version, in meaning, effect, and tone. There is, however, a fascinating change at the end of the tale. In the Wife of Bath's Tale, when the lady transforms, the knight sees 'That she so fair was, and so yong therto' (1251). She is explicitly young and beautiful. But in *The Wife of Willesden*, when the lady transforms, she turns into Alvita herself, a woman described in the cast list as in her mid-fifties. The stage direction after the transformation refers to her 'middle-aged beauteousness' (98).

This is an explicit rejection of the idea that youth and beauty go hand in hand, a rejection of the romance fantasy that the Wife of Bath's Tale (at least briefly) subscribes to at this point. Alvita also declares that she is more beautiful than Beyoncé, Jourdan Dunn, or Naomi (97). All three are Black women known for their beauty. They are also of various ages—Beyoncé was born in 1981, Dunn in 1990, and Naomi Campbell in 1970. Beauty is again decoupled from age as, in a move of which Alison would surely have approved, Smith emphasises that ageing should not make women invisible or remove them from a world of sexual activity and attractiveness. Not only in the world of eighteenth-century Jamaican folklore, but also in the contemporary moment in Brent, a middle-aged woman, represented by Alvita, can symbolise beauty.

Smith ends her play with a Chaucerian Retraction, comically mirroring the end of the *Canterbury Tales*. She praises Chaucer, accepts blame for anything she did wrong, and adds a general apology for many other issues in previous books, such as 'all the swearing and cultural appropriation in my first book' (103), asking for mercy in her last words, as Chaucer asks for salvation in his final sentence.[34] In the last stage direction, 'The AUTHOR joins ALVITA in a how-low-can-you-go dance-off as the lights fade, and the scene ends' (104). This moment encapsulates what authors across time have done with Alison of Bath, dancing with her in a wild exchange of energy, passion, and ideas, a dance now imbued with more traditions and innovations, but still centred in an extraordinary fourteenth-century text. Alison's footsteps are, if anything, beating louder in the twenty-first century than ever before.

Acknowledgements

I wrote much of this book during the first year of the pandemic, a strange era when time and space seemed to work differently. Thinking back to those intense days of home school, one walk a day, and the frantic search for flour, my deepest thanks go, even more than usual, to the three people who share my home—Elliot, Cecilia, and Peter. You fill my life with light. And I've done much of the revision of the book with a cocker pug called Kastor on my knee, an addition who has made our house even happier, though also even messier.

The rest of my family probably remain amazed that I continue to make a career out of Chaucer, but I think they are pleased for me too. Thank you Katie, Damon, Michael and Ruby, Bernard and Diane, Moira, Rita, and families and, of course, Mum and Dad, unfailing supporters and cheerleaders since 1976.

Books are made by communities—people who will listen to fledgling ideas, read bits and pieces, offer up their own work for discussion, or 'just' be interested. There are many different communities that have helped me to bring this book into being, even though for so much of its gestation we were only able to interact virtually, from our strange isolations.

At Princeton University Press, Ben Tate remains the best of editors. Thank you, Ben, for always backing me. The rest of the Princeton team are also extraordinarily enthusiastic, helpful, and engaged believers in what I do. And the passion of George Capel, my agent, is a consistent bedrock of support for my work. Thank you.

At Oxford, there are so many people to thank. Here are just a few: fellow medievalists, particularly Vincent Gillespie, Dan Wakelin, Helen Swift, Nick Perkins, Mark Williams, Carolyne Larrington, and Francis Leneghan; fellow life-writers such as Robert Douglas-Fairhurst, Laurie Maguire, Bart van Es, Elleke Boehmer, Marina McKay, Hermione Lee, Sophie Ratcliffe, Joe Moshenska; brilliant colleagues including Emma Smith, Adam Smyth, Katie Murphy, Nick Gaskill, Helen Small, Ros Ballaster, and Lorna Hutson. And all the rest of you—this is a great place to work.

The interdisciplinary community at Jesus College, led by Nigel Shadbolt, provides another intellectual home that I feel very lucky to have, and my undergraduate students there and at Oriel are invariably wonderful. And graduate students and postdocs are the future of the field; incisive interlocutors from that group include Jack Colley, Micah McKay, Peter Buchanan, Ellie Myerson, Pamela Kask, Shelley Williams, Rebecca Menmuir, Hannah Bower, and Lucy Fleming. Special thanks go to Felicity Brown, who provided invaluable research assistance to me while I was writing this book. I could not have hoped for a more thoughtful and committed assistant. You were amazing.

There is also a wonderful international community of scholars who have helped to make me the scholar that I am—it is hard to single people out, as there are so many of you, particularly from the New Chaucer Society, whose work and conversation have helped me so much. I feel lucky to be part of such a warm and intellectually rigorous group.

The anonymous readers for the Press have my eternal gratitude for the time and thought that they put into engaging with my manuscript. Peer review work is time-consuming and can be fairly thankless—so thank you. You made this book better.

My earliest reader was my dear friend Paul Strohm, one of the most important people in my life. Thank you—your careful reading helped me so much at a crucial point, just as you have helped me with both my other monographs. And particular thanks to Anthony Bale, another very dear friend and colleague, with whom I've been discussing Chaucer over cocktails for over two decades. Thank you to many other friends too, whom I have seen much less in these strange Covid years, but who remain just as important—especially Isabel Davis, Rachel Wevill, Tim Phillips, Claire Harman, Alex Gillespie, Ned Fletcher, and Natalie Walker.

The thoughtful readers of my last book, *Chaucer: A European Life*, have shaped this book too. The responses to that book—often in handwritten letters, or lovely conversations at festivals—consolidated my desire to do more of a certain kind of writing, to create research-based books that reach a wide audience and move beyond universities. I know I'm lucky that there are readers who like that kind of book and will come with me on my idiosyncratic intellectual journeys. I hope you like this book too.

Notes

Introduction

1. William Blake, *The Complete Poetry and Prose of William Blake*, ed. David V. Erdman (Berkeley: University of California Press, 1982), 537; D. W. Robertson, *A Preface to Chaucer* (Princeton: Princeton University Press, 1962), 317.

2. Class is a modern concept; medieval people certainly thought about order and classification within society but used words such as 'estate.' As such terms do not resonate today, I have used the word 'class' where I think it is helpful.

3. Calendar of the Plea and Memoranda Rolls of the City of London: Volume 2, 1364–1381. London: His Majesty's Stationery Office, London, 1929, Roll A 14: 1368–69. https://www.british-history.ac.uk/plea-memoranda-rolls/vol2/pp96-113.

4. For these women, see Anne F. Sutton, 'Two Dozen and More Silkwomen of Fifteenth Century London,' *Ricardian* 16 (2006): 1–8.

5. David Harry, *Constructing a Civic Community in Late Medieval London: The Common Profit, Charity and Commemoration* (Woodbridge: Boydell and Brewer, 2019).

6. See Natalie Zemon Davis's seminal account of the literary qualities of documentary texts, *Fiction in the Archives* (Stanford: Stanford University Press, 1987). See also Hayden White, *The Content of the Form: Narrative Discourse and Historical Representation* (Baltimore, MD: Johns Hopkins, 1987).

7. Alain Renoir, 'Thebes, Troy, Criseyde, and Pandarus: An Instance of Chaucerian Irony,' *Studia Neophilologica* 32 (1960): 14–17; Leah Schwebel, 'What's in Criseyde's Book?' *Chaucer Review* 54:1 (2019): 91–115.

8. Geoffrey Chaucer, *The Riverside Chaucer*, ed. Larry Benson, F. N. Robinson, and Christopher Cannon, 3rd ed. (Oxford: Oxford University Press, 2008). All references to Chaucer's texts are to this edition unless otherwise specified.

9. See Anthony Bale, *Margery Kempe: A Mixed Life* (London: Reaktion Books, 2021).

10. Lynn Staley, *Margery Kempe's Dissenting Fictions* (University Park: Pennsylvania State University Press, 1994).

11. See Sebastian Sobecki, '"The writyng of this tretys": Margery Kempe's Son and the Authorship of Her Book,' *Studies in the Age of Chaucer* 37 (2015): 257–283; and Anthony Bale, 'Richard Salthouse of Norwich and the Scribe of *The Book of Margery Kempe*,' *Chaucer Review* 52 (2017): 173–187.

12. Ted Hughes, 'Chaucer,' in *Birthday Letters* (London: Faber, 1998). See also James Robinson, 'Hughes and the Middle Ages,' in Terry Gifford (ed.), *Ted Hughes in Context* (Cambridge: Cambridge University Press, 2018), 209–218.

13. James Simpson argues that the Wife of Bath's Prologue and Tale is an open, 'not yet' text that can only be interpreted in a longer history, in 'The Not Yet Wife of Bath's Prologue and Tale,' in Jennifer Jahner and Ingrid Nelson (eds.), *Gender, Poetry, and the Form of Thought in Later Medieval Literature: Essays in Honor of Elizabeth A. Robertson* (Bethlehem, PA: Lehigh University Press, 2022), 201–221.

Prologue to Part I. 'Beaten for a Book': Literary Form and Lived Experience

1. See for instance Rosemary Horrox (ed. and trans.), *The Black Death* (Manchester: Manchester University Press, 2013). For the Statute of Labourers and sumptuary laws, see Christopher Given-Wilson (ed.), *Parliament Rolls of Medieval England, 1275–1504* (Woodbridge: Boydell and Brewer, 2005), Edward III: February 1351, item 47; and Edward III: October 1363, item 25.

2. Caroline Barron has argued forcefully for the idea that there was a golden age for women in late medieval London, in 'The Golden Age of Women in Medieval London,' *Reading Medieval Studies* 15 (1989): 35–58. Jeremy Goldberg, focusing on evidence from York, concurs that there was a golden age; see P.J.P Goldberg, *Women, Work, and Life-Cycle in a Medieval Economy: Women in York and Yorkshire c. 1300–1520* (Oxford: Oxford University Press, 1992), 336–337. This view is not universal: Marjorie McIntosh writes that she agrees that women had more economic opportunities post-plague, but thinks that their situation was still less than 'rosy' (30). Marjorie Keniston McIntosh, *Working Women in English Society, 1300–1620* (Cambridge: Cambridge University Press, 2005), 28–34. Judith M. Bennett critiques the golden age idea forcefully, but even she concedes that 'it seems possible that the labour shortages of the decades that followed the Black Death improved the wage-earning potential of women,' and that women might have been able to negotiate better pay and equal pay during these decades, although she sees this as a more temporary improvement. Judith M. Bennett, 'Medieval Women, Modern Women: Across the Great Divide,' in David Aers (ed.), *Culture and History, 1350–1600: Essays on English Communities, Identities and Writing* (Detroit: Wayne University Press, 1992), 147–175, especially 162. See also Judith M Bennett, *Ale, Beer, and*

Brewsters in England: Women's Work in a Changing World 1300–1600 (Oxford: Oxford University Press, 1996).

3. Barron, 'Golden Age,' 36, 40.

4. Marion Turner, *Chaucer: A European Life* (Princeton, NJ: Princeton University Press, 2019), 458–465.

5. See Cordelia Beattie, *Medieval Single Women: The Politics of Social Classification in Late Medieval England* (Oxford: Oxford University Press, 2007), 3, 147–148.

6. Georges Duby, 'Histoire sociale et idéologie des sociétiés,' in Jacques Le Goff and P. Nora (eds.), *Faire de l'histoire* (Paris: Guillimard, 1974), 1: 147–168, 148.

7. Elaine Treharne, 'The Stereotype Confirmed?: Chaucer's Wife of Bath,' in Elaine Treharne (ed.), *Writing Gender and Genre in Medieval Literature: Approaches to Old and Middle English Texts* (Cambridge: D. S. Brewer: 2002), 93–116.

8. Virginia Woolf, *A Room of One's Own and Three Guineas* (Oxford: Oxford University Press, 1992), 39.

9. Ralph Hanna III and Traugott Lawler (eds.), *Jankyn's Book of Wikked Wyves. Vol. 1: The Primary Texts* (Athens: University of Georgia Press, 1997), 88.

10. Joseph L. Baird and John Robert Kane, *La Querelle de la Rose: Letters and Documents* (Chapel Hill: University of North Carolina Press, 1978), 136. See discussion in Marilyn Desmond, 'The Querelle de la Rose and the Ethics of Reading,' in Barbara K. Altmann and Deborah L. McGrady (eds.), *Christine de Pizan: A Casebook* (New York: Routledge, 2003), 167–180, 171. See also Kathryn Gravdal, *Ravishing Maidens: Writing Rape in Medieval French Literature and Law* (Philadelphia: University of Pennsylvania Press, 1991).

11. See Otto Gerhard Oexle, 'Perceiving Social Reality in the Early and High Middle Ages: A Contribution to the History of Social Knowledge,' in Bernhard Jussen (ed.), *Ordering Medieval Society: Perspectives on Intellectual and Practical Modes of Shaping Social Relations*, trans. Pamela Selwyn (Philadelphia: University of Pennsylvania Press, 2001), 92–143, 92–100; and Beattie, *Medieval Single Women*, 1–5.

Chapter 1. The Invention of Character

1. Harold Bloom, *The Western Canon: The Books and School of the Ages* (London: Macmillan, 1995), 113, 115; Warren Ginsberg, *The Cast of Character: The Representation of Personality in Ancient and Medieval Literature* (Toronto: University of Toronto Press, 1983), 134; A. C. Spearing, *Medieval Autographies: The "I" of the Text* (Notre Dame, IN: University of Notre Dame Press, 2012), 77.

2. Jill Mann, *Chaucer and Medieval Estates Satire: The Literature of Social Classes and the General Prologue to the Canterbury Tales* (Cambridge: Cambridge University Press, 1973), xi, 2, 8.

3. Elizabeth Fowler, *Literary Character: The Human Figure in Early English Writing* (Ithaca, NY: Cornell University Press, 2003), 10, 36, 34–35.

4. Antonina Harbus, *Cognitive Approaches to Old English Poetry* (Woodbridge: Boydell and Brewer, 2012).

5. R. N. Swanson, *The Twelfth-Century Renaissance* (Manchester: Manchester University Press, 1999); Alex J. Novikoff (ed.), *The Twelfth-Century Renaissance: A Reader* (Toronto: University of Toronto Press, 2017); Laura Ashe, *The Oxford English Literary History. Vol. 1: 1000–1350: Conquest and Transformation* (Oxford: Oxford University Press, 2017).

6. Karen Winstead, *The Oxford History of Life-Writing* (Oxford: Oxford University Press, 2017), 1:5.

7. On confession see Christopher Cannon, *Middle English Literature: A Cultural History* (Cambridge: Polity, 2008), 27–35; Mary Flowers Braswell, *The Medieval Sinner: Characterization and Confession in the Literature of the English Middle Ages* (Rutherford, NJ: Farleigh Dickinson University Press, 1983); John Ganim, 'Chaucer, Boccaccio, Confession, and Subjectivity,' in Leonard Michael Koff and Brenda Dean Schildgen (eds.), *The 'Decameron' and the 'Canterbury Tales': New Essays on an Old Question* (Madison, NJ: Fairleigh Dickinson University Press, 2000), 128–147.

8. See Sarah Kay, Terence Cave, and Malcolm Bowie, *A Short History of French Literature* (Oxford: Oxford University Press, 2003), 75–80.

9. For Machaut's development of the genre and of his narratorial persona, see Deborah McGrady, 'Guillaume de Machaut,' in Simon Gaunt and Sarah Kay (eds.), *The Cambridge Companion to Medieval French Literature* (Cambridge: Cambridge University Press, 2009), 109–122; Kevin Brownlee, *Poetic Identity in Guillaume de Machaut* (Madison: University of Wisconsin Press, 1984); Helen Swift, 'The Poetic I,' and Anne-Helene Miller, 'Guillaume de Machaut and the Forms of Pre-Humanism in Fourteenth-Century France,' both in Deborah McGrady and Jennifer Bain (eds.), *A Companion to Guillaume de Machaut* (Leiden: Brill, 2012), 15–32 and 33–48.

10. Jerry Root, *'Space to Speke,' The Confessional Subject in Medieval Literature* (New York: Peter Laing, 1997), 126.

11. Michel Zink, *The Invention of Literary Subjectivity*, trans. Davis Sices (Baltimore, MD: Johns Hopkins, 1999), 140.

12. Spearing, *Medieval Autographies*, 7–9.

13. See Turner, *Chaucer: A European Life*, 130–131.

14. Christopher Cannon, *From Literacy to Literature: England, 1300–1400* (Oxford: Oxford University Press, 2016), 119–124.

15. Spearing comments that this 'varied collection of nonlyrical first-person discourses is quite unparalleled in any earlier Middle English writing,' terming it a 'new and striking phenomenon.' *Medieval Autographies*, 53.

16. Fowler, *Literary Character*, 34–35.

17. It is important to note that Justinus has been arguing *against* marriage.

18. I borrow the term 'bookrunner' from Jasper Fforde's Thursday Next series. See *The Eyre Affair* (London: Hodder and Stoughton, 2001).

19. J. M. Manly, *Some New Light on Chaucer: Lectures Delivered at the Lowell Institute* (London: Bell, 1926), 227, 231.

20. Donald Howard, *Chaucer: His Life, His Works, His World* (New York: Dutton, 1987), 447, 96.

21. Dolores Palomo, 'The Fate of the Wife of Bath's "Bad Husbands,"' *Chaucer Review* 9:4 (1975): 303–319; Beryl Rowland, 'On the Timely Death of the Wife of Bath's Fourth Husband,' *Archiv* 209 (1972–1973): 273–282.

22. Donald B. Sands, 'The Non-Comic, Non-Tragic Wife: Chaucer's Dame Alys as Sociopath,' *Chaucer Review* 12:3 (1978): 171–182, 171.

23. Harry Berger Jr., '"What Did the King Know and When Did He Know It?" Shakespearean Discourses and Psychoanalysis,' *South Atlantic Quarterly* 88:4 (1989): 811–862, 823; L.C. Knights, *How Many Children Had Lady Macbeth? An Essay in the Theory and Practice of Shakespeare Criticism* (Cambridge: Minority Press, 1933), 6–7.

24. See David A. Brewer, *The Afterlife of Character, 1726–1825* (Philadelphia: University of Pennsylvania Press, 2005), 3.

25. This is not Ganim's own view but his description of determinist and poststructuralist thought. John Ganim, 'Identity and Subjecthood,' in Steve Ellis (ed.), *Chaucer: An Oxford Guide* (Oxford: Oxford University Press, 2005), 224–238, 225.

26. Lee Patterson, '"For the Wyves Love of Bathe": Feminine Rhetoric and Poetic Resolution in the *Roman de la Rose* and the *Canterbury Tales*,' *Speculum* 58:3 (1983): 656–695, 658.

27. Brewer, *Afterlife*, 3.

28. Blakey Vermeule, *Why Do We Care About Literary Characters?* (Baltimore: Johns Hopkins University Press, 2010), 246; Martha Nussbaum, *Poetic Justice: The Literary Imagination and Public Life* (Boston: Beacon Press, 1995).

29. See also Uri Margolin, 'Character,' in David Herman (ed.), *The Cambridge Companion to Narrative* (Cambridge: Cambridge University Press, 2007), 67, 77–78.

30. 'Hire browe broun, hire yen [eyes] blake / [...] With middel [waist] small and wel ymake / [...] Hire swire [neck] is whittere than the swan' [14, 16, 28]. The poem (also known as 'Bytuene Mersh and Aueril') is easily available online and in multiple editions, including John Hirsh (ed.), *Medieval Lyric* (Oxford: Blackwell, 2005), 101–102.

31. For a discussion of the involvement of women in medieval drama, see Katie Normington, '"Faming of the Shrews": Medieval Drama and Feminist Approaches,' *Yearbook of English Studies* 43 (2013): 105–120.

32. Mann, *Chaucer and Medieval Estates Satire*.

33. For discussion see Lawrence Besserman, 'Lay Piety and Impiety: The Role of Noah in the Chester Play of Noah's Flood,' in Eva von Contzen and Chanita Goodblatt (eds.), *Enacting the Bible in Medieval and Early Modern Drama* (Manchester: Manchester University Press, 2020), 13–27.

34. James I. Wimsatt, *Chaucer and His French Contemporaries: Natural Music in the Fourteenth Century* (Toronto: University of Toronto Press, 1991), 205. See also John Scattergood, 'The Love Lyric before Chaucer,' in Thomas G. Duncan (ed.), *A Companion to the Middle English Lyric* (Cambridge: D. S. Brewer, 2005), 39–67; William W. Kibler and James I. Wimsatt (eds.), 'The Development of the Pastourelle in the Fourteenth Century: An Edition of Fifteen Poems with an Analysis,' *Mediaeval Studies* 45 (1983): 22–78.

35. Carolyn Dinshaw, *Chaucer's Sexual Poetics* (Madison: University of Wisconsin Press, 1989).

36. Discussed in Dinshaw, *Chaucer's Sexual Poetics*, 22–25.

37. R. Howard Bloch, *Medieval Misogyny and the Invention of Western Romantic Love* (Chicago: University of Chicago Press, 1991), 50–51.

38. Saint Augustine of Hippo, *Confessions*, trans. Henry Chadwick (Oxford University Press, 2008), 1:13:15.

39. Marilynn Desmond, *Reading Dido: Gender, Textuality, and the Medieval 'Aeneid'* (Minneapolis: University of Minnesota Press, 1994).

40. He tells Dido's story in the *House of Fame* and in the *Legend of Good Women*. On the *Legend of Good Women*, see especially Carolyn Collette, *The Legend of Good Women: Context and Reception* (Cambridge: D. S. Brewer, 2006) and *Rethinking Chaucer's Legend of Good Women* (York: York University Press, 2014). See also Suzanne Hagedorn, *Abandoned Women: Rewriting the Classics in Dante, Boccaccio, and Chaucer* (Ann Arbor: University of Michigan Press, 2004). On Chaucer's re-shaping of Criseyde see, for instance, James Simpson, 'Chaucer as a European Writer,' in Seth Lerer (ed.), *The Yale Companion to Chaucer* (New Haven: Yale University Press, 2006), 55–86, 75–76.

41. Middle English Dictionary, https://quod.lib.umich.edu/m/middle-english-dictionary/dictionary.

42. La Vielle's speech is lines 12902–12918 in *La Roman de la Rose*, conveniently cited in Robert M. Correale and Mary Hamel (eds.), *Sources and Analogues of 'The Canterbury Tales'* (Cambridge: D. S. Brewer, 2005), 2:372–373.

43. See for instance, Bloom's comments on her as a 'great vitalist,' with a 'rage to live' who 'has only life in her.' *Western Canon*, 112, 113, 115.

44. On the Wife of Bath's memory see H. Marshall Leicester, *The Disenchanted Self: Representing the Subject in 'The Canterbury Tales'* (Berkeley: University of Cali-

fornia Press, 1990), 82–113; for further discussion of the Wife of Bath and time see Sachi Shimomura, *Odd Bodies and Visible Ends in Medieval Literature* (New York: Palgrave Macmillan, 2006), chap. 3.

45. This is discussed by Lee Patterson, *Chaucer and the Subject of History* (Madison: University of Wisconsin Press, 1991), 308.

46. See chapter 7 for further discussion of this image.

47. R. Pratt, 'The Order of the Canterbury Tales,' *PMLA* 66:6 (1951): 1141–1167. For further discussion of the textual confusion at this point in manuscripts of the *Tales*, see chapter 3.

48. Alastair Minnis, *Fallible Authors* (Philadelphia: University of Pennsylvania Press, 2011), 253.

49. Correale and Hamel, *Sources and Analogues*, 2:388.

50. Correale and Hamel, *Sources and Analogues*, 2:398.

51. See chapter 6 for a discussion of a scribe's attempt to whip up readerly outrage at this comment.

52. For Jerome's use of the example see Correale and Hamel, *Sources and Analogues*, 2:366.

53. For a discussion of the Wife of Bath's deployment of multiple genres and traditions see Susan Crane, 'Alison's Incapacity and Poetic Instability in the Wife of Bath's Tale,' *PMLA* 102:1 (1987): 20–28.

54. See Christopher Cannon, '*Raptus* in the Chaumpaigne Release and a Newly Discovered Document Concerning the Life of Geoffrey Chaucer,' *Speculum* 68 (1993): 74–94; Susan S. Morrison, 'The Use of Biography in Medieval Literary Criticism: The Case of Geoffrey Chaucer and Cecily Chaumpaigne,' *Chaucer Review* 34 (1999): 69–86; Samantha Katz Seal and Nicole Sidhu, 'New Feminist Approaches to Chaucer Introduction,' *Chaucer Review* 54 (2019): 224–229; Sebastian Sobecki, 'Wards and Widows: *Troilus and Criseyde* and New Documents on Chaucer's Life,' *ELH* 86 (2019): 413–440.

55. Correale and Hamel, *Sources and Analogues*, 2:405–409. In chapter 8, I discuss some of the global origins of this story.

56. For a discussion of the tradition, see S. Elizabeth Passmore and Susan Carter, *The English 'Loathly Lady' Tales: Boundaries, Traditions, Motifs* (Kalamazoo, MI: Medieval Institute Publications, 2007).

57. See Carissa M. Harris, *Obscene Pedagogies: Transgressive Talk and Sexual Education in Late Medieval Britain* (Ithaca, NY: Cornell University Press, 2018), 104.

58. Minnis, *Fallible Authors*, 294.

59. See further discussion in chapter 8.

60. Discussed in detail in chapter 4.

61. Minnis, *Fallible Authors*, 311.

62. Mann, *Chaucer and Medieval Estates Satire*, 8.

63. Margolin, 'Character,' 67–69, 77–78.

64. Fowler, *Literary Character*, 94.

Chapter 2. Working Women

1. David Herlihy, *Opera Muliebria: Women and Work in Medieval Europe* (London: McGraw-Hill, 1990), xi.

2. Caroline Barron, 'Golden Age'; McIntosh, *Working Women*, 28–34. For further references see note 2 in the prologue to this section.

3. For Lydia, see Acts of the Apostles 16:14–15 and 40. See also biography of Tom Wright, *St Paul: A Biography* (London: SPCK, 2018), 179.

4. For Phoebe see Wright, *St Paul*, 327.

5. I discuss Paula in more detail below, in chapter 3. For Jerome and Paula, see Andrew Cain, 'Jerome's *Epitaphium Paulae*: Hagiography, Pilgrimage and the Cult of St Paula,' *Journal of Early Christian Studies* 18:1 (2010): 105–139.

6. Kay E. Lacey, 'Women and Work in Fourteenth and Fifteenth Century London,' in Lindsey Charles and Lorna Duffin (eds.), *Women and Work in Pre-Industrial England* (Abingdon: Routledge, 2013 [1985]), 24–82.

7. Goldberg, *Women, Work, and Life-Cycle*, 368, 93.

8. See T. H. Lloyd, *The English Wool-Trade in the Middle Ages* (Cambridge: Cambridge University Press, 1977); Alwyn Ruddock, *Italian Merchants and Shipping in Southampton* (Southampton: University College, 1951).

9. See Turner, *Chaucer: A European Life*, 151–155.

10. Mary Carruthers, 'The Wife of Bath and the Painting of Lions,' *PMLA* 94:2 (1979): 209–222, 209–210.

11. Maryanne Kowaleski, 'Women's Work in a Market Town: Exeter in the Late Fourteenth Century,' in Barbara Hanawalt (ed.), *Women and Work in Pre-Industrial Europe* (Bloomington: Indiana University Press, 1986), 145–164, 152.

12. Carruthers, 'Wife of Bath,' 210.

13. For further discussion of the Wife of Bath and inheritance see Samantha Katz Seal, *Father Chaucer: Generating Authority in 'The Canterbury Tales'* (Oxford: Oxford University Press, 2019), pp. 57–91; and Lee Patterson, *Temporal Circumstances: Form and History in the Canterbury Tales* (New York: Palgrave Macmillan, 2006), 43.

14. Woolf, *Room of One's Own*, 149.

15. See, for instance, McIntosh, *Working Women*, 46; and Goldberg, *Women, Work, and Life-Cycle*, 327–328.

16. Jan Luiten van Zanden, Sarah Carmichael, and Tine de Moor, *Capital Women: The European Marriage Pattern, Female Empowerment and Economic Development in Western Europe, 1300–1800* (Oxford: Oxford University Press: 2019), 38.

17. Iris Origo, 'The Domestic Enemy: The Eastern Slaves in Tuscany in the Fourteenth and Fifteenth Centuries,' *Speculum* 30:3 (1955): 321–366, 324.

18. Origo, 'Domestic Enemy,' 336.

19. Van Zanden et al., *Capital Women*, 35.

20. Goldberg, *Women, Work, and Life-Cycle*, 327.

21. P.J.P Goldberg, 'Migration, Youth, and Gender in Later Medieval England,' in *Youth in the Middle Ages*, ed. P.J.P Goldberg and Felicity Riddy (York: York Medieval Press, 2004), 86, 97.

22. See Beattie, *Medieval Single Women*; and Maryanne Kowaleski, 'Singlewomen in Medieval and Early Modern Europe: The Demographic Perspective,' in Judith M. Bennett and Amy M. Froide (ed.), *Singlewomen in the European Past, 1250–1800* (Philadelphia: University of Pennsylvania Press, 1999), 38–81. Kowaleski discusses the Mediterranean marriage pattern that resulted in far fewer lifelong single women (50), and European Jewish communities, in which lifelong single women were 'virtually non-existent' (62), contrasting such communities with the situation in England, possibly Flanders, and some Continental towns where there is evidence of 'fairly large concentrations of singlewomen,' in the later Middle Ages' (64).

23. George Shuffelton (ed.), 'Item 4, How the Good Wife Taught Her Daughter,' in *Codex Ashmole 61: A Compilation of Popular Middle English Verse* (Kalamazoo, MI: Medieval Institute Publications, 2008). https://d.lib.rochester.edu/teams/text /shuffelton-codex-ashmole-61-how-the-good-wife-taught-her-daughter.

24. Felicity Riddy, 'Mother Knows Best: Reading Social Change in a Courtesy Text,' *Speculum* 71:1 (1996): 66–86, 85–86.

25. Van Zanden et al., *Capital Women*; Kowaleski, 'Singlewomen.'

26. Van Zanden et al., *Capital Women*, 45.

27. Van Zanden et al., *Capital Women*, 11.

28. For further discussion of the evolution of marriage as a sacrament, and the issues of consent and consummation see P. Reynolds, *How Marriage Became One of the Sacraments: The Sacramental Theology of Marriage from Its Medieval Origins to the Council of Trent* (Cambridge: Cambridge University Press, 2016), especially 157–243 and Bloch, *Medieval Misogyny*, 183–186.

29. Van Zanden et al., *Capital Women*, 26, 30–31, 24.

30. McIntosh, *Working Women*, 8.

31. Goldberg, 'Migration,' 86, 97.

32. Goldberg, *Women, Work, and Life-Cycle*, 12; R. H. Hilton, *The English Peasantry in the Later Middle Ages: The Ford Lectures for 1973, and Related Studies* (Oxford: Clarendon Press, 1975) 102–103; Lord Beveridge, 'Westminster Wages in the Manorial Era,' *Economic History Review* 8:1 (1955): 18–35.

33. Van Zanden et al., *Capital Women*, 10.

34. See the prologue to this section for more discussion and references.

35. Goldberg, *Women, Work, and Life-Cycle*, 93; Barbara Hanawalt, *The Wealth of Wives: Women, Law, and Economy in Late Medieval London* (Oxford: Oxford University Press, 2007), 174.

36. Goldberg, *Women, Work, and Life-Cycle*, 132.

37. Hilton, *English Peasantry*, 102–103; Goldberg, *Women, Work, and Life-Cycle*, 125. The ship was the Anneys de Yhork, left by Nichola de Irby in her will in 1395.

38. Margery Kempe, *The Book of Margery Kempe*, ed. Barry Windeatt (Cambridge: D. S. Brewer, 2000), chap. 2.

39. Elspeth Veale, 'Matilda Penne, Skinner (d. 1392–3),' in Caroline M. Barron and Anne F. Sutton (eds.), *Medieval London Widows, 1300–1500* (London: Bloomsbury, 1994), 47–54.

40. Christine de Pizan, *The Treasure of the City of Ladies; or, The Book of the Three Virtues*, trans. Sarah Lawson, rev. ed. (London: Penguin, 2003), 110.

41. Christine de Pizan, *Treasure*, 110–112.

42. Rowena E. Archer, '"How ladies . . . who live on their manors ought to manage their households and estates": Women as Landholders and Administrators in the Later Middle Ages,' in P.J.P. Goldberg (ed.), *Woman Is a Worthy Wight: Women in English Society c. 1200–1500* (Stroud: Alan Sutton, 1992), 149–181, 150.

43. William de la Pole's will can be found in J. W. Clay (ed.). *North Country Wills* (Durham: Andrews, 1912), 50–51. The letter from William to John is printed in Norman Davis (ed.), *Paston Letters and Papers of the Fifteenth Century*, Early English Text Society s.s. 20–22, 3 vols. (Oxford: Oxford University Press, 2004), 3:82–83, 83.

44. John Paston III to Margaret Paston, between 1482 and 1484. Davis (ed.), *Paston Letters*, 1:621.

45. Carol M. Meale, 'Reading Women's Culture in Fifteenth-Century England: The Case of Alice Chaucer,' in Piero Boitani and Anna Torti (eds.), *Mediaevalitas: Reading the Middle Ages* (Woodbridge: D. S. Brewer, 1996), 81–102, 93. See also the relevant entries in the *Oxford Dictionary of National Biography* (Oxford University Press, 2004).

46. John Watts, *Henry VI and the Politics of Kingship* (Cambridge: Cambridge University Press, 1996), 205–254.

47. Joseph Stevenson (ed.), *Letters and papers illustrative of the wars of the English in France during the reign of Henry the Sixth, King of England* (London: Longman and Green, 1864), 2:768.

48. Given-Wilson (ed.), *Parliament Rolls*, Henry VI: November 1450, item 16.

49. Stevenson (ed.), *Letters and papers*, 2:770.

50. Harris Nicolas (ed.), *Proceedings and Ordinances of the Privy Council*, 7 vols. (London: Printed by G. Eyre and A. Spottiswoode, 1834–1837), 6:245–6.

51. Helen Castor, *Blood and Roses: The Paston Family and the Wars of the Roses* (London: Faber and Faber, 2004), 81, 147–148, 189–190.

52. Davis (ed.), *Paston Letters*, 1:323.

53. Castor, *Blood and Roses*, 147.

54. Alice's father, Thomas Chaucer, was first cousin to the Beaufort children of John of Gaunt and Katherine Swynford. The eldest of those Beaufort children, John, was the grandfather of Margaret Beaufort, mother of Henry Tudor. John's sister, Joan, was the grandmother of the Yorkist Edward IV and Richard III. The Beauforts were half-siblings of Henry IV, and therefore great-aunts and great-uncles to Henry VI.

55. Calendar of the Plea and Memoranda Rolls of the City of London, vol. 2, 1364–1381. (London: HMSO, 1929), https://www.british-history.ac.uk/plea-memoranda-rolls/vol2/pp96-113. See also Goldberg, 'Migration, Youth, and Gender,' 224; and Marian K. Dale, 'The London Silkwomen of the Fifteenth Century,' in *Economic History Review* 4:3 (1933): 324–335.

56. Woolf, *Room of One's Own*, 106–109.

57. Sutton, 'Two Dozen and More Silkwomen,' 6.

58. See Veale, 'Matilda Penne,' 49.

59. Christine de Pizan, *Le Livre de la mutacion de Fortune*, ed. S. Solente (Paris: A. & J. Picard, 1959–1966). See translation of these lines and discussion in Marilynn Desmond, 'Christine De Pizan,' in Simon Gaunt and Sarah Kay (eds.), *The Cambridge Companion to Medieval French Literature* (Cambridge: Cambridge University Press, 2008), 123–136, 128.

Chapter 3. The Marriage Market

1. Hanawalt, *Wealth of Wives*, 45.

2. Dorigen's version is somewhat comic in its excessiveness, and she conspicuously does not follow these women's example.

3. Bonnie Thurston, *The Widows: A Women's Ministry in the Early Church* (Minneapolis: Thurston Press, 1989), 11.

4. B. Jussen, 'Virgins—Widows—Spouses: On the language of moral distinction as applied to women and men in the Middle Ages,' *History of the Family* 7 (2002): 13–32, 15.

5. Barron, 'Golden Age,' 36–38.

6. Hanawalt, *Wealth of Wives*, 6–7, 12, 20.

7. Hanawalt, *Wealth of Wives*, 68, 113–114.

8. Carole Rawcliffe, 'Margaret Stodeye, Lady Philipot (d. 1431),' in Barron and Sutton (eds.), *Medieval London Widows*, 85–98.

9. W. J. Hardy and W. Page, *A Calendar to the Feet of Fines for London and Middlesex, vol. 1: Richard I—Richard III* (London: Hardy and Page, 1892), 143.

10. In *Letter-Book H*, fol. 1 b, the guardianship of Thomas and Idonea, the children of John Belyngham, and of John, a child with whom Margaret was 'enceinte at the time of her husband's death' is granted to John Philipot. Reginald R. Sharpe (ed.),

Calendar of Letter-Books of the City of London: H, 1375–1399 (London: His Majesty's Stationery Office, 1907).

11. Martin Crow and Clair Olson (eds.), *Chaucer Life-Records* (Oxford: Clarendon Press, 1966), 8; Turner, *Chaucer: A European Life*, 118.

12. John Stodeye's will, from 22 March 1376, refers to Margaret as married to John Philipot. Reginald R. Sharpe (ed.), *Calendar of Wills Proved and Enrolled in the Court of Husting, London: Part 2, 1358–1688* (London: Her Majesty's Stationery Office, 1890), Roll 104 (123).

13. For Brembre, see especially Pamela Nightingale, *A Medieval Mercantile Community: The Grocers' Company and the Politics and Trade of London, 1000–1485* (New Haven: Yale University Press, 1995), 194–262.

14. Sharpe, *Calendar of Wills*, 25 July 1389.

15. *Calendar of the Patent Rolls Preserved In the Public Record Office: Richard II, vol. 5 1391–1396* (London: HMSO, 1891), 4.

16. Guildhall Library, London, MS 9531/3, f. 346v. See also Rawcliffe, 'Margaret Stodeye,' 96.

17. Rowena E. Archer, 'Neville [married names Mowbray, Strangways, Beaumont, Woodville], Katherine, duchess of Norfolk (c. 1400–1483),' in ODNB, https://ezproxy-prd.bodleian.ox.ac.uk:2102/10.1093/ref:odnb/54432.

18. Cecily and Richard were the parents of Edward IV and Richard III. Cecily too was a book owner, and she and her husband owned a copy of Christine's *Cité des Dames*. See A.S.G. Edwards, 'Northern Magnates and Their Books,' *Textual Cultures* 7:1 (2012): 176–186, 177.

19. William Worcester termed it a 'maritagium diabolicum.' See Stevenson (ed.), *Letters and papers*, 2:783.

20. Rowena E. Archer, 'Chaucer [married names Phelip, Montagu, de la Pole], Alice, duchess of Suffolk (c. 1404–1475),' in ODNB, https://ezproxy-prd.bodleian.ox.ac.uk:2102/10.1093/ref:odnb/54434.

21. H. C. Maxwell Lyte, *Calendar of Close Rolls: Richard II, vol. 5: 1392–1396* (London: His Majesty's Stationery Office, 1925), 446; Turner, *Chaucer: A European Life*, 449–450.

22. See chapter 2 for further discussion.

23. Margaret Paston to John Paston II, attrib. 15 November, 1470, in Davis (ed.), *Paston Letters*, 1:356–357, 357.

24. The letter from William to John is printed in Davis (ed.), *Paston Letters*, 3:82–83.

25. Mary Carruthers, 'The Wife of Bath and the Painting of Lions,' *PMLA* 94:2 (1979): 209–222, 213–4.

26. The original text is Saint Augustine, 'Tractate 15,' in Jacques-Paul Migne, *Patrologia Latina* 35 (Paris, 1845), cols. 1510–1522. The translation is by John W. Rettig,

Tractates on the Gospel of John, vol. 79 (Washington, DC: Catholic University of America Press, 1988). See discussion in Robert Longsworth, 'The Wife of Bath and the Samaritan Woman,' *Chaucer Review* 34:4 (2000): 372–387.

27. Tertullian, *Cum Samaritinae maritum negat, ut adulterum ostendat numerosum maritum*, in Jacques-Paul Migne, *Patrologia Latina* 2 (Paris, 1844), col. 940B.

28. Warren S. Smith, 'The Wife of Bath Debates Jerome,' *Chaucer Review* 32:2 (1997): 129–145, 134–135.

29. Hanna and Lawler (eds.), *Jankyn's Book of Wikked Wyves*, 27.

30. Wright, *St Paul*, 424.

31. Hanna and Lawler (eds.), *Jankyn's Book of Wikked Wyves*, 18, 19–20, 17.

32. The significance of this specific reference is also discussed by Carruthers, 'Painting of Lions,' 211.

33. Andrew Cain, 'Jerome's *Epitaphium Paulae*: Hagiography, Pilgrimage and the Cult of St Paula,' *Journal of Early Christian Studies* 18:1 (2010): 105–139.

34. James A. Brundage, 'Widows and Remarriage: Moral Conflicts and Their Resolution in Classical Canon Law,' in Sue Sheridan Walker (ed.), *Wife and Widow in Medieval England* (Ann Arbor: University of Michigan Press, 1993), 17–31. For further discussion of the evolution of marriage as a sacrament, see Reynolds, *How Marriage Became One of the Sacraments*, especially 157–243.

35. Rawcliffe, 'Margaret Stodeye,' 97.

36. See Karma Lochrie, *Margery Kempe and Translations of the Flesh* (Philadelphia: University of Pennsylvania Press, 1994), 220–225.

37. Lee Patterson makes the case for the Parson-Wife of Bath interaction as a re-enactment of the Monk-Miller. '"For the Wyves love of Bathe": Feminine Rhetoric and Poetic Resolution in the *Roman de la Rose* and the *Canterbury Tales*,' *Speculum* 58:3 (1983): 656–693, 685.

38. R. Pratt, 'The Order of the Canterbury Tales,' *PMLA* 66:6 (1951), 1141–1167.

39. This is known as the Bradshaw Shift. George R. Keiser, 'In Defence of the Bradshaw Shift,' *Chaucer Review* 12:4 (1978): 191–201. We know that the Shipman's Tale was intended for the Wife of Bath due to its use of the female voice in the opening lines.

40. The lowest class pilgrim—the Plowman—does not tell a tale.

41. This is discussed in chapter 8.

Chapter 4. The Female Storyteller

1. 'Avianus,' in J. Wight Duff and Arnold M. Duff (ed. and trans.), *Minor Latin Poets* (Cambridge, MA: Harvard University Press, 1934), 669–749, 718–721.

2. Kamila Shamsie, 'Let's Have a Year of Publishing Only by Women—A Provocation.' Guardian, 5 June 2015, https://www.theguardian.com/books/2015/jun/05/kamila-shamsie-2018-year-publishing-women-no-new-books-men.

3. Richard de Bury, 'The Complaint of Books against the Clergy Already Promoted,' in *Philobiblon*, trans. E. C. Thomas (London: Kegan Paul, 1888), chap. 4.

4. See discussion in Jill Mann, *From Aesop to Reynard: Beast Literature in Medieval Britain* (Oxford: Oxford University Press, 2009), 92–93.

5. David Wallace, *Chaucerian Polity: Absolutist Lineages and Associational Forms in England and Italy* (Stanford: Stanford University Press, 1997), 377.

6. See Joan M. Ferrante, *To the Glory of Her Sex: Women's Roles in the Composition of Medieval Texts* (Bloomington: Indiana University Press, 1997), 8, 14.

7. Woolf, *Room of One's Own*, 63.

8. Diane Watt, *Women, Writing, and Religion in England and Beyond, 650–1100* (London: Bloomsbury, 2020), 2–4.

9. Jean Devaux, 'From the Court of Hainault to the Court of England: The Example of Jean Froissart,' in C. T. Allmand (ed.), *War, Government and Power in Late Medieval France* (Liverpool: Liverpool University Press, 2000), 1–20; Jean Froissart, *Le Joli Buisson de Jonece*, ed. Anthime Fourrier (Geneva: Droz, 1975), line 237.

10. Turner, *Chaucer: A European Life*, 95–119.

11. Nicola McDonald, 'Chaucer's *Legend of Good Women*, Ladies at Court and the Female Reader,' *Chaucer Review* 35:1 (2000): 22–42; and 'Games Medieval Women Play,' in *The Legend of Good Women: Context and Reception*, ed. Carolyn P. Collette (Cambridge: D. S. Brewer, 2006), 176–197.

12. Carole M. Meale, '"alle the bokes that I have of latyn, englisch, and frensch": Laywomen and their books in late medieval England,' in Carole M. Meale (ed.), *Women and Literature in Britain 1150–1500*, 2nd ed. (Cambridge: Cambridge University Press, 1996), 128–158, 136–141; Karen K. Jambeck, 'Patterns of Women's Literary Patronage: England, 1200–ca. 1475,' in *The Cultural Patronage of Medieval Women*, ed. Jane Hall McCash (Athens: University of Georgia Press, 1996), 228–265, 233, 235, 239.

13. Durham, University Library, MS Cosin V.iii.9.

14. MS Cosin V.iii.9, fol. 95r.

15. See discussion by David Watt in *The Making of Thomas Hoccleve's Series* (Liverpool: Liverpool University Press, 2014), esp. 54–55. See also Sebastian J. Langdell, *Thomas Hoccleve: Religious Reform, Transnational Poetics, and the Invention of Chaucer* (Liverpool: Liverpool University Press, 2018), 33–34.

16. Meale, '"alle the bokes,"' 145.

17. Jambeck, 'Patterns,' 239–241; Meale, '"alle the bokes,"' 136.

18. Karen Jambeck, 'The Library of Alice Chaucer,' *Profane Arts* 7:2 (1998): 106–135, 133.

19. Meale, 'Reading Women's Culture,' 81–101; Jambeck, 'Library of Alice Chaucer,' 133–134.

20. Oxford, St John's College, MS 56.

21. Meale, 'Reading Women's Culture,' 91–92.

22. John Goodall, *God's House at Ewelme: Life, Devotion and Architecture in a Fifteenth-century Almshouse* (Aldershot: Ashgate, 2001), 11–12; H. Anstey (ed.), *Epistolae Academicae Oxon*, 2 vols., OHS 35–36 (Oxford: Oxford Historical Society, 1898), 1:303, 326, 2:369–370.

23. Martin Michael Crow, 'John of Angoulême and His Chaucer Manuscript,' *Speculum* 17:1 (1942): 86–99, 89 n.5; Ralph Hanna and A.S.G. Edwards, 'Rotheley, the De Vere Circle, and the Ellesmere Chaucer,' *Huntington Library Quarterly* 58:1 (1995): 11–35, 16–17.

24. Meale, '"alle the bokes,"' 142.

25. Diane Watt, *Women, Writing, and Religion*, 2.

26. Guillaume de Lorris and Jean de Meun, *The Romance of the Rose*, trans. Frances Horgan (Oxford: Oxford University Press, 1994), 134–135.

27. For a discussion of the three traditions of misogamy—ascetic, philosophic, and popular, see Glenda McLeod and Katharina Wilson, 'A Clerk in Name Only—A Clerk in All But Name. The Misogamous Tradition and "La Cite des Dames,"' in Margarette Zimmerman and Dina De Rentiis (eds.), *The City of Scholars: New Approaches to Christine de Pizan* (Berlin: De Gruyter, 1994), 67–76, 68.

28. Betty Radice (trans.), *The Letters of Abelard and Heloise*, revised by M. T. Clanchy (London: Penguin Random House, 2003).

29. Constant J. Mews, *Abelard and Heloise* (Oxford: Oxford University Press, 2005), 8; Barbara Newman, 'Authority, authenticity, and the repression of Heloise,' *JMEMS* 22:2 (Spring 1992): 121–157, 130.

30. Peter the Venerable, 'Letter (115) to Heloise,' in Radice (trans.), *Letters of Abelard and Heloise*, 217–223, 218.

31. Hugh Metel, Letter 16, trans. M. T. Clanchy, in Constant J. Mews (ed.), 'Hugh Metel, Heloise and Peter Abelard,' *Viator* 32 (2001): 89.

32. See discussion in Mews, *Abelard and Heloise*, 15–17.

33. Newman, 'Authority,' 125.

34. Newman, 'Authority,' 122–125.

35. See Barbara Newman (ed. and trans.), *Making Love in the Twelfth Century: Letters of Two Lovers in Context* (Philadelphia: University of Pennsylvania Press, 2016).

36. See the discussion of the erotic letters between the abbot Baudri of Bourgueil and the nun Constance of Angers in Katherine Kong, *Lettering the Self in Medieval and Early Modern France* (Woodbridge: Boydell and Brewer, 2017), 15–54.

37. Mews, *Abelard and Heloise*, 70–71.

38. Newman, 'Authority,' 127.

39. For discussion of these sixteenth-century editions see Lochrie, *Margery Kempe*, 220–225.

40. Hilton Kelliher, 'The Rediscovery Of Margery Kempe: A Footnote,' *British Library Journal* 23:2 (1997): 259–263, 260–261.

41. Charity Cannon Willard, *Christine de Pizan: Her Life and Works* (New York: Perseus Books, 1984).

42. Christine de Pizan, *The Book of the City of Ladies*, trans. Rosalind Brown-Grant (London: Penguin, 1999), 5–11.

43. 's'on me dit li livre en sont tuit plein / [. . .] / Je leur respons que les livres ne firent / Pas les femmes'; 'Mais se femmes eussent li livre fait / Je sçay de vray qu'aultrement fust du fait' (ll. 409–411 and 417–418); in Thelma S. Fenster and Mary Carpenter Erler (eds.), *Poems of Cupid, God of Love: Christine de Pizan's 'Epistre au dieu d'amours' and 'Dit de la Rose,' Thomas Hoccleve's 'The Letter of Cupid,' Editions and Translations, with George Sewell's 'The Proclamation of Cupid'* (Leiden: E. J. Brill, 1990), 54–55.

44. Baird and Kane, *La Querelle de la Rose*, 136.

45. Fenster and Erler (eds.), *Poems of Cupid*, 52–53.

46. The first comment is by Gontier Col, the second by Jean du Montreuil, both cited in Baird and Kane, *La Querelle de la Rose*, 60, 153. This is also discussed by Willard, *Christine de Pizan*, 84, 86.

47. For Christine as female clerk, see Lori Walters, 'Chivalry and the (En)Gendered Poetic Self, Petrarchan Models in the "Cent Balades,"' in Zimmerman and de Rentis, *City of Scholars*, 43–66; and McLeod and Wilson, 'A Clerk in Name Only,' 75.

48. Kevin Brownlee, 'Discourses of the Self: Christine de Pizan and the Rose,' *Romantic Review* 79:1 (1988): 199–221.

49. For an argument focusing more on their differences, see S. H. Rigby, 'The Wife of Bath, Christine de Pizan, and the Medieval Case for Women,' *Chaucer Review* 35:2 (2000): 133–165.

50. Paul Strohm, *Social Chaucer* (Cambridge, MA: Harvard University Press, 1989), 41–46, Turner, *Chaucer: A European Life*, 377–382.

51. See J. C. Laidlaw, 'Christine de Pizan, the Earl of Salisbury, and Henry IV,' *French Studies* 36 (1982): 129–143.

52. See also Theresa Coletti, 'Paths of Long Study: Reading Chaucer and Christine de Pizan in Tandem,' *Studies in the Age of Chaucer* 28 (2006): 1–40.

53. Laidlaw, 'Christine de Pizan,' 133, 139.

54. This was discussed in chapter 2.

55. See chapter 2.

56. Willard, *Christine*, 186.

57. Jennifer Summit, *Lost Property: The Woman Writer and English Literary History, 1380–1589* (Chicago: University of Chicago Press, 2000), 61.

58. Stephen Scrope, *The Epistle of Othea to Hector; or, The Boke of Knyghthode, Translated from the French of Christine de Pisan with a Dedication to Sir John Fastolf, K.G.*, ed.

George F. Warner (London: J. B. Nichols and Sons, 1904), 3. See also Misty Schieberle, 'Rethinking Gender and Language in Stephen Scrope's Epistle of Othea 1,' *Journal of the Early Book Society for the Study of Manuscripts and Printing History* 21 (2018): 97–121, 322.

59. Summit, *Lost Property*, 72–75. For the original Latin, see William Worcester, *The Boke of Noblesse*, ed. J. G. Nichols (London: Roxburghe Club, 1860), 54, n. 151: 'Notandum est quod Cristina [fuit] domina præclara natu et moribus, et manebat in domo religiosarum dominarum apud Passye prope Parys; et ita virtuosa fuit quod ipsa exhibuit plures clericos studentes in universitate Parisiensi, et compilare fecit plures libros virtuosos.'

Chapter 5. The Wandering Woman

1. See Anthony Bale and Sebastian Sobecki (eds.), *Medieval English Travel: A Critical Anthology* (Oxford: Oxford University Press, 2019), 397–400.

2. Saint Augustine, *De Doctrina Christiana*, bk. 1, chap. 4, http://ezproxy-prd .bodleian.ox.ac.uk:2855/llta/pages/Toc.aspx?ctx=545701.

3. John Lydgate, *Payne and Sorowe of Evyll Maryage*, 119, in *The Trials and Joys of Marriage*, ed. Eve Salisbury (Kalamazoo, MI: Medieval Institute Publications, 2002), https://d.lib.rochester.edu/teams/text/salisbury-trials-and-joys-payne-and-sorowe -of-evyll-maryage.

4. T. F. Mustanoja (ed.), *The Good Wife Taught Her Daughter, The Good Wife Wold a Pylgrymage, The Thewis of Gud Women* (Helsinki: Academia Scientiarum Fennica, 1948).

5. Felix Fabri, *The Book of Wanderings of Brother Felix Fabri*, trans. Aubrey Stewart (London: Palestine Pilgrims' Text Society, 1896), 11–12, 153, 166–167.

6. Jonathan Sumption, *Pilgrimage: An Image of Medieval Religion* (London: Faber and Faber, 1974), 111–112, 141–143, 170.

7. Susan Signe Morrison, *Women Pilgrims in Later Medieval England: Private Piety as Public Performance* (New York: Routledge, 2000), 17.

8. See the classic account in R. W. Southern, *The Making of the Middle Ages* (New Haven, CT: Yale University Press, 1953), 219–257. See also Swanson, *Twelfth Century Renaissance*, and the essays in Robert Louis Benson, Giles Constable, and Carol Dana Lanham (eds.), *Renaissance and Renewal in the Twelfth Century* (Toronto: University of Toronto Press, 1999).

9. George B. Parks, *The English Traveller to Italy: The Middle Ages (to 1525)* (Rome: Edizioni di Storia e Letteratura, 1954), 376.

10. Sumption, *Pilgrimage*, 228–229.

11. Sumption, *Pilgrimage*, 286.

12. For a wide range of documents see Bale and Sobecki, *Medieval English Travel*; for what to take on the boat, see Sumption, *Pilgrimage*, 26–227; for the rivers of Spain,

see Jeanne Krochalis, Alison Stones, Annie Shaver-Crandell, and Paula Lieber Gerson, *The Pilgrim's Guide to Santiago de Compostela: A Critical Edition* (London: H. Miller, 1998), 2:19.

13. Morrison, *Women Pilgrims*, 2.

14. Ronald C. Finucane, *Miracles and Pilgrims: Popular Beliefs in Medieval England* (London: Dent, 1977), 126–129.

15. To explore the window see https://stainedglass-navigator.yorkglazierstrust .org/window/pilgrimage-window.

16. Calendar of Close Rolls, Edward III, vol. 9: 1349–1354 (London, His Majesty's Stationery Office, 1906), 8 September 1350, membrane 11d.

17. *Calendar of the Patent Rolls Preserved In the Public Record Office, Henry IV, vol. 2: 1401–1405* (London: HMSO, 1891), 14 March 1403, membrane 33.

18. For a comparison, see Sylvia Schein, 'Bridget of Sweden, Margery Kempe and Women's Jerusalem Pilgrimages in the Middle Ages,' *Mediterranean Historical Review* 14:1 (1999), 44–58.

19. See Margaret Harvey, *The English in Rome, 1362–1420: Portrait of an Expatriate Community* (Cambridge: Cambridge University Press, 2000), 128. For William Swan's letters referring to Alice, see his letterbook, in British Library, MS Cotton Cleopatra E iv.

20. Girolamo Golubovich, *Biblioteca Bio-Bibliografica della Terra Santa e dell'Oriente francescano*, 5 vols. (Quaracchi: Collegio di S Bonaventura, 1906–1927), 5:60–68, 105–109, 156–159, 196–199, 218. See also Anthony Luttrell, 'Englishwomen as Pilgrims to Jerusalem: Isolda Parewastell, 1365,' in Julia Bolton Holloway, Constance S. Wright, and Joan Bechtold (eds.), *Equally in God's Name: Women in the Middle Ages* (New York: P. Lang, 1990), 184–197, 187.

21. Ephraim Emerton (ed. and trans.), *The Letters of Saint Boniface* (New York: Columbia University Press, 1940), 140.

22. Thomas Wright (ed.), *The Book of the Knight of La Tour Landry* (London: Kegan Paul, 1906), 50.

23. Christine de Pizan, *Treasure of the City of Ladies*, 135.

24. Van Beuningen Collection, Cothen, The Netherlands, Inv. no. 2184. H.J.E Van Beuningen and A.M. Koldeweij (eds.), *Heilig en Profaan. 1000 laatmiddeleeuwse insignes uit de collectie H.J.E. van Beuningen*, Rotterdam Papers 8 (Cothen: Stichting Middeleeuwse religieuze en profane insignes, 1993), cat. no. 663. This badge is discussed in Leigh Ann Craig, *Wandering Women and Holy Matrons: Women as Pilgrims in the Later Middle Ages* (Leiden: Brill, 2009), 21–22.

25. Morrison, *Women Pilgrims*, 124.

26. Laura F. Hodges, 'The Wife of Bath's Costumes: Reading the Subtexts,' *Chaucer Review* 27:4 (1993): 359–376, 365–367.

27. Joseph Fr. Michaud and Joseph Toussaint Reinaud (eds.), *Bibliothèque des Croisades* (Paris: A L'Imprimerie Royale, 1829), 3:369–375. See also Paul Gerhardt Schmidt (ed.), 'Peregrinatio periculosa: Thomas von Froidmont über die Jerusalem-Fahrten seiner Schwester Margareta,' in Ulrich Justus Stache, Wolfgang Maaz and Fritz Wagner (eds.), *Kontinuität und Wandel: Lateinische Poesie von Naevius bis Baudelaire, Franco Munaro zum 65. Geburtstag* (Hildesheim: Weidmann, 1986), 461–485; Morrison, *Women Pilgrims*, 21; and http://www.umilta.net/jerusalem.html.

28. Rev. F. C. Hingeston, *The Register of Edmund Stafford (AD 1395–1419): An Index and Abstract of Its Contents* (G. Bell and Sons, 1886), 308.

29. Morrison, *Women Pilgrims*, 20.

30. Celia M. Lewis, 'History, Mission, and Crusade in the *Canterbury Tales*,' *Chaucer Review* 42:4 (2008): 353–82.

31. Archivio Vaticano, Reg. Supp. 45, fol. 55–55v (15 January 1366), printed and translated in Luttrell, 'Englishwomen as Pilgrims,' 191–192.

32. Luttrell, 'Englishwomen as Pilgrims,' 189.

33. For further discussion of Kempe's pilgrimages see, for instance, Anthony Goodman, *Margery Kempe and Her World* (London: Longman, 2002); Clarissa Atkinson, *Mystic and Pilgrim: The Book and the World of Margery Kempe* (Ithaca, NY: Cornell University Press, 2003); John H. Arnold and Katherine A. Lewis (eds.), *A Companion to the Book of Margery Kempe* (Cambridge: D. S. Brewer, 2004); and Terence N. Bowers, 'Margery Kempe as Traveler,' *Studies in Philology* 97:1 (2000): 1–28.

34. The only discussion of the maid of which I am aware is Diane Watt, 'Margery Kempe,' in L. H. McAvoy et al. (eds.), *The History of British Women's Writing, 700–1500* (Basingstoke: Palgrave Macmillan, 2012), 232–240, 236–238.

35. See earlier discussion of service in chapter 2.

36. For Kempe's interest in *imitatio Christi*, and in depicting herself as a martyr see, for instance, Sarah Salih, *Versions of Virginity in Late Medieval England* (Cambridge: D. S. Brewer, 2001); and Lochrie, *Margery Kempe*.

37. The Shepherds bought the house from Antonio Smerucci, and then sold it on to William Chandler of York, representing the community of the English at Rome. As the Shepherds continued to run the hospice, it is clear that their original purpose in buying it was for the community. See Harvey, *English in Rome*, 10–11.

38. Harvey, *English in Rome*, 30, 57–39, 65, 69, 76, 112.

39. Parks, *English Traveler to Italy*, 372.

40. Krochalis et al., *Pilgrim's Guide*, 2:11.

41. Krochalis et al., *Pilgrim's Guide*, 2:29–31.

42. Rory G. Critten, 'The *Manières de langage* as Evidence for the Use of Spoken French within Fifteenth-Century England,' *Forum for Modern Language Studies* 55:2 (April 2019): 121–137.

43. P. Meyer (ed.), *La Manière de Langage qui Enseigne Parler et a Écrire Le Français: Modèles de Conversations Composés en Angleterre a la Fin du XIV Siècle* (Paris: Librairie A. Franck, 1873), 404 (translation mine, with thanks to Helen Swift).

44. Meyer, *Manière*, 401 (translation mine). Chaucer's Cook also has a mormal, which does not prevent his going on pilgrimage.

45. P. Rickard, 'Anglois Coué and L'Anglois Qui Couve,' *French Studies* 7 (1953): 48–55.

46. Ludwig Pfandl, 'Itinerarum Hispanicum Hieronymi Monetarii, 1494–1495,' *Revue Hispanique* 48 (1920): 1–179, 94; discussed in Sumption, *Pilgrimage*, 202.

47. Krochalis et al., *Pilgrim's Guide*, 2:73.

48. Hodges, 'Wife of Bath's Costumes,' 366.

49. John Bowers (ed.), 'The Canterbury Interlude and Merchant's Tale of Beryn,' in *The Canterbury Tales: Fifteenth-Century Continuations and Additions* (Kalamazoo, MI: Medieval Institute Publications, 1992), https://d.lib.rochester.edu/teams/text /bowers-canterbury-tales-fifteenth-century-interlude-and-merchants-tale-of-beryn -introduction.

50. For medieval interpretation of the garden of the *Song of Songs* as Mary's body, see Ann Astell, *The Song of Songs in the Middle Ages* (Ithaca, NY: Cornell University Press, 1995); and Brian E. Daley, 'The Closed Garden and Sealed Fountain: Song of Songs 4.12 in the Late Medieval Iconography of Mary,' in Elizabeth MacDougall (ed.), *Medieval Gardens* (Washington, DC: Dumbarton Oaks, 1986), 254–278, esp. 263–267. For Chaucer and gardens see Turner, *Chaucer: A European Life*, chap. 14; and Laura Howes, *Chaucer's Gardens and the Language of Convention* (Gainesville: University Press of Florida, 1997), 83–109, esp. 100–101.

Prologue to Part II. 'Now Merrier and Extra Mature'

1. https://www.thecheeseshed.com/from-the-mongers-mouth/new-wyfe-of -bath.

2. https://www.theliterarygiftcompany.com/products/wife-of-bath-soap.

3. Margaret Atwood, *The Handmaid's Tale* (London: Penguin Random House, 2017), xi.

4. Atwood, *Handmaid's Tale*, 303.

Chapter 6. Silencing Alison

1. Constance and Griselda are the heroines of the Man of Law's Tale and the Clerk's Tale respectively, but appeared in other texts both before and after Chaucer's versions. Piers Plowman is best known from Langland's poem, but also appears in

other texts associated with the Revolt of 1381. See especially Steven Justice, *Writing and Rebellion: England in 1381* (Berkeley: University of California Press, 1994).

2. Thomas Hoccleve, *Dialogue with a Friend*, in *My Compleinte and Other Poems*, ed. Roger Ellis (Liverpool: Liverpool University Press, 2001), line 694; John Lydgate, *A Mumming at Hertford*, in *Minor Poems of John Lydgate*, ed. Henry Noble Mac-Cracken, Early English Text Society extra ser. 107, o.s. 192 (London: Oxford University Press, 1911–1934; reprinted 1961), vol. 2, 676–680, l. 168; William Dunbar, *Tua Mariit Wemen and the Wedo*, https://digital.nls.uk/firstscottishbooks/page/?folio =77; John Skelton, *Phyllyp Sparowe*, in *The Complete English Poems*, ed. V. J. Scatter-good (Harmondsworth: Penguin Books, 1983), 71–105, ll. 618–627.

3. The Wife of Bath's influence can be seen in Edmund Spenser, *The Faerie Queene Disposed into Twelue Bookes, Fashioning XII: Morall Vertues* (London: Printed for William Ponsonbie, 1596); Robert Greene, *Greenes Vision Written at the Instant of his Death* (London: Thomas Newman, 1592); John Fletcher, *Women Pleased*, in *Comedies and Tragedies Written by Francis Beaumont and Iohn Fletcher*, Dddddd1^r–Ffffff3^v (London: Humphrey Robinson, 1647). For further discussion of the Wife of Bath, Spenser, and Fletcher, see Helen Cooper, 'The Shape-shiftings of the Wife of Bath, 1395–1670,' in Ruth Morse and Barry Windeatt (eds.), *Chaucer Traditions: Studies in Honour of Derek Brewer* (Cambridge: Cambridge University Press, 1990), 168–184, 173–180 and, for an analysis of Greene's vision, see Jeremy Dimmick, 'Gower, Chaucer and the Art of Repentance in Robert Greene's *Vision*,' *Review of English Studies*, n.s., 57:231 (2006): 456–473. For the Wife of Bath's influence on Shakespeare, see chapter 7. In the early eighteenth century, Gay wrote a play about the Wife of Bath for which Pope almost certainly wrote the epilogue, while Dryden translated the Wife of Bath's Tale. Pope also produced an abridged translation of the Wife of Bath's Prologue. See below for further discussion of Gay, Pope, and Dryden's versions of the Wife, and for Pope's authorship of the epilogue, see Calhoun Winton, *John Gay and the London Theatre* (Lexington: University Press of Kentucky, 1993), 39.

4. Kenneth Clarke comments that the scene is 'humorously reminiscent of Paolo and Francesca,' comparing their burning passion with the burning of the book. *Chaucer and Italian Textuality* (Oxford: Oxford University Press, 2011), 150.

5. See Rita Copeland's magisterial 'Why Women Can't Read: Medieval Herme-neutics, Statutory Law, and the Lollard Heresy Trials,' in Zipporah Batshaw Wiseman and Susan Sage Heinzelman, *Representing Women: Law, Literature, and Femi-nism* (Durham, NC: Duke University Press, 1994), 253–286. For a discussion of the long-standing stereotype of Jews as literal readers see Jeremy Cohen, *Living Letters of the Law: Ideas of the Jew in Medieval Christianity* (Berkeley: University of California Press, 1999), 59.

6. See Dinshaw, *Chaucer's Sexual Poetics*, 3–27 and 113–131.

7. John Leo, 'Toxic Feminism on the Big Screen,' *US News and World Report*, 110:22 (October 6, 1991), 22, 20. See also discussion by Rita Felski in 'Identifying with Characters,' in Amanda Anderson, Toril Moi, and Rita Felski (eds.), *Character: Three Inquiries in Literary Studies* (Chicago: University of Chicago Press, 2019), 77–126, 99.

8. Transcriptions of all the glosses on all the manuscripts are provided by Stephen Partridge, 'Glosses in the Manuscripts of the *Canterbury Tales*: An Edition and Commentary' (PhD diss., Harvard University, 1992).

9. Partridge, 'Glosses,' sec. III-2 (not paginated).

10. For discussion of the Ellesmere glossing, see Clarke, *Chaucer and Italian Textuality*, 130–151; and Susan Schibanoff, 'The New Reader and Female Textuality in Two Early Commentaries on Chaucer,' *Studies in the Age of Chaucer* 10 (1988): 71–108. For another view see Graham D. Caie, 'The Significance of the Early Chaucer Manuscript Glosses (with Special Reference to "The Wife of Bath's Prologue"),' *Chaucer Review* 10:4 (1976): 350–360.

11. MS Additional 5140 has been fully digitised and can be viewed at http://www.bl.uk/manuscripts/Viewer.aspx?ref=add_ms_5140_fs001r. MS Egerton 2864 has also been digitised and can be viewed at http://www.bl.uk/manuscripts/Viewer.aspx?ref=egerton_ms_2864_f092r.

12. Schibanoff, 'New Reader,' 78–79.

13. This is reminiscent of the allegorical interpretation of the story of Walter and Griselda, in which the abuser (Walter) stands for God. This is how Petrarch reads the story, and the Clerk refers to this interpretation in his version (1142–1212). See Wallace, *Chaucerian Polity*, 261–98, for a detailed discussion of Petrarch's politics, poetics, and treatment of the Griselda story.

14. My transcription, with thanks to Daniel Wakelin. Partridge here has misread 'due' as 'duc'.

15. See Schibanoff, 'New Reader,' 80.

16. See Betsy Bowden, *The Wife of Bath in Afterlife: Ballads to Blake* (Bethlehem, PA: Lehigh University Press, 2017), 1–19. Bowden also prints versions of both the earlier and the later ballad in appendices A1 and A2, 307–328. Cooper also discusses the Wanton Wife in 'Shape-shiftings,' 180–182; and in 'After Chaucer,' *Studies in the Age of Chaucer* 25 (2003): 3–24.

17. Edward Arber (ed.), *A Transcript of the Register of the Company of Stationers of London, 1554–1640* (London: 1875–1877), 2:831.

18. J. S. Burn, *The High Commission: Notices of the Court and Its Proceedings* (London: J. R. Smith, 1865), 47.

19. For an account of ballad culture and the intersections between oral, written, and printed texts in the early modern period see Adam Fox, *Oral and Literate Culture in England, 1500–1700* (Oxford: Oxford University Press, 2002).

20. Hyder E. Rollins, 'The Black-Letter Broadside Ballad,' *PMLA* 34:2 (1919): 258–339, 285–286.

21. 'disorderly, adj. and n.' meaning 2a, OED Online, https://ezproxy-prd.bodleian .ox.ac.uk:2446/view/Entry/54865?rskey=h9dadx&result=1.

22. British Library, London, 11630.ee.15 [28].

23. Bowden, *Wife of Bath in Afterlife*, 5.

24. On 12 June, the Lord Keeper criticised 'the Abuses of the Times, committed by lewd and idle Persons, by the Way of Libells, in taxing their Doings and Actions that were in Authority.' He specifically 'spoke of the earl of Essex,' saying that 'some wicked Persons intermedled by libelling, to find Fault with the Doings of her Majestie.' Arthur Collins, *Letters and Memorials of State* (London: T. Osborne, 1746), 2:202.

25. See the ODNB for a useful summary of his life. Paul E. J. Hammer, 'Devereux, Robert, second earl of Essex (1565–1601),' in ODNB, https://ezproxy-prd.bodleian .ox.ac.uk:2102/10.1093/ref:odnb/7565.

26. Ernest Kuhl made the connection between the Wanton Wife and the earl of Essex, in 'The Wanton Wife of Bath and Queen Elizabeth,' *Studies in Philology* 26:2 (1929): 177–183.

27. See discussion in Jonathan Bate, *Soul of the Age: The Life, Mind, and World of William Shakespeare* (London: Penguin, 2008), 160–263.

28. Mary Anne Everett Greene (ed.), *Calendar of State Papers Domestic Series: Elizabeth* (London: Longman, 1869), 275:449.

29. Bate, *Soul of the Age*, 249–253, 278, 281–286.

30. See Jason Scott-Warren, 'Was Elizabeth I Richard II? The Authenticity of Lambarde's "Conversation,"' *Review of English Studies* 64 (2013): 208–230.

31. Winton, *John Gay and the London Theatre*, 28–39, 146–147, quote at 147. See also Andrew Higl, 'The Wife of Bath Retold: From the Medieval to the Postmodern,' in *Inhabited by Stories: Critical Essays on Tales Retold*, ed. Nancy Barton-Smith and Danette DiMario (Newcastle: Cambridge Scholars Publishing, 2012), 294–313.

32. John Gay, *The Wife of Bath, a Comedy: As It Is Acted at the Theatre-Royal in Drury-Lane, by Her Majesty's Servants; by Mr. Gay* (London: Printed for Bernard Lintott, 1713).

33. John Gay, *The Wife of Bath, a Comedy; As It Is Acted at the Theatre-Royal in Lincoln's-Inn-Fields; Written by Mr. Gay, Revised and Altered by the Author* (London: Printed for Bernard Lintot, 1730).

34. Candace Barrington, *American Chaucers* (Basingstoke: Palgrave Macmillan, 2007), 61–62.

35. I discuss MacKaye's play in more detail in chapter 8.

36. John Dryden, 'Preface' to *Fables: Ancient and Modern* (London: Jacob Tonson, 1700), 8, 11.

37. Joseph Warton, *An Essay on the Genius and Writings of Pope* (London: J. Dodsley, 1782), 2:69.

Chapter 7. When Shakespeare Met Alison

1. See Helen Cooper, *Shakespeare and the Medieval World* (London: Bloomsbury Arden Shakespeare, 2010), esp. pp. 204–234; and E. Talbot Donaldson, *The Swan at the Well* (New Haven, CT: Yale University Press, 1985).

2. See Ann Thompson, *Shakespeare's Chaucer: A Study in Literary Origins* (Liverpool: Liverpool University Press, 1978), 16. On Jonson see especially Robert C. Evans, 'Ben Jonson's Chaucer,' *English Literary Renaissance* 19:3 (1989), 324–245; and Kathryn Jacobs and D'Andra White, 'Ben Jonson on Shakespeare's Chaucer,' *Chaucer Review* 50 (2015), 198–215. On Marlowe see Loren Cressler, 'Asinine Heroism and the Mediation of Empire in Chaucer, Marlowe, and Shakespeare,' *Modern Language Quarterly* 81:3 (2020): 319–347. On Spenser see Anne Higgins, 'Spenser Reading Chaucer: Another Look at the "Faerie Queene" Allusions,' *Journal of English and Germanic Philology* 89:1 (1990): 17–36. See also Philip Sidney, *A Defence of Poetry*, ed. J. A. van Dortsten (Oxford: Oxford University Press, 1966).

3. On antiquarians see Megan L. Cook, *The Poet and the Antiquaries: Chaucerian Scholarship and the Rise of Literary History, 1532–1635* (Philadelphia: University of Pennsylvania Press, 2019).

4. For the significance of the 'Works' see Cooper, *Shakespeare and the Medieval World*, 205.

5. John Foxe, *The Acts and Monuments of John Foxe* (London: R. B. Seeley and W. Burnside, 1837–1841), 4:249. For discussion see Holly Crocker, 'John Foxe's Chaucer: Affecting Form in Post-Historicist Criticism,' *New Medieval Literatures* 15 (2013): 149–182.

6. For discussion see Cooper, 'Shape-shiftings,' 173–175.

7. On Chaucer as father see Seth Lerer, *Chaucer and His Readers: Imagining the Author in Late Medieval England* (Princeton, NJ: Princeton University Press, 1993).

8. Richard B. Brathwait, *Richard Brathwait's Comments in 1665 upon Chaucer's Tales of the Miller and the Wife of Bath*, ed. C.F.E. Spurgeon (London: Kegan Paul, Trench, Trubner, 1901).

9. See Donna N. Murphy, 'The Cobbler of Canterbury and Robert Greene,' *Notes and Queries* 57:3 (2010): 349–352.

10. *The cobler of caunterburie, or an inuectiue against tarltons newes out of purgatorie A merrier iest then a clownes iigge, and fitter for gentlemens humors; published with the cost of a dickar of cowe hides* (London: Printed by Robert Robinson, 1590), 67.

11. Jeremy Dimmick, 'Gower, Chaucer and the Art of Repentance in Robert Greene's *Vision*,' *Review of English Studies*, n.s., 57 (2006): 456–473.

12. See Harold Bloom, *The Anxiety of Influence: A Theory of Poetry* (Oxford: Oxford University Press, 1975).

13. See Misha Teramura, 'The Anxiety of *Auctoritas*: Chaucer and *The Two Noble Kinsmen*,' *Shakespeare Quarterly* 63:4 (2012): 544–576.

14. Thompson, *Shakespeare's Chaucer*, 220–221.

15. Laurie Maguire and Emma Smith, 'What Is a Source? Or, How Shakespeare Read His Marlowe,' *Shakespeare Survey* 68 (2015): 15–31, 30.

16. Cooper, 'After Chaucer,' 17.

17. Cooper, *Shakespeare and the Medieval World*, 210.

18. Cooper, *Shakespeare and the Medieval World*, 212–218; 'After Chaucer,' 17.

19. Melissa Emerson Walter, *The Italian Novella and Shakespeare's Comic Heroines* (Toronto: University of Toronto Press, 2019), 81–83, 16.

20. Jonathan Goldberg, 'What Do Women Want? The Merry Wives of Windsor,' *Criticism* 51:3 (2009): 367–383.

21. William Shakespeare, *Richard II*, in G. Blakemore Evans and J. J. M. Tobin (eds.), *The Riverside Shakespeare*, 2nd ed. (Boston: Houghton Mifflin, 1997), I.iii.294–295; Wife of Bath's Tale, 1139–1143. See Thompson, *Shakespeare's Chaucer*, 77.

22. On Shakespeare's 'inspired misremembering,' see Colin Burrow, 'Shakespeare and Humanistic Culture,' in Charles Martindale and A. B. Taylor (ed.), *Shakespeare and the Classics* (Cambridge: Cambridge University Press, 2004), 9–28, 14.

23. Shakespeare, *Alls Well that Ends Well*, II.iii.123–135; Wife of Bath's Tale, 1146–1164.

24. Bloom, *Western Canon*, 112.

25. Jeanne Addison Roberts, 'Falstaff in Windsor Forest: Villain or Victim?' *Shakespeare Quarterly* 26:1 (1975), 8–15, 8.

26. Bloom, *Western Canon*, 47.

27. Harold Bloom, *Falstaff: Give Me Life* (New York: Scribner, 2017), 1.

28. Laurie A. Finke, 'Falstaff, the Wife of Bath, and the Sweet Smoke of Rhetoric,' in E. Talbot Donaldson and Judith J. Kollmann (eds.), *Chaucerian Shakespeare: Adaptation and Transformation* (Detroit: Michigan Consortium for Medieval and Early Modern Studies, 1983), 7–24, 11–12.

29. Beatrice Groves, '"The ears of profiting": Listening to Falstaff's Biblical Quotations,' in Julie Maxwell and Kate Rumbold (eds.), *Shakespeare and Quotation* (Cambridge: Cambridge University Press, 2018), 60–71, 61; Hannibal Hamlin, *The Bible in Shakespeare* (Oxford: Oxford University Press, 2013), 234.

30. Donaldson terms them both 'gross solipsists' of 'enormous vitality,' Donaldson, *Swan at the Well*, 129.

31. Anne Barton, *Essays Mainly Shakespearean* (Cambridge: Cambridge University Press, 1994), 70–74.

32. Bloom, *Western Canon*, 112.

33. Evelyn Gajowski and Phyllis Rackin, *The Merry Wives of Windsor: New Critical Essays* (London: Routledge, 2015), 1–4.

34. Phyllis Rackin, *Shakespeare and Women* (Oxford University Press, 2005), 51.

35. Graham Holderness, 'Cleaning House: The Courtly and the Popular in *The Merry Wives of Windsor*,' *Critical Survey* 22:1 (2010): 26–40, 27.

36. Harriet Phillips, 'Late Falstaff, the Merry World, and *The Merry Wives of Windsor*,' *Shakespeare* 10 (2014): 111–137.

37. Skimmington rides often involved cross-dressing and usually were enacted to humiliate cuckolds. Charivari tended to involve women being ducked and beaten, and were usually supposed to punish whores or adulteresses. In the *Merry Wives*, Falstaff is the victim of both kinds of ritual. See Natasha Korda, *Shakespeare's Domestic Economies: Gender and Property in Early Modern England* (Philadelphia: University of Pennsylvania Press, 2002), 94; and Martin Ingram, 'Flyting, Polemics, Charivaris,' in Martin Ingram et al. (eds), *The Cambridge Guide to the Worlds of Shakespeare* (Cambridge: Cambridge University Press, 2019), 516–523.

38. For Falstaff's association with grease more generally see M. P. Tilley, 'Two Shakespearean Notes,' *Journal of English and Germanic Philology* 24:3 (July 1925): 315–324.

39. It occurs in two manuscripts of the *Temple of Glas* (a text that is heavily influenced by Chaucer, most notably by the *House of Fame*), in the context of a woman complaining about a husband's jealousy, saying that because of this jealousy, he is 'fryed in his owen grese' (349). The lines are quoted in the note to line 335–369 of J. Allan Mitchell's edition: John Lydgate, *The Temple of Glass*, ed. J. Allan Mitchell (Kalamazoo, MI: Medieval Institute Publications, 2007), https://d.lib.rochester.edu/teams/text/mitchell-lydgate-temple-of-glas. It also appears as a proverb in John Heywood, *A dialogue conteinyng the nomber in effect of all the prouerbes in the englishe tongue compacte in a matter concernyng two maner of mariages, made and set foorth by Iohn Heywood* (London: Thomas Berthelet, 1546), pt. 1, chap. 11.

40. J. A. Bryant Jr, 'Falstaff and the Renewal of Winter,' *PMLA* 89:2 (1974): 296–301; Jan Lawson Hinely, 'Comic Scapegoats and the Falstaff of the Merry Wives of Windsor,' *Shakespeare Studies* 15 (1982): 37–54; and Roberts, 'Falstaff in Windsor Forest.'

41. For a discussion of players' association with a blurring of gender, see Patricia Parker, *Shakespeare from the Margins: Language, Culture, Context* (Chicago: University of Chicago Press, 1996), 143.

42. Goldberg discusses Ford's horror at 'women doing things that men don't understand and can't do,' 'What Do Women Want?' 376.

43. Withingson argues that Falstaff is 'relentlessly effeminised' and becomes a 'conflation' of 'pejorative female stereotypes,' in Phil Withingson, 'Putting the City into Shakespeare's City Comedy,' in David Armitage et al. (eds.), *Shakespeare and*

Early Modern Political Thought (Cambridge: Cambridge University Press, 2010), 197–216, 210.

44. See Peter Stallybrass and Allon White, *The Politics and Poetics of Transgression* (London: Methuen, 1986).

45. http://www.nationaltrustcollections.org.uk/object/486148.

46. https://artuk.org/discover/artworks/group-of-five-women-mocking-an-effaced-figure-falstaff-in-the-laundry-basket-mocked-by-women-219657.

47. http://www.hellenicaworld.com/Art/Paintings/en/Part8654.html.

Chapter 8. Alison Abroad

1. See discussion in Thomas A. Kirby, 'Theodore Roosevelt on Chaucer and a Chaucerian,' *Modern Language Notes* 68:1 (1953): 34–37.

2. For a discussion of Pasolini's use of Italian translations, and his attention to dialect and language in the film see Louise D'Arcens, 'The Thunder after the Lightning: Language and Pasolini's Medievalist Poetics,' in *postmedieval* 6:2 (2015): 191–199.

3. Voltaire, *Contes en vers et en prose*, ed. Sylvain Menant (Paris: Bordas, 1992), 1:331–346.

4. Bowden, *Wife of Bath in Afterlife*, 142.

5. Candace Barrington traces the earliest example of American ownership of Chaucer folio editions to Daniel Russell's 1679 will in *American Chaucers*, 5.

6. For an overview, see https://oliviagiovetti.substack.com/p/force-majeured. For her attempt to establish her right to sue, see https://casetext.com/case/arndt-ober-v-metropolitan-opera-co-1. See also Barrington, *American Chaucers*, 43–44.

7. Donald Clive Stuart, 'The Source of Two of Voltaire's "Contes en Vers,"' *Modern Language Review* 12:2 (1917): 177–181, 177.

8. Ian Davidson, *Voltaire: A Life* (New York: Pegasus Books, 2010), 317–326.

9. Roger Pearson, 'Introduction,' in Voltaire, *Candide and Other Stories*, trans. Roger Pearson (Oxford: Oxford University Press, 2006), vii–xliii, xxvi.

10. Bowden, *Wife of Bath in Afterlife*, 135–136.

11. Davidson, *Voltaire*, 58–66.

12. The letter is dated 1 December 1763 and is cited in Stuart, 'Source of Two of Voltaire's "Contes en Vers,"' 177.

13. Translations are from Voltaire, *Candide and Other Stories*. *Ce qui plaît aux dames*, translated as 'What Pleases the Ladies,' appears on 178–189.

14. See my earlier discussion in chapter 6.

15. For the text see appendix B1 in Bowden, *Wife of Bath in Afterlife*.

16. Note, however, that the 'our' is not in Voltaire's original—i.e., the modern translation strengthens our identification here.

17. The translations for the rest of this paragraph are my own, literal translations. Pearson's translation is freer, and as such sometimes inserts puns that are not there in the original.

18. Bowden, *Wife of Bath in Afterlife*, 206.

19. Ananda K. Coomaraswamy, 'On the Loathly Bride,' *Speculum* 20:4 (1945): 391–404.

20. The story is summarised in G. H. Maynadier, *The Wife of Bath's Tale; Its Sources and Analogues* (London: D. Nutt, 1901), 27–29.

21. Coomaraswamy, 'On the Loathly Bride,' 393–400.

22. Bowden, *Wife of Bath in Afterlife*, 142–143.

23. See Eleanor Farjeon, *Tales from Chaucer: Done into Prose* (London: Medici Society, 1930), 93. See also Velma Bourgeois Richmond, *Chaucer as Children's Literature: Retellings from the Victorian and Edwardian Eras* (Jefferson, North Carolina: McFarland and Co., 2004), Candace Barrington, 'Retelling Chaucer's Wife of Bath for Modern Children: Picture Books and Evolving Feminism,' in Karen A. Ritzenhoff and Katherine A. Hermes (eds.), *Sex and Sexuality in a Feminist World* (Newcastle upon Tyne: Cambridge Scholars Publishing, 2009), 26–51; and Kathryn L. Lynch, 'Katharine Lee Bates and Chaucer's American Children,' *Chaucer Review* 56:2 (2021): 95–118.

24. Charles Cowden Clarke, *Tales from Chaucer* (London: Everyman's Library, 1911).

25. Blake, *Complete Poetry and Prose*, 537.

26. Archives of Doe Library, University of California, Berkeley. The poster is discussed in Richmond, *Chaucer as Children's Literature*, 151.

27. Martin Greene, 'The Dialectic of Adaptation: The Canterbury Tales of Pier Paolo Pasolini,' *Literature/Film Quarterly* 4:1 (1976): 46–53, 46.

28. Pier Paolo Pasolini, 'Trilogy of Life Rejected' (written 15 June 1975; published 9 November 1975). Published in *Lutheran Letters*, trans. Stuart Hood (New York: Caracanet Press, 1983), 49–52, 49. See also D'Arcens, 'Thunder after the Lightning'; she comments on Pasolini's interest in 'bodies asserting their materiality in a kind of folk defiance of social and institutional oppression,' 193.

29. Pasolini, 'Trilogy of Life Rejected,' 51.

30. For a discussion of Pasolini's ideological relationship to the sub-proletariat, see Fabio Vighi, 'Pasolini and Exclusion: Žižek, Agamben and the Modern Sub-Proletariat,' *Theory, Culture & Society* 20:5 (2003): 99–121.

31. Discussed by Naomi Greene, *Pier Paolo Pasolini: Cinema as Heresy* (Princeton, NJ: Princeton University Press, 1990), 217.

32. Carol L. Robinson, 'Celluloid Criticism: Pasolini's Contribution to a Chaucerian Debate,' in Leslie J. Workman (ed.), *Medievalism in Europe* (Woodbridge: Boydell and Brewer, 1994), 115–126, 124. Tison Pugh reads Pasolini somewhat more

sympathetically: see 'Chaucerian Fabliaux, Cinematic Fabliau: Pier Paolo Pasolini's I racconti di Canterbury,' in *Literature/Film Quarterly* 32 (2004): 199–206.

33. Jürgen Wasim Frembgen, 'Honour, Shame, and Bodily Mutilation: Cutting Off the Nose among Tribal Societies in Pakistan,' *Journal of the Royal Asiatic Society* 16:3 (2006): 243–260, 245.

34. For overviews see Jill Raitt, 'The "Vagina Dentata" and the "Immaculatus Uterus Divini Fonti,"' *Journal of the American Academy of Religion* 48:3 (1980): 415–431; Verrier Elwin, 'The Vagina Dentata Legend,' *British Journal of Medical Psychology* 19 (1943): 439–53; Wolfgang Lederer, *The Fear of Women* (New York: Harcourt, 1968).

35. http://encyklopediateatru.pl/sztuki/7994/opowiesci-kanterberyjskie.

36. https://www.jansawka.com///index.html.

37. Although some have suggested that the figures represent contemporary Polish political figures (https://collections.vam.ac.uk/item/O75992/the-canterbuty-tales -poster-sawka-jan/), I have not found any direct connections, and conversations with Polish colleagues have confirmed that they do not seem to represent specific individuals. Sebastian Sobecki has helpfully advised me on this issue.

38. https://collections.vam.ac.uk/item/O75992/the-canterbury-tales-poster -sawka-jan/.

39. https://globalchaucers.wordpress.com/category/translations/.

40. http://www.agendabh.com.br/maite-proenca-em-a-mulher-de-bath/.

Chapter 9. Alison and the Novel

1. Joyce Coleman, *Public Reading and the Reading Public in Late Medieval England and France* (Cambridge: Cambridge University Press, 2005).

2. Conversation recorded by Arthur Power. Arthur Power, *Conversations with James Joyce* (London: Millington, 1974), 95.

3. Lucia Boldrini, 'Introduction: Middayevil Joyce,' in Lucia Boldrini (ed.), *Medieval Joyce* (Amsterdam, NY: Rodopi, 2002), 11–44, 11.

4. James Joyce, *Ulysses: The 1922 Text*, ed. Jeri Johnson (Oxford: Oxford University Press, 1993), 367, 371. Further references are to this edition and appear in the text.

5. Johnson notes 'We will misread if we assume that the history of styles follows the growth of the foetus in any teleologically progressive way,' *Ulysses*, 907.

6. See Lucia Boldrini, 'Translating the Middle Ages: Modernism and the Ideal of the Common Language,' *Translation and Literature* 12:1 (2003): 41–68.

7. Conversation with Frank Budgen. Frank Budgen, *James Joyce and the Making of Ulysses* (Bloomington: Indiana University Press, 1960 [1934]), 181.

8. The comments come from Louis Gillet's 'Preface' in Geoffrey Chaucer, *A Chaucer A B C, initial letters designed and illuminated by Lucia Joyce with a preface by Louis Gillet* (Paris: Obelisk Press, 1936), i.

9. See Helen Cooper, 'Joyce's Other Father: The Case for Chaucer,' in Boldrini (ed.), *Medieval Joyce*, 143–163, 146–147.

10. See Alessa Johns, 'Joyce and Chaucer: The Historical Significance of Similarities Between *Ulysses* and the *Canterbury Tales*' (unpublished MA thesis, McGill University, 1985), 3.

11. Joyce mentions this in a letter on 23 October, 1932. See Richard Ellmann, *James Joyce*, rev. ed. (Oxford: Oxford University Press, 1982), 658.

12. Budgen, *James Joyce and the Making of Ulysses*, 181.

13. Chaucer, *A Chaucer A B C*.

14. For instance, see Richard Ellmann, *Ulysses on the Liffey* (Oxford: Oxford University Press, 1986), 163.

15. Stewart Justman, *The Springs of Liberty: The Satiric Tradition and Freedom of Speech* (Evanston, IL: Northwestern University Press, 1999), 98; Cooper, 'Joyce's Other Father,' 159.

16. John H. Lammers, 'The Archetypal Molly Bloom, Joyce's Frail Wife of Bath,' *James Joyce Quarterly* 25:4 (Summer 1998), 487–502, 488, Lewis M. Schwartz, 'Eccles Street and Canterbury: An Approach to Molly Bloom,' *Twentieth-Century Literature* 15:3 (1969): 155–165, 155; Johns, 'Joyce and Chaucer,' i, 6.

17. Chaucer, *A Chaucer ABC*, i. For Joyce's praise, see Stuart Gilbert and Richard Ellmann (eds.), *Letters of James Joyce* (London: Viking Press, 1966 [1957]), 1:337.

18. Letter from Joyce to Frank Budgen, 16 August 1921, Gilbert and Ellmann, *Letters*, 1:170. The final sentence inverts Mephistopheles' statement from Goethe's *Faust*: I am the spirit that always denies.

19. Letter from Joyce to Harriet Shaw Weaver, 8 February 1922, Gilbert and Ellmann, *Letters*, 1:180. Bloch comments that 'in the early centuries of Christianity among the church fathers, the flesh becomes gendered as specifically feminine,' *Medieval Misogyny*, 46.

20. Lammers, 'Archetypal Molly,' 488; Schwartz, 'Eccles Street and Canterbury,' 156.

21. Umberto Eco, *The Middle Ages of James Joyce: The Aesthetic of Chaosmos* (Tulsa: University of Oklahoma Press, 1982), 26.

22. Charles E. Noad, 'The Tolkien Society—the early days,' in Henry Gee (ed.), *Mallorn* (London: Tolkien Society, 2010), 50:15–24.

23. Vera Chapman, *The Wife of Bath* (London: Rex Collings, 1978).

24. The *Middle English Dictionary* suggests, '?means of relief for lovers; ?means of contraception or abortion' as a definition for the phrase in this context. In contrast,

an article on this phrase considers all kinds of possible meanings, including (at some length) the idea that it implies that Alison poisoned her husband, without considering contraception as a possibility. See Martin Puhvel, 'The Wife of Bath's "Remedies of Love,"' *Chaucer Review* 20:4 (1986): 307–312.

25. On medieval birth control see John Riddle, *Contraception and Abortion from the Ancient World to the Renaissance* (Cambridge, MA: Harvard University Press, 1992); P.P.A. Biller, 'Birth-Control in the West in the Thirteenth and Early Fourteenth Centuries,' *Past and Present* 94 (1982): 3–26; Danielle Jacquart and Claude Thomasset, *Sexuality and Medicine in the Middle Ages* (Princeton, NJ: Princeton University Press, 1988); and Robert Jutte, *Contraception: A History* (Cambridge: Polity Press, 2008).

26. Caroline Bergvall, *Alisoun Sings* (New York: Nightboat Books, 2019).

27. Beyoncé is a Black American singer, Gina Miller a prominent campaigner against Brexit, Mary Beard a Cambridge classicist, Judith Butler an American feminist and theorist mainly known for her work on gender, Audre Lorde (deceased) a Black poet and activist, Diane Abbott a Black British MP, and Arundhati Roy an Indian campaigner and novelist. All are known for speaking out against authorities and oppression in varying ways; many are frequently attacked on social media in extremely misogynist and aggressive ways.

28. On Rykener's case see Carolyn Dinshaw, *Getting Medieval: Sexualities and Communities, Pre- and Postmodern* (Durham, NC: Duke University Press, 1999), 100–142; Ruth Evans, 'Production of Space in Chaucer's London,' in Ardis Butterfield (ed.), *Chaucer and the City* (Woodbridge: D. S. Brewer, 2006), 41–56; P.J.P. Goldberg, 'John Rykener, Richard II, and the Governance of London,' *Leeds Studies in English* 45 (2014): 49–70; R. M. Karras and D. L. Boyd, 'The Interrogation of a Male Transvestite Prostitute in Fourteenth-Century London,' *GLQ: A Journal of Lesbian and Gay Studies* 1 (1995): 459–465; R. M. Karras and D. L. Boyd, '"Ut cum muliere": A Male Transvestite Prostitute in Fourteenth-Century London,' in Louise Fradenburg and Carla Freccero (eds.), *Premodern Sexualities* (London: Routledge, 1996), 99–116; R. M. Karras and T. Linkinen, 'John/Eleanor Rykener Revisited,' in L. E. Doggett and D. E. O'Sullivan (eds.), *Founding Feminisms in Medieval Studies: Essays in Honor of E. Jane Burns* (Cambridge: D. S. Brewer, 2016), 111–124.

Chapter 10. Black Alisons: Wives of Brixton, Bafa, and Willesden

1. Kathleen Forni, *Chaucer's Afterlife: Adaptations in Recent Popular Culture* (Jefferson, NC: McFarland, 2013), 106–121, 106.

2. Marilyn Nelson, 'The Cachoeira Tales,' in *The Cachoeira Tales and Other Poems* (Baton Rouge: Louisiana State University Press, 2005), 11–54, 11.

3. Nelson, *Cachoeira Tales*, 13.

4. David Wallace discusses her affinities with the Clerk as well as the Wife of Bath in 'New Chaucer Topographies,' *Studies in the Age of Chaucer* 29 (2007): 3–19, 13. The ski-slope story is told on pp. 45–46 of Nelson, *Cachoeira Tales*.

5. Nelson, *Cachoeira Tales*, 15.

6. https://literature.britishcouncil.org/writer/jean-binta-breeze.

7. Jean 'Binta' Breeze, *The Arrival of Brighteye and Other Poems* (Newcastle upon Tyne: Bloodaxe Books, 2000).

8. https://www.youtube.com/watch?v=MiyKat1QzbQ.

9. http://www.transculturalwriting.com/radiophonics/contents/writerson writing/patienceagbabi/thewifeofbafa-analysis/index.html.

10. Patience Agbabi, *Telling Tales* (London: Canongate, 2014).

11. Zadie Smith, *The Wife of Willesden* (London: Penguin Random House, 2021), 10.

12. June 1948 is thus seen as a marker of a new era in Black British identity and poetry. See Jahan Ramazani, 'Black British Poetry and the Translocal,' in Neil Corcoran (ed.), *The Cambridge Companion to Twentieth-Century English Poetry* (Cambridge: Cambridge University Press, 2007), 200–214, 201.

13. See, for instance, Amelia Gentleman, *The Windrush Betrayal: Exposing the Hostile Environment* (London: Guardian Faber Publishing, 2019); and Colin Grant, *Homecoming: Voices of the Windrush Generation* (London: Jonathan Cape, 2019).

14. Zadie Smith, 'Introduction: From Chaucerian to North Weezian (via Twitter),' in *The Wife of Willesden*, ix–xvi, xii.

15. Caroline Barron, *London in the Later Middle Ages: Government and People 1200–1500* (Oxford: Oxford University Press, 2004), 97; Paul Freedman, *Out of the East: Spices and the Medieval Imagination* (New Haven: Yale University Press, 2007), 1–11.

16. Turner, *Chaucer: A European Life*, 95–119.

17. Turner, *Chaucer: A European Life*, 437, n. 70.

18. Bernadine Evaristo, *The Emperor's Babe* (London: Penguin, 2001).

19. See discussion by Ramazani, who notes that Evaristo 'takes a cross-racial, polyglot England to be fundamental'; see 'Black British Poetry,' 210–211.

20. See National Archives, E 122/71/4; and Turner, *Chaucer: A European Life*, 189.

21. T.F.T. Baker (ed.), *A History of the County of Middlesex, vol. 7: Acton, Chiswick, Ealing and Brentford, West Twyford, Willesden* (London: Victoria County History, 1982), https://www.british-history.ac.uk/vch/middx/vol7/pp236-241#fnn36.

22. Over the last twenty years in particular, a great deal of scholarship has been published about postcolonialism and the Middle Ages. For a discussion of several major books in the field, see Simon Gaunt, 'Can the Middle Ages be Postcolonial?' *Comparative Literature* 61:2 (Spring, 2009): 160–176. For a recent influential discus-

sion of race in the medieval era see Geraldine Heng, *The Invention of Race in the Middle Ages* (Cambridge: Cambridge University Press, 2018).

23. John H. Fisher, 'Chancery and the Emergence of Standard Written English in the Fifteenth Century,' *Speculum* 52:4 (1977): 870–899.

24. On aurality and orality see Coleman, *Public Reading and the Reading Public*. There has also long been a tendency amongst some colonialists and historiographers to suggest reductive similarities between colonial subjects and medieval people. For an intelligent discussion and critique of this position see Kathleen Davis, who argues that 'the genealogies of "the Middle Ages" and of colonialism are intimately entwined' and that 'Europe's "medieval" past and cultural others, mainly colonized non-Christians, were defined as religious, static, and ahistorical'; see *Periodization and Sovereignty: How Ideas of Feudalism and Secularization Govern the Politics of Time* (Philadelphia, University of Pennsylvania Press, 2008), 20, 77. See also Dinshaw, *Getting Medieval*, 18–19.

25. Manuela Coppola, 'A Tale of Two Wives: The Transnational Poetry of Patience Agbabi and Jean 'Binta' Breeze,' *Journal of Postcolonial Writing* 52:3 (2016): 305–318.

26. Darcus Howe discusses this in his London walk, 'Black Sabbath,' in Andrew White (ed.), *Time Out London Walks* (London: Penguin, 2002), 166–173, 169; see discussion in Wallace, 'New Chaucer Topographies,' 10.

27. http://www.transculturalwriting.com/radiophonics/contents/writerson writing/patienceagbabi/thewifeofbafa-analysis/index.html.

28. For a fascinating discussion of teaching Breeze and Agbabi's texts, see Jonathan Hsy, 'Teaching the Wife of Bath through Adaptation,' https://globalchaucers .wordpress.com/2014/11/21/teaching-the-wife-of-bath-through-adaptation/.

29. Aarthi Vaddi, 'Narratives of Migration, Immigration, and Interconnection,' in David James (ed.), *The Cambridge Companion to British Fiction since 1945* (Cambridge: Cambridge University Press, 2015), 61–76, 74.

30. Jordan Peterson *Twelve Rules for Life: An Antidote to Chaos* (London: Allen Lane, 2018); Warren Farrell, *The Myth of Male Power* (New York: Simon and Schuster, 1993); Neil Strauss, *The Game: Penetrating the Secret Society of Pick-Up Artists* (Edinburgh: Canongate, 2007); and Steve Moxon, *The Woman Racket: The New Science Explaining How the Sexes Relate at Work, at Play and in Society* (Exeter: Imprint Academic, 2008).

31. Homi K. Bhabha, *The Location of Culture* (London: Routledge, 2004), 145–147.

32. Karla Gottlieb, *The Mother of Us All: A History of Queen Nanny, Leader of the Windward Jamaican Maroons* (Trenton, NJ: Africa World Press, 2000); Mavis Campbell, *The Maroons of Jamaica 1655–1796: a History of Resistance, Collaboration &*

Betrayal (Granby, MA: Bergin & Garvey, 1988); and Richard Price (ed.), *Maroon Societies: Rebel Slave Communities in the Americas* (Baltimore, MD: Johns Hopkins University Press, 1996).

33. Breeze, *Arrival of Brighteye*, 67–71.

34. Zadie Smith's first book was *White Teeth* (London: Hamish Hamilton, 2000).

Bibliography

Manuscript and Documentary Sources

British Library, London, MS Cotton Cleopatra E iv.

British Library, London, MS 5140.

British Library, London, 11630.ee.15.

Durham, University Library. MS Cosin V.iii.9.

Guildhall Library, London. MS 9531/3.

National Archives. E 122/71/4.

St John's College, Oxford. MS 56.

Doe Library Archives, University of California, Berkeley.

Primary Sources

Agbabi, Patience. *Telling Tales*. London: Canongate, 2014.

Anonymous. *The cobler of caunterburie, or an inuectiue against tarltons newes out of purgatorie A merrier iest then a clownes iigge, and fitter for gentlemens humors; published with the cost of a dickar of cowe hides*. London: Printed by Robert Robinson, 1590.

Anstey, H., ed. *Epistolae Academicae Oxon*. OHS 35–36. 2 vols. Oxford: Oxford Historical Society, 1898.

Arber, Edward, ed. *A Transcript of the Register of the Company of Stationers of London, 1554–1640*. 5 vols. London, 1875–1877.

Atwood, Margaret. *The Handmaid's Tale*. London: Penguin Random House, 2017.

Augustine, of Hippo, Saint. *Confessions*. Translated by Henry Chadwick. Oxford: Oxford University Press, 2008.

———. *De Doctrina Christiana*. Turnhout: Brepols Publishers. http://ezproxy-prd .bodleian.ox.ac.uk:2855/llta/pages/Toc.aspx?ctx=545701.

———. 'Tractate 15.' In *Patrologia Latina* 35, edited by Jacques-Paul Migne. Paris, 1845.

Baird, Joseph L., and John Robert Kane. *La Querelle de la Rose: Letters and Documents*. Chapel Hill: University of North Carolina Press, 1978.

Bergvall, Caroline. *Alisoun Sings*. New York: Nightboat Books, 2019.

Blake, William. *The Complete Poetry and Prose of William Blake*. Edited by David V. Erdman. Berkeley: University of California Press, 1982.

Bowers, John, ed. 'The Canterbury Interlude and Merchant's Tale of Beryn.' In *The Canterbury Tales: Fifteenth-Century Continuations and Additions*, 55–196. Kalamazoo, MI: Medieval Institute Publications, 1992.

Brathwait, Richard B. *Richard Brathwait's Comments in 1665 upon Chaucer's Tales of the Miller and the Wife of Bath*. Edited by C.F.E. Spurgeon. London: Kegan Paul, Trench, Trubner, 1901.

Breeze, Jean 'Binta.' *The Arrival of Brighteye and Other Poems*. Newcastle upon Tyne: Bloodaxe Books, 2000.

Burn, J. S. *The High Commission: Notices of the Court and Its Proceedings*. London: J. R. Smith, 1865.

Calendar of Close Rolls: Richard II. Vol. 5: 1392–1396. London: His Majesty's Stationery Office, 1925.

Calendar of Close Rolls. Edward III, vol. 9: 1349–1354. London: His Majesty's Stationery Office, 1906.

Calendar of the Patent Rolls Preserved In the Public Record Office: Henry IV. Vol. 2: 1401–1405. London: His Majesty's Stationery Office, 1891.

Calendar of the Patent Rolls Preserved In the Public Record Office: Richard II. Vol. 5: 1391–1396. London: His Majesty's Stationery Office, 1891.

Calendar of the Plea and Memoranda Rolls of the City of London. Vol. 2: 1364–1381. London: His Majesty's Stationery Office, 1929.

Chapman, Vera. *The Wife of Bath*. London: Rex Collings, 1978.

Chaucer, Geoffrey. *A Chaucer A B C, initial letters designed and illuminated by Lucia Joyce with a preface by Louis Gillet*. Paris: Obelisk Press, 1936.

———. *The Riverside Chaucer*. Edited by Larry Benson, F. N. Robinson, and Christopher Cannon. 3rd ed. Oxford: Oxford University Press, 2008.

Collins, Arthur. *Letters and Memorials of State, in the reigns of Queen Mary, Queen Elizabeth, King James, King Charles the First, part of the reign of King Charles the Second, and Oliver's usurpation*. London: Printed for T. Osborne, 1746.

Correale, Robert M. and Mary Hamel, eds. *Sources and Analogues of 'The Canterbury Tales.'* 2 vols. Cambridge: D. S. Brewer, 2005.

Cowden Clarke, Charles. *Tales from Chaucer*. London: Everyman's Library, 1911.

Crow, Martin, and Clair Olson, eds. *Chaucer Life-Records*. Oxford: Clarendon Press, 1966.

Evaristo, Bernadine. *The Emperor's Babe*. London: Penguin, 2001.

Davis, Norman, ed. *Paston Letters and Papers of the Fifteenth Century*. Early English Text Society, s.s. 20, 21, 22. 3 vols. Oxford: Oxford University Press, 1983.

de Bury, Richard. *Philobiblon*, trans. E. C. Thomas. London: Kegan Paul, 1888.

Dryden, John. *Fables: Ancient and Modern*. London: Jacob Tonson, 1700.

Duff, J. Wight, and Arnold M. Duff, ed. and trans. 'Avianus.' In *Minor Latin Poets*, 669–749. Loeb Classical Library. Cambridge, MA: Harvard University Press, 1934.

Dunbar, William. *Tua Mariit Wemen and the Wedo*. https://digital.nls.uk/firstscottish books/page/?folio=177.

Ephraim, Emerton, ed. and trans. *The Letters of Saint Boniface*. New York: Columbia University Press, 1940.

Fabri, Felix. *The Book of Wanderings of Brother Felix Fabri*. Translated by Aubrey Stewart. London: Palestine Pilgrims' Text Society, 1896.

Farjeon, Eleanor. *Tales from Chaucer: Done into Prose*. London: Medici Society, 1930.

Fenster, Thelma S., and Mary Carpenter Erler, eds. *Poems of Cupid, God of Love: Christine de Pizan's 'Epistre au dieu d'amours' and 'Dit de la Rose,' Thomas Hoccleve's 'The Letter of Cupid,' Editions and Translations, with George Sewell's 'The Proclamation of Cupid.'* Leiden: E. J. Brill, 1990.

Fforde, Jasper. *The Eyre Affair*. London: Hodder and Stoughton, 2001.

Fletcher, John. *Women Pleased*. In *Comedies and Tragedies Written by Francis Beaumont and Iohn Fletcher*, Ddddddi^r–Ffffff3^v. London: Humphrey Robinson, 1647.

Foxe, John. *The Acts and Monuments of John Foxe*. London: R. B. Seeley and W. Burnside, 1837–1841.

Froissart, Jean. *Le Joli Buisson de Jonece*. Edited by Anthime Fourrier. Geneva: Droz, 1975.

Gay, John. *The Wife of Bath, a Comedy: As It Is Acted at the Theatre-Royal in Drury-Lane, by Her Majesty's Servants; by Mr. Gay*. London: Printed for Bernard Lintott, 1713.

———. *The Wife of Bath, a Comedy: As It Is Acted at the Theatre-Royal in Lincoln's-Inn-Fields; Written by Mr. Gay, Revised and Altered by the Author*. London: Printed for Bernard Lintot, 1730.

Gilbert, Stuart, and Richard Ellmann, eds. *Letters of James Joyce*. 3 vols. London: Viking Press, 1957.

Given-Wilson, Christopher, ed. *Parliament Rolls of Medieval England, 1275–1504*. 16 vols. Woodbridge: Boydell and Brewer, 2005.

Greene, Mary Anne Everett, ed. *Calendar of State Papers Domestic Series: Elizabeth*. Vol. 275. London: Longman, 1869.

Greene, Robert. *Greenes Vision Written at the Instant of his Death*. London: Thomas Newman, 1592.

Hardy, W. J., and W. Page, eds. *A Calendar to the Feet of Fines for London and Middlesex. Vol. 1: Richard I—Richard III*. London: Hardy and Page, 1892.

Harris, Nicolas, ed. *Proceedings and Ordinances of the Privy Council*. 7 vols. London: G. Eyre and A. Spottiswoode, 1834–1837.

Heywood, John. *A dialogue conteinyng the number in effect of all the prouerbes in the englishe tongue compacte in a matter concernyng two maner of mariages, made and set foorth by Iohn Heywood.* London: Thomas Berthelet, 1546.

Hirsh, John, ed. *Medieval Lyric.* Oxford: Blackwell, 2005.

Hoccleve, Thomas. *My Compleinte and Other Poems.* Edited by Roger Ellis. Liverpool: Liverpool University Press, 2001.

Hughes, Ted. *Birthday Letters.* London: Faber, 1998.

Joyce, James. *Ulysses: The 1922 Text.* Edited by Jeri Johnson. Oxford: Oxford University Press, 1993.

Kempe, Margery. *The Book of Margery Kempe.* Edited by Barry Windeatt. Cambridge: D. S. Brewer, 2000.

Krochalis, Jeanne, Alison Stones, Annie Shaver-Crandell, and Paula Lieber Gerson. *The Pilgrim's Guide to Santiago de Compostela: A Critical Edition.* London: H. Miller, 1998.

Lorris, Guillaume de, and Jean de Meun. *The Romance of the Rose.* Translated by Frances Horgan. Oxford: Oxford University Press, 1994.

Luttrell, Anthony, trans. *Archivio Vaticano, Reg. Supp. 45, fol. 55–55v.* In *Equally in God's Name: Women in the Middle Ages,* edited by Julia Bolton Holloway, Constance S. Wright, and Joan Bechtold, 191–192. New York: P. Lang, 1990.

Lydgate, John. *A Mumming at Hertford.* In *Minor Poems of John Lydgate,* edited by Henry Noble MacCracken, vol. 2, 676–680. Early English Text Society extra series 107; original series 192. London: Oxford University Press, 1911–1934; reprinted 1961.

———. *Payne and Sorowe of Evyll Maryage.* In *The Trials and Joys of Marriage,* edited by Eve Salisbury. Kalamazoo, MI: Medieval Institute Publications, 2002. https://d.lib.rochester.edu/teams/text/salisbury-trials-and-joys-payne-and -sorowe-of-evyll-maryage.

———. *The Temple of Glas.* Edited by J. Allan Mitchell. Kalamazoo, MI: Medieval Institute Publications, 2007. https://d.lib.rochester.edu/teams/text/mitchell -lydgate-temple-of-glas.

Maynadier, G. H. *The Wife of Bath's Tale: Its Sources and Analogues.* London: D. Nutt, 1901.

Metel, Hugh. Letter 16 (transl.). In Constant J. Mews, 'Hugh Metel, Heloise and Peter Abelard: The Letters of an Augustinian Canon and the Challenge of Innovation in Twelfth-Century Lorraine.' *Viator* 32 (2001):59–91.

Mustanoja, T. F., ed. *The Good Wife Taught Her Daughter, The Good Wife Wold a Pylgrymage, The Thewis of Gud Women.* Helsinki: Academia Scientiarum Fennica, 1948.

Nelson, Marilyn. 'The Cachoeira Tales.' In *The Cachoeira Tales and Other Poems,* 11–54. Baton Rouge: Louisiana State University Press, 2005.

Pasolini, Pier Paolo. 'Trilogy of Life Rejected,' written 15 June 1975, published 9 November 1975. In *Lutheran Letters*, translated by Stuart Hood, 49–52. New York: Caracanet Press, 1983.

Peter the Venerable. 'Letter (115) to Heloise.' In *The Letters of Abelard and Heloise*, translated by Betty Radice, revised by M. T. Clanchy, 217–223. London: Penguin Random House, 2003.

Pfandl, Ludwig. 'Itinerarum Hispanicum Hieronymi Monetarii, 1494–1495.' *Revue Hispanique* 48 (1920): 1–179.

Pizan, Christine de. *Le Livre de la mutacion de Fortune*. Edited by S. Solente. 4 vols. Paris: A. & J. Picard, 1959–1966.

———. *The Book of the City of Ladies*. Translated by Rosalind Brown-Grant. London: Penguin, 1999.

———. *The Treasure of the City of Ladies; or, The Book of the Three Virtues*. Translated by Sarah Lawson, rev. ed. London: Penguin, 2003.

Pole, William de la, 'Will.' In *North Country Wills*, edited by J. W. Clay, 50–51. Durham: Andrews, 1912.

Radice, Betty, trans. *The Letters of Abelard and Heloise*. Revised by M. T. Clanchy. London: Penguin Random House, 2003.

Rettig, John W. *Tractates on the Gospel of John*. Washington, DC: Catholic University of America Press, 1988.

Schmidt, Paul Gerhardt, ed. 'Peregrinatio periculosa: Thomas von Froidmont über die Jerusalem-Fahrten seiner Schwester Margareta.' In *Kontinuität und Wandel: Lateinische Poesie von Naevius bis Baudelaire, Franco Munaro zum 65. Geburtstag*, edited by Ulrich Justus Stache, Wolfgang Maaz, and Fritz Wagner. Hildesheim: Weidmann, 1986, 461–85.

Scrope, Stephen. *The Epistle of Othea to Hector; or, The Boke of Knyghthode, Translated from the French of Christine de Pisan with a Dedication to Sir John Fastolf, K.G.* Edited by George F. Warner. London: J. B. Nichols and Sons, 1904.

Shakespeare, William. *The Riverside Shakespeare*, 2nd ed. Edited by G. Blakemore Evans and J. J. M. Tobin. Boston: Houghton Mifflin, 1997.

Sharpe, Reginald R., ed. *Letter-Book H*. In *Calendar of Letter-Books of the City of London: H, 1375–1399*. London: His Majesty's Stationery Office, 1907.

———, ed. *Calendar of Wills, Proved and Enrolled in the Court of Husting*. London, Her Majesty's Stationery Office, 1890.

Shuffelton, George, ed. 'Item 4, How the Good Wife Taught Her Daughter.' In *Codex Ashmole 61: A Compilation of Popular Middle English Verse*. Kalamazoo, MI: Medieval Institute Publications, 2008. https://d.lib.rochester.edu/teams/text/shuffelton-codex-ashmole-61-how-the-good-wife-taught-her-daughter.

Sidney, Philip. *A Defence of Poetry*. Edited by J. A. van Dortsten. Oxford: Oxford University Press, 1966.

Skelton, John. *Phyllyp Sparowe*. In *The Complete English Poems*, edited by V. J. Scattergood, 618–627. Harmondsworth: Penguin Books, 1983.

Smith, Zadie. *White Teeth*. London: Hamish Hamilton, 2000.

———. *The Wife of Willesden*. London: Penguin Random House, 2021.

Spenser, Edmund. *The Faerie Queene Disposed into Twelue Bookes, Fashioning XII Morall Vertues*. London: Printed for William Ponsonbie, 1596.

Stevenson, Joseph, ed. *Letters and papers illustrative of the wars of the English in France during the reign of Henry the Sixth, King of England*. 2 vols. London: Longman and Green, 1864.

Stewart, Aubrey, trans. *The Book of Wanderings of Brother Felix Fabri*. London: Palestine Pilgrims' Text Society, 1896.

Tertullian. *Cum Samaritinae maritum negat, ut adulterum ostendat numerosum maritum*. In *Patrologia Latina* 2, edited by Jacques-Paul Migne. Paris, 1864.

Van Beuningen, H.J.E., and A. M. Koldeweij, eds. *Heilig en Profaan. 1000 laatmiddeleeuwse insignes uit de collectie H.J.E. van Beuningen*. Rotterdam Papers 8. Cothen: Stichting Middeleeuwse religieuze en profane insignes, 1993.

Voltaire. *Contes en vers et en prose*. Edited by Sylvain Menant. 2 vols. Paris: Bordas, 1992.

———. *Candide and Other Stories*. Translated by Roger Pearson. Oxford: Oxford University Press, 2006.

Warton, Joseph. *An Essay on the Genius and Writings of Pope*, vol. 2. London: J. Dodsley, 1782.

Woolf, Virginia. *A Room of One's Own and Three Guineas*. Oxford: Oxford University Press, 1992.

Worcester, William. *The Boke of Noblesse*. Edited by J. G. Nichols. London: Roxburghe Club, 1860.

Wright, Thomas, ed. *The Book of the Knight of La Tour Landry*. London: Kegan Paul, 1906.

Electronic Sources

http://www.agendabh.com.br/maite-proenca-em-a-mulher-de-bath/.

https://artuk.org/discover/artworks/group-of-five-women-mocking-an-effaced-figure-falstaff-in-the-laundry-basket-mocked-by-women-219657.

http://www.bl.uk/manuscripts/Viewer.aspx?ref=add_ms_5140_fs001r.

https://www.british-history.ac.uk/vch/middx/vol7/pp236-241#fnn36.

https://casetext.com/case/arndt-ober-v-metropolitan-opera-co-1.

https://collections.vam.ac.uk/item/O75992/the-canterbuty-tales-poster-sawka-jan/.

http://encyklopediateatru.pl/sztuki/7994/opowiesci-kanterberyjskie.

https://ezproxy-prd.bodleian.ox.ac.uk:2102/10.1093/ref:odnb/54432.

https://ezproxy-prd.bodleian.ox.ac.uk:2102/10.1093/ref:odnb/54434.

https://globalchaucers.wordpress.com/category/translations/.

http://www.hellenicaworld.com/Art/Paintings/en/Part8654.html.

https://www.jansawka.com///index.html.

https://literature.britishcouncil.org/writer/jean-binta-breeze.

http://www.nationaltrustcollections.org.uk/object/486148.

https://oliviagiovetti.substack.com/p/force-majeured.

https://stainedglass-navigator.yorkglazierstrust.org/window/pilgrimage-window.

https://www.thecheeseshed.com/from-the-mongers-mouth/new-wyfe-of-bath.

https://www.theliterarygiftcompany.com/products/wife-of-bath-soap.

http://www.transculturalwriting.com/radiophonics/contents/writersonwriting
     /patienceagbabi/thewifeofbafa-analysis/index.html.

http://www.umilta.net/jerusalem.html.

https://www.youtube.com/watch?v=MiyKat1QzbQ.

Secondary Sources

Archer, Rowena E. 'Chaucer [married names Phelip, Montagu, de la Pole], Alice,
     duchess of Suffolk (c. 1404–1475).' In *Oxford Dictionary of National Biography*.
     Oxford University Press, 2004. https://ezproxy-prd.bodleian.ox.ac.uk:2102/10
     .1093/ref:odnb/54434.

———. '"How ladies . . . who live on their manors ought to manage their households
     and estates": Women as Landholders and Administrators in the Later Middle
     Ages.' In *Woman Is a Worthy Wight: Women in English Society c. 1200–1500*, edited
     by P.J.P. Goldberg, 149–181. Stroud: Alan Sutton, 1992.

———. 'Neville [married names Mowbray, Strangways, Beaumont, Woodville],
     Katherine, duchess of Norfolk (c. 1400–1483).' In *Oxford Dictionary of National
     Biography*. Oxford University Press, 2004. https://ezproxy-prd.bodleian.ox.ac
     .uk:2102/10.1093/ref:odnb/54432.

Arnold, John H., and Katherine A. Lewis, eds. *A Companion to the Book of Margery
     Kempe*. Cambridge: D. S. Brewer, 2004.

Ashe, Laura. *The Oxford English Literary History. Vol. 1: 1000–1350, Conquest and Trans-
     formation*. Oxford: Oxford University Press, 2017.

Astell, Ann. *The Song of Songs in the Middle Ages*. Ithaca, NY: Cornell University
     Press, 1995.

Atkinson, Clarissa. *Mystic and Pilgrim: The Book and the World of Margery Kempe*.
     Ithaca, NY: Cornell University Press, 2003.

Baker, T.F.T., ed. *A History of the County of Middlesex, vol. 7: Acton, Chiswick, Ealing
     and Brentford, West Twyford, Willesden*. London: Victoria County History, 1982,
     https://www.british-history.ac.uk/vch/middx/vol7/pp236-241#fnn36.

Bale, Anthony. *Margery Kempe: A Mixed Life*. London: Reaktion Books, 2021.

———. 'Richard Salthouse of Norwich and the Scribe of *The Book of Margery Kempe*.' *Chaucer Review* 52:2 (2017): 173–187.

Bale, Anthony, and Sebastian Sobecki, eds. *Medieval English Travel: A Critical Anthology*. Oxford: Oxford University Press, 2019.

Barrington, Candace. *American Chaucers*. Basingstoke: Palgrave Macmillan, 2007.

———. 'Retelling Chaucer's Wife of Bath for Modern Children: Picture Books and Evolving Feminism.' In *Sex and Sexuality in a Feminist World*, edited by Karen A. Ritzenhoff and Katherine A. Hermes, 26–51. Newcastle upon Tyne: Cambridge Scholars Publishing, 2009.

Barron, Caroline. 'The Golden Age of Women in Medieval London.' *Reading Medieval Studies* 15 (1989): 35–58.

———. *London in the Later Middle Ages: Government and People 1200–1500*. Oxford: Oxford University Press, 2004.

Barton, Anne. *Essays Mainly Shakespearean*. Cambridge: Cambridge University Press, 1994.

Bate, Jonathan. *Soul of the Age: The Life, Mind, and World of William Shakespeare*. London: Penguin, 2008.

Beattie, Cordelia. *Medieval Single Women: The Politics of Social Classification in Late Medieval England*. Oxford: Oxford University Press, 2007.

Bennett, Judith M. *Ale, Beer, and Brewsters in England: Women's Work in a Changing World, 1300–1600*. Oxford: Oxford University Press, 1996.

———. 'Medieval Women, Modern Women: Across the Great Divide.' In *Culture and History, 1350–1600: Essays on English Communities, Identities and Writing*, edited by David Aers, 147–175. Detroit: Wayne University Press, 1992.

Benson, Robert Louis, Giles Constable, and Carol Dana Lanham, eds. *Renaissance and Renewal in the Twelfth Century*. Toronto: University of Toronto Press, 1999.

Berger, Harry, Jr. '"What Did the King Know and When Did He Know It?" Shakespearean Discourses and Psychoanalysis.' *South Atlantic Quarterly* 88:4 (1989): 811–862.

Besserman, Lawrence. 'Lay Piety and Impiety: The Role of Noah in the Chester Play of Noah's Flood.' In *Enacting the Bible in Medieval and Early Modern Drama*, edited by Eva von Contzen and Chanita Goodblatt, 13–27. Manchester: Manchester University Press, 2020.

Beveridge, Lord. 'Westminster Wages in the Manorial Era.' *Economic History Review* 8:1 (1955): 18–35.

Bhaba, Homi K. *The Location of Culture*. London: Routledge, 2004.

Biller, P.P.A. 'Birth-Control in the West in the Thirteenth and Early Fourteenth Centuries.' *Past and Present* 94 (1982): 3–26.

Bloch, R. Howard. *Medieval Misogyny and the Invention of Western Romantic Love*. Chicago: University of Chicago Press, 1991.

Bloom, Harold. *The Anxiety of Influence: A Theory of Poetry*. Oxford: Oxford University Press, 1975.

———. *Falstaff: Give Me Life*. New York: Scribner, 2017.

———. *The Western Canon: The Books and School of the Ages*. London: Macmillan, 1995.

Boldrini, Lucia. 'Introduction: Middayevil Joyce.' In *Medieval Joyce*, edited by Lucia Boldrini, 11–44. Amsterdam, NY: Rodopi, 2002.

———. 'Translating the Middle Ages: Modernism and the Ideal of the Common Language.' *Translation and Literature* 12:1 (2003): 41–68.

Bowden, Betsy. *The Wife of Bath in Afterlife: Ballads to Blake*. Bethlehem, PA: Lehigh University Press, 2017.

Bowers, Terence N. 'Margery Kempe as Traveler.' *Studies in Philology* 97:1 (2000): 1–28.

Brewer, David A. *The Afterlife of Character, 1726–1825*. Philadelphia: University of Pennsylvania Press, 2005.

Brownlee, Kevin, 'Discourses of the Self: Christine de Pizan and the Rose.' *Romantic Review* 79:1 (1988): 199–221.

———. *Poetic Identity in Guillaume de Machaut*. Madison: University of Wisconsin Press, 1984.

Brundage, James A. 'Widows and Remarriage: Moral Conflicts and Their Resolution in Classical Canon Law.' In *Wife and Widow in Medieval England*, edited by Sue Sheridan Walker, 17–31. Ann Arbor: University of Michigan Press, 1993.

Bryant, J. A., Jr. 'Falstaff and the Renewal of Winter.' *PMLA* 89:2 (1974): 296–301.

Budgen, Frank. *James Joyce and the Making of Ulysses*. Bloomington: Indiana University Press, 1960 [first printed 1934].

Burrow, Colin. 'Shakespeare and Humanistic Culture.' In *Shakespeare and the Classics*, edited by Charles Martindale and A. B. Taylor, 9–28. Cambridge: Cambridge University Press, 2004.

Caie, Graham D. 'The Significance of the Early Chaucer Manuscript Glosses (with Special Reference to "The Wife of Bath's Prologue").' *Chaucer Review* 10:4 (1976): 350–360.

Cain, Andrew. 'Jerome's *Epitaphium Paulae*: Hagiography, Pilgrimage and the Cult of St Paula.' *Journal of Early Christian Studies* 18:1 (2010): 105–139.

Campbell, Mavis. *The Maroons of Jamaica 1655–1796: A History of Resistance, Collaboration & Betrayal*. Granby, MA: Bergin & Garvey, 1988.

Cannon, Christopher. *From Literacy to Literature: England, 1300–1400*. Oxford: Oxford University Press, 2016.

———. *Middle English Literature: A Cultural History*. Cambridge: Polity, 2008.

———. '*Raptus* in the Chaumpaigne Release and a Newly Discovered Document Concerning the Life of Geoffrey Chaucer.' *Speculum* 68 (1993): 74–94.

Carruthers, Mary. 'The Wife of Bath and the Painting of Lions.' *PMLA* 94:2 (1979): 209–222.

Castor, Helen. *Blood and Roses: The Paston Family and the Wars of the Roses*. London: Faber and Faber, 2004.

Clarke, Kenneth. *Chaucer and Italian Textuality*. Oxford: Oxford University Press, 2011.

Cohen, Jeremy. *Living Letters of the Law: Ideas of the Jew in Medieval Christianity*. Berkeley: University of California Press, 1999.

Coleman, Joyce. *Public Reading and the Reading Public in Late Medieval England and France*. Cambridge: Cambridge University Press, 2005.

Coletti, Theresa. 'Paths of Long Study: Reading Chaucer and Christine de Pizan in Tandem.' *Studies in the Age of Chaucer* 28 (2006): 1–40.

Collette, Carolyn. *The Legend of Good Women: Context and Reception*. Cambridge: D. S. Brewer, 2006.

———. *Rethinking Chaucer's Legend of Good Women*. York: York University Press, 2014.

Cook, Megan L. *The Poet and the Antiquaries: Chaucerian Scholarship and the Rise of Literary History, 1532–1635*. Philadelphia: University of Pennsylvania Press, 2019.

Coomaraswamy, Ananda K. 'On the Loathly Bride.' *Speculum* 20:4 (1945): 391–404.

Cooper, Helen. 'After Chaucer.' *Studies in the Age of Chaucer* 25 (2003): 3–24.

———. 'Joyce's Other Father: The Case for Chaucer.' In *Medieval Joyce*, edited by Lucia Boldrini, 143–163. Amsterdam, NY: Rodopi, 2002.

———. *Shakespeare and the Medieval World*. London: Bloomsbury Arden Shakespeare, 2010.

———. 'The Shape-Shiftings of the Wife of Bath, 1395–1670.' In *Chaucer Traditions: Studies in Honour of Derek Brewer*, edited by Ruth Morse and Barry Windeatt, 168–184. Cambridge: Cambridge University Press, 1990.

Copeland, Rita. 'Why Women Can't Read: Medieval Hermeneutics, Statutory Law, and the Lollard Heresy Trials.' In *Representing Women: Law, Literature, and Feminism*, edited by Zipporah Batshaw Wiseman and Susan Sage Heinzelman, 253–286. Durham, NC: Duke University Press, 1994.

Coppola, Manuela. 'A Tale of Two Wives: The Transnational Poetry of Patience Agbabi and Jean 'Binta' Breeze.' *Journal of Postcolonial Writing* 52:3 (2016): 305–318.

Craig, Leigh Ann. *Wandering Women and Holy Matrons: Women as Pilgrims in the Later Middle Ages*. Leiden: Brill, 2009.

Crane, Susan. 'Alison's Incapacity and Poetic Instability in the Wife of Bath's Tale.' *PMLA* 102:1 (January 1987): 20–28.

Cressler, Loren. 'Asinine Heroism and the Mediation of Empire in Chaucer, Marlowe, and Shakespeare.' *Modern Language Quarterly* 81:3 (September 2020): 319–347.

Critten, Rory G. 'The *Manières de Langage* as Evidence for the Use of Spoken French within Fifteenth-Century England.' *Forum for Modern Language Studies* 55:2 (April 2019): 121–137.

Crocker, Holly. 'John Foxe's Chaucer: Affecting Form in Post-Historicist Criticism.' *New Medieval Literatures* 15 (2013): 149–182.

Crow, Martin Michael. 'John of Angoulême and His Chaucer Manuscript.' *Speculum* 17:1 (1942): 86–99.

Dale, Marian K. 'The London Silkwomen of the Fifteenth Century.' In *Economic History Review* 4:3 (1933): 324–335.

Daley, Brian E. 'The Closed Garden and Sealed Fountain: Song of Songs 4.12 in the Late Medieval Iconography of Mary.' In *Medieval Gardens*, edited by Elizabeth MacDougall, 254–278. Washington, DC: Dumbarton Oaks, 1986.

D'Arcens, Louise. 'The Thunder after the Lightning: Language and Pasolini's Medievalist Poetics.' *postmedieval* 6:2 (2015): 191–199.

Davidson, Ian. *Voltaire: A Life*. New York: Pegasus Books, 2010.

Davis, Kathleen. *Periodization and Sovereignty: How Ideas of Feudalism and Secularization Govern the Politics of Time*. Philadelphia: University of Pennsylvania Press, 2008.

Davis, Natalie Zemon. *Fiction in the Archives*. Stanford: Stanford University Press, 1987.

Desmond, Marilynn. 'Christine De Pizan.' In *The Cambridge Companion to Medieval French Literature*, edited by Simon Gaunt and Sarah Kay, 123–136. Cambridge: Cambridge University Press, 2008.

———. 'The Querelle de la Rose and the Ethics of Reading.' In *Christine de Pizan: A Casebook*, edited by Barbara K. Altmann and Deborah L. McGrady. New York: Routledge, 2003.

———. *Reading Dido: Gender, Textuality, and the Medieval 'Aeneid.'* Minneapolis: University of Minnesota Press, 1994.

Devaux, Jean. 'From the Court of Hainault to the Court of England: The Example of Jean Froissart.' In *War, Government and Power in Late Medieval France*, edited by C. T. Allmand, 1–20. Liverpool: Liverpool University Press, 2000.

Dimmick, Jeremy. 'Gower, Chaucer and the Art of Repentance in Robert Greene's *Vision.' Review of English Studies*, n.s., 57:231 (2006): 456–473.

Dinshaw, Carolyn. *Chaucer's Sexual Poetics*. Madison: University of Wisconsin Press, 1989.

———. *Getting Medieval: Sexualities and Communities, Pre- and Postmodern.* Durham, NC: Duke University Press, 1999.

Duby, Georges. 'Histoire sociale et idéologie des sociétiés.' In *Faire de l'histoire*, edited by Jacques Le Goff and P. Nora. 3 vols. 1:147–168. Paris: Guillimard, 1974.

Eco, Umberto. *The Middle Ages of James Joyce: The Aesthetic of Chaosmos.* Tulsa: University of Oklahoma Press, 1982.

Edwards, A.S.G. 'Northern Magnates and Their Books.' *Textual Cultures* 7:1 (2012): 176–186.

Ellmann, Richard. *James Joyce.* Rev. ed. Oxford: Oxford University Press, 1982.

———. *Ulysses on the Liffey.* Oxford: Oxford University Press, 1986.

Elwin, Verrier. 'The Vagina Dentata Legend.' *British Journal of Medical Psychology* 19 (1943): 439–453.

Evans, Robert C. 'Ben Jonson's Chaucer.' *English Literary Renaissance* 19:3 (Autumn 1989): 324–345.

Evans, Ruth. 'Production of Space in Chaucer's London.' In *Chaucer and the City*, edited by Ardis Butterfield, 41–56. Woodbridge: D. S. Brewer, 2006.

Farrell, Warren. *The Myth of Male Power: Why Men Are the Disposable Sex.* New York: Simon and Schuster, 1993.

Felski, Rita. 'Identifying with Characters.' In *Character: Three Inquiries in Literary Studies*, edited by Amanda Anderson, Rita Felski, and Toril Moi, 77–126. Chicago: University of Chicago Press, 2019.

Ferrante, Joan M. *To the Glory of Her Sex: Women's Roles in the Composition of Medieval Texts.* Bloomington: Indiana University Press, 1997.

Finke, Laurie A. 'Falstaff, the Wife of Bath, and the Sweet Smoke of Rhetoric.' In *Chaucerian Shakespeare: Adaptation and Transformation*, edited by E. Talbot Donaldson and Judith J. Kollmann, 7–24. Detroit: Michigan Consortium for Medieval and Early Modern Studies, 1983.

Finucane, Ronald C. *Miracles and Pilgrims: Popular Beliefs in Medieval England.* London: Dent, 1977.

Fisher, John H. 'Chancery and the Emergence of Standard Written English in the Fifteenth Century.' *Speculum* 52:4 (1977): 870–899.

Flowers Braswell, Mary. *The Medieval Sinner: Characterization and Confession in the Literature of the English Middle Ages.* Rutherford, NJ: Farleigh Dickinson University Press, 1983.

Forni, Kathleen. *Chaucer's Afterlife: Adaptations in Recent Popular Culture.* Jefferson, NC: McFarland, 2013.

Fowler, Elizabeth. *Literary Character: The Human Figure in Early English Writing.* Ithaca, NY: Cornell University Press, 2003.

Fox, Adam. *Oral and Literate Culture in England, 1500–1700*. Oxford: Oxford University Press, 2002.

Freedman, Paul. *Out of the East: Spices and the Medieval Imagination*. New Haven: Yale University Press, 2007.

Frembgen, Jürgen Wasim. 'Honour, Shame, and Bodily Mutilation: Cutting Off the Nose among Tribal Societies in Pakistan.' *Journal of the Royal Asiatic Society* 16:3 (2006): 243–260.

Gajowski, Evelyn, and Phyllis Rackin. *The Merry Wives of Windsor: New Critical Essays*. London: Routledge, 2015.

Ganim, John. 'Chaucer, Boccaccio, Confession, and Subjectivity.' In *The 'Decameron' and the 'Canterbury Tales': New Essays on an Old Question*, edited by Leonard Michael Koff and Brenda Dean Schildgen, 128–147. Madison, NJ: Fairleigh Dickinson University Press, 2000.

———. 'Identity and Subjecthood.' In *Chaucer: An Oxford Guide*, edited by Steve Ellis, 224–238. Oxford: Oxford University Press, 2005.

Gaunt, Simon. 'Can the Middle Ages Be Postcolonial?' *Comparative Literature* 61:2 (Spring 2009): 160–176.

Gentleman, Amelia. *The Windrush Betrayal: Exposing the Hostile Environment*. London: Guardian Faber Publishing, 2019.

Ginsberg, Warren. *The Cast of Character: The Representation of Personality in Ancient and Medieval Literature*. Toronto: University of Toronto Press, 1983.

Goldberg, Jonathan. 'What Do Women Want? The Merry Wives of Windsor.' *Criticism* 51:3 (2009): 367–383.

Goldberg, P.J.P. 'John Rykener, Richard II, and the Governance of London.' *Leeds Studies in English* 45 (2014): 49–70.

———. 'Migration, Youth, and Gender in Later Medieval England.' In *Youth in the Middle Ages*, edited by P.J.P Goldberg and Felicity Riddy, 85–99. York: York Medieval Press, 2004.

———. *Women, Work, and Life-Cycle in a Medieval Economy: Women in York and Yorkshire c. 1300–1520*. Oxford: Oxford University Press, 1992.

Golubovich, Girolamo. *Biblioteca Bio-Bibliografica della Terra Santa e dell'Oriente francescano*. 5 vols. Quaracchi: Collegio di S Bonaventura, 1906–1927.

Goodall, John. *God's House at Ewelme: Life, Devotion and Architecture in a Fifteenth-century Almshouse*. Aldershot: Ashgate, 2001.

Goodman, Anthony. *Margery Kempe and Her World*. London: Longman, 2002.

Gottlieb, Karla. *The Mother of Us All: A History of Queen Nanny, Leader of the Windward Jamaican Maroons*. Trenton, NJ: Africa World Press, 2000.

Grant, Colin. *Homecoming: Voices of the Windrush Generation*. London: Jonathan Cape, 2019.

Gravdal, Kathryn. *Ravishing Maidens: Writing Rape in Medieval French Literature and Law*. Philadelphia: University of Pennsylvania Press, 1991.

Greene, Martin. 'The Dialectic of Adaptation: The Canterbury Tales of Pier Paolo Pasolini.' *Literature/Film Quarterly* 4:1 (Winter 1976): 46–53.

Greene, Naomi. *Pier Paolo Pasolini: Cinema as Heresy*. Princeton, NJ: Princeton University Press, 1990.

Groves, Beatrice. '"The ears of profiting": Listening to Falstaff's Biblical Quotations.' In *Shakespeare and Quotation*, edited by Julie Maxwell and Kate Rumbold, 60–71. Cambridge: Cambridge University Press, 2018.

Hagedorn, Suzanne. *Abandoned Women: Rewriting the Classics in Dante, Boccaccio, and Chaucer*. Ann Arbor: University of Michigan Press, 2004.

Hamlin, Hannibal. *The Bible in Shakespeare*. Oxford: Oxford University Press, 2013.

Hammer, Paul E. J. 'Devereux, Robert, second earl of Essex (1565–1601).' In *Oxford Dictionary of National Biography*. Oxford University Press, 2004. https://ezproxy-prd.bodleian.ox.ac.uk:2102/10.1093/ref:odnb/7565.

Hanawalt, Barbara. *The Wealth of Wives: Women, Law, and Economy in Late Medieval London*. Oxford: Oxford University Press, 2007.

Hanna, Ralph, and A.S.G. Edwards. 'Rotheley, the De Vere Circle, and the Ellesmere Chaucer.' *Huntington Library Quarterly* 58:1 (1995): 11–35.

Hanna, Ralph, and Traugott Lawler, eds. *Jankyn's Book of Wikked Wyves. Vol. 1: The Primary Texts*. Chaucer Library. Athens: University of Georgia Press, 1997.

Harbus, Antonina. *Cognitive Approaches to Old English Poetry*. Woodbridge: Boydell and Brewer, 2012.

Harris, Carissa M. *Obscene Pedagogies: Transgressive Talk and Sexual Education in Late Medieval Britain*. Ithaca, NY: Cornell University Press, 2018.

Harry, David. *Constructing a Civic Community in Late Medieval London: The Common Profit, Charity and Commemoration*. Woodbridge: Boydell and Brewer, 2019.

Harvey, Margaret. *The English in Rome, 1362–1420: Portrait of an Expatriate Community*. Cambridge: Cambridge University Press, 2000.

Heng, Geraldine. *The Invention of Race in the Middle Ages*. Cambridge: Cambridge University Press, 2018.

Herlihy, David. *Opera Muliebria: Women and Work in Medieval Europe*. New York: McGraw-Hill, 1990.

Higgins, Anne. 'Spenser Reading Chaucer: Another Look at the "Faerie Queene" Allusions.' *Journal of English and Germanic Philology* 89:1 (1990): 17–36.

Higl, Andrew. 'The Wife of Bath Retold: From the Medieval to the Postmodern.' In *Inhabited by Stories: Critical Essays on Tales Retold*, edited by Nancy Barton-Smith and Danette DiMario, 294–313. Newcastle: Cambridge Scholars Publishing, 2012.

Hilton, R. H. *The English Peasantry in the Later Middle Ages: The Ford Lectures for 1973, and Related Studies*. Oxford: Clarendon Press, 1975.

Hinely, Jan Lawson. 'Comic Scapegoats and the Falstaff of the Merry Wives of Windsor.' *Shakespeare Studies* 15 (1982): 37–54.

Hingeston, Rev. F. C. *The Register of Edmund Stafford (AD 1395–1419): An Index and Abstract of Its Contents.* London: G. Bell and Sons, 1886.

Hodges, Laura F. 'The Wife of Bath's Costumes: Reading the Subtexts.' *Chaucer Review* 27:4 (1993): 359–376.

Holderness, Graham. 'Cleaning House: The Courtly and the Popular in *The Merry Wives of Windsor.' Critical Survey* 22:1 (2010): 26–40.

Horrox, Rosemary, ed. and trans. *The Black Death.* Manchester: Manchester University Press, 2013.

Howard, Donald. *Chaucer: His Life, His Works, His World.* New York: Dutton, 1987.

Howe, Darcus. 'Black Sabbath.' In *Time Out London Walks*, edited by Andrew White, 166–173. London: Penguin, 2002.

Howes, Laura. *Chaucer's Gardens and the Language of Convention.* Gainesville: University Press of Florida, 1997.

Hsy, Jonathan. 'Teaching the Wife of Bath through Adaptation.' https://globalchaucers.wordpress.com/2014/11/21/teaching-the-wife-of-bath-through-adaptation/.

Ingram, Martin. 'Flyting, Polemics, Charivaris.' In *The Cambridge Guide to the Worlds of Shakespeare*, edited by Martin Ingram et al., 516–523. Cambridge: Cambridge University Press, 2019.

Jacobs, Kathryn, and D'Andra White. 'Ben Jonson on Shakespeare's Chaucer.' *Chaucer Review* 50 (2015): 198–215.

Jacquart, Danielle, and Claude Thomasset. *Sexuality and Medicine in the Middle Ages.* Princeton, NJ: Princeton University Press, 1988.

Jambeck, Karen K. 'Patterns of Women's Literary Patronage: England, 1200–ca. 1475.' In *The Cultural Patronage of Medieval Women*, edited by Jane Hall McCash, 228–265. Athens: University of Georgia Press, 1996.

———. 'The Library of Alice Chaucer.' *Profane Arts* 7:2 (1998): 106–135.

Johns, Alessa. 'Joyce and Chaucer: The Historical Significance of Similarities between *Ulysses* and the *Canterbury Tales.'* Unpublished MA thesis, McGill University, 1985.

Jussen, B. 'Virgins—Widows—Spouses: On the language of moral distinction as applied to women and men in the Middle Ages.' *History of the Family* 7 (2002): 13–32.

Justice, Steven. *Writing and Rebellion: England in 1381.* Berkeley: University of California Press, 1994.

Justman, Stewart. *The Springs of Liberty: The Satiric Tradition and Freedom of Speech.* Evanston, IL: Northwestern University Press, 1999.

Jutte, Robert. *Contraception: A History.* Cambridge: Polity Press, 2008.

Karras, R. M., and D. L. Boyd. 'The Interrogation of a Male Transvestite Prostitute in Fourteenth-Century London.' *GLQ: A Journal of Lesbian and Gay Studies* 1 (1995): 459–465.

———. '"Ut cum muliere": A Male Transvestite Prostitute in Fourteenth-Century London.' In *Premodern Sexualities*, edited by Louise Fradenburg and Carla Freccero, 99–116. London: Routledge, 1996.

Karras, R. M., and T. Linkinen. 'John/Eleanor Rykener Revisited.' In *Founding Feminisms in Medieval Studies: Essays in Honor of E. Jane Burns*, edited by L. E. Doggett and D. E. O'Sullivan, 111–124. Cambridge: D. S. Brewer, 2016.

Katz Seal, Samantha. *Father Chaucer: Generating Authority in 'The Canterbury Tales.'* Oxford: Oxford University Press, 2019.

Kay, Sarah, Terence Cave, and Malcolm Bowie. *A Short History of French Literature.* Oxford: Oxford University Press, 2003.

Keiser, George R. 'In Defence of the Bradshaw Shift.' *Chaucer Review* 12:4 (1978): 191–201.

Kelliher, Hilton. 'The Rediscovery of Margery Kempe: A Footnote.' *British Library Journal* 23:2 (1997): 259–263.

Kibler, William W., and James I. Wimsatt, eds. 'The Development of the Pastourelle in the Fourteenth Century: An Edition of Fifteen Poems with an Analysis.' *Mediaeval Studies* 45 (1983): 22–78.

Kirby, Thomas A. 'Theodore Roosevelt on Chaucer and a Chaucerian.' *Modern Language Notes* 68:1 (1953): 34–37.

Knights, L. C. *How Many Children Had Lady Macbeth? An Essay in the Theory and Practice of Shakespeare Criticism.* Cambridge: Minority Press, 1933.

Kong, Katherine. *Lettering the Self in Medieval and Early Modern France.* Woodbridge: Boydell and Brewer, 2017.

Korda, Natasha. *Shakespeare's Domestic Economies: Gender and Property in Early Modern England.* Philadelphia: University of Pennsylvania Press, 2002.

Kowaleski, Maryanne. 'Singlewomen in Medieval and Early Modern Europe: The Demographic Perspective.' In *Singlewomen in the European Past, 1250–1800*, edited by Judith M. Bennett and Amy M. Froide, 38–81. Philadelphia: University of Pennsylvania Press, 1999.

———. 'Women's Work in a Market Town: Exeter in the Late Fourteenth Century.' In *Women and Work in Pre-Industrial Europe*, edited by Barbara Hanawalt, 145–164. Bloomington: Indiana University Press, 1986.

Kuhl, Ernest. 'The Wanton Wife of Bath and Queen Elizabeth.' *Studies in Philology* 26:2 (April 1929): 177–183.

Lacey, Kay E. 'Women and Work in Fourteenth and Fifteenth Century London.' In *Women and Work in Pre-Industrial England*, edited Lindsey Charles and Lorna Duffin, 24–82. Abingdon: Routledge, 2013 [1985].

Laidlaw, J. C. 'Christine de Pizan, the Earl of Salisbury, and Henry IV.' *French Studies* 36 (1982): 129–143.

Lammers, John H. 'The Archetypal Molly Bloom, Joyce's Frail Wife of Bath.' *James Joyce Quarterly* 25:4 (Summer 1998): 487–502.

Langdell, Sebastian J. *Thomas Hoccleve: Religious Reform, Transnational Poetics, and the Invention of Chaucer*. Liverpool: Liverpool University Press, 2018.

Lederer, Wolfgang. *The Fear of Women*. New York: Harcourt, 1968.

Leicester, H. Marshall. *The Disenchanted Self: Representing the Subject in 'The Canterbury Tales.'* Berkeley: University of California Press, 1990.

Leo, John. 'Toxic Feminism on the Big Screen.' *US News and World Report* 110:22 (October 6, 1991): 20.

Lerer, Seth. *Chaucer and His Readers: Imagining the Author in Late Medieval England*. Princeton, NJ: Princeton University Press, 1993.

Lewis, Celia M. 'History, Mission, and Crusade in the *Canterbury Tales*.' *Chaucer Review* 42:4 (2008): 353–382.

Lloyd, T. H. *The English Wool-Trade in the Middle Ages*. Cambridge: Cambridge University Press, 1977.

Lochrie, Karma. *Margery Kempe and Translations of the Flesh*. Philadelphia: University of Pennsylvania Press, 1994.

Longsworth, Robert. 'The Wife of Bath and the Samaritan Woman.' *Chaucer Review* 34:4 (2000): 372–387.

Luttrell, Anthony. 'Englishwomen as Pilgrims to Jerusalem: Isolda Parewastell, 1365.' In *Equally in God's Name: Women in the Middle Ages*, edited by Julia Bolton Holloway, Constance S. Wright, and Joan Bechtold, 184–197. New York: P. Lang, 1990.

Lynch, Kathryn L. 'Katharine Lee Bates and Chaucer's American Children.' *Chaucer Review* 56:2 (2021): 95–118.

Maguire, Laurie, and Emma Smith. 'What Is a Source? Or, How Shakespeare Read His Marlowe.' *Shakespeare Survey* 68 (2015): 15–31.

Manly, J. M. *Some New Light on Chaucer: Lectures Delivered at the Lowell Institute*. London: Bell, 1926.

Mann, Jill. *Chaucer and Medieval Estates Satire: The Literature of Social Classes and the General Prologue to the Canterbury Tales*. Cambridge: Cambridge University Press, 1973.

———. *From Aesop to Reynard: Beast Literature in Medieval Britain*. Oxford: Oxford University Press, 2009.

Margolin, Uri. 'Character.' In *The Cambridge Companion to Narrative*, edited by David Herman, 66–79. Cambridge: Cambridge University Press, 2007.

McDonald, Nicola. 'Chaucer's *Legend of Good Women*, Ladies at Court and the Female Reader.' *Chaucer Review* 35:1 (2000): 22–42.

————. 'Games Medieval Women Play.' In *The Legend of Good Women: Context and Reception*, edited by Carolyn P. Collette, 176–197. Cambridge: D. S. Brewer, 2006.

McGrady, Deborah. 'Guillaume de Machaut.' In *The Cambridge Companion to Medieval French Literature*, edited by Simon Gaunt and Sarah Kay, 109–22. Cambridge: Cambridge University Press, 2009.

McIntosh, Marjorie Keniston. *Working Women in English Society, 1300–1620*. Cambridge: Cambridge University Press, 2005.

McLeod, Glenda, and Katharina Wilson. 'A Clerk in Name Only—A Clerk in All but Name. The Misogamous Tradition and "La Cite des Dames."' In *The City of Scholars: New Approaches to Christine de Pizan*, edited by Margarette Zimmerman and Dina De Rentiis, 67–76. Berlin: De Gruyter, 1994.

Meale, Carol M. '"alle the bokes that I have of latyn, englisch, and frensch": Laywomen and Their Books in Late Medieval England.' In *Women and Literature in Britain, 1150–1500*, edited by Carole M. Meale, 128–158. 2nd ed. Cambridge: Cambridge University Press, 1996.

————. 'Reading Women's Culture in Fifteenth-Century England: The Case of Alice Chaucer.' In *Mediaevalitas: Reading the Middle Ages,* edited by Piero Boitani and Anna Torti, 81–102. Woodbridge: D. S. Brewer, 1996.

Mews, Constant J. *Abelard and Heloise.* Oxford: Oxford University Press, 2005.

Meyer, P., ed. *La Manière de Langage qui Enseigne Parler et a Écrire Le Français: Modèles de Conversations Composés en Angleterre a la Fin du XIV Siècle*. Paris: Librairie A. Franck, 1873.

Michaud, Joseph, Fr., and Joseph Toussaint Reinaud, eds. *Bibliothéque des Croisades.* Paris: A L'Imprimerie Royale, 1829.

Miller, Anne-Helene. 'Guillaume de Machaut and the Forms of Pre-Humanism in Fourteenth-Century France.' In *A Companion to Guillaume de Machaut*, edited by Deborah McGrady and Jennifer Bain, 33–48. Leiden: Brill, 2012.

Minnis, Alastair. *Fallible Authors*. Philadelphia: University of Pennsylvania Press, 2011.

Morrison, Susan Signe. 'The Use of Biography in Medieval Literary Criticism: The Case of Geoffrey Chaucer and Cecily Chaumpaigne.' *Chaucer Review* 34 (1999): 69–86.

————. *Women Pilgrims in Later Medieval England: Private Piety as Public Performance*. New York: Routledge, 2000.

Moxon, Steve. *The Woman Racket: The New Science Explaining How the Sexes Relate at Work, at Play and in Society*. Exeter: Imprint Academic, 2008.

Murphy, Donna N. 'The Cobbler of Canterbury and Robert Greene.' *Notes and Queries* 57:3 (2010): 349–352.

Newman, Barbara. 'Authority, authenticity, and the repression of Heloise.' *JMEMS* 22:2 (Spring 1992): 121–157.

————, ed. and trans. *Making Love in the Twelfth Century: Letters of Two Lovers in Context*. Philadelphia: University of Pennsylvania Press, 2016.

Nightingale, Pamela. *A Medieval Mercantile Community: The Grocers' Company and the Politics and Trade of London, 1000–1485*. New Haven, CT: Yale University Press, 1995.

Noad, Charles E. 'The Tolkien Society—the early days.' In *Mallorn*, vol. 50, edited by Henry Gee, 15–24. London: Tolkien Society, 2010.

Normington, Katie. '"Faming of the Shrews": Medieval Drama and Feminist Approaches.' *Yearbook of English Studies* 43 (2013): 105–120.

Novikoff, Alex J., ed. *The Twelfth-Century Renaissance: A Reader*. Toronto: University of Toronto Press, 2017.

Nussbaum, Martha. *Poetic Justice: The Literary Imagination and Public Life*. Boston: Beacon Press, 1995.

Oexle, Otto Gerhard. 'Perceiving Social Reality in the Early and High Middle Ages: A Contribution to the History of Social Knowledge.' In *Ordering Medieval Society: Perspectives on Intellectual and Practical Modes of Shaping Social Relations*, edited by Bernhard Jussen, translated by Pamela Selwyn. Philadelphia: University of Pennsylvania Press, 2001.

Origo, Iris. 'The Domestic Enemy: The Eastern Slaves in Tuscany in the Fourteenth and Fifteenth Centuries.' *Speculum* 30:3 (1955): 321–366.

Palomo, Dolores. 'The Fate of the Wife of Bath's "Bad Husbands."' *Chaucer Review* 9:4 (1975): 303–319.

Parker, Patricia. *Shakespeare from the Margins: Language, Culture, Context*. Chicago: University of Chicago Press, 1996.

Parks, George B. *The English Traveller to Italy: The Middle Ages (to 1525)*. Rome: Edizioni di Storia e Letteratura, 1954.

Partridge, Stephen. 'Glosses in the Manuscripts of the *Canterbury Tales*: An Edition and Commentary. PhD dissertation, Harvard University, 1992.

Passmore, S. Elizabeth, and Susan Carter. *The English 'Loathly Lady' Tales: Boundaries, Traditions, Motifs*. Kalamazoo, MI: Medieval Institute Publications, 2007.

Patterson, Lee. *Chaucer and the Subject of History*. Madison: University of Wisconsin Press, 1991.

————. '"For the Wyves Love of Bathe": Feminine Rhetoric and Poetic Resolution in the *Roman de la Rose* and the *Canterbury Tales*.' *Speculum* 58:3 (1983): 656–695.

————. *Temporal Circumstances: Form and History in the Canterbury Tales*. New York: Palgrave Macmillan, 2006.

Peterson, Jordan. *Twelve Rules for Life: An Antidote to Chaos*. London: Allen Lane, 2018.

Phillips, Harriet. 'Late Falstaff, the Merry World, and *The Merry Wives of Windsor*.' *Shakespeare* 10 (2014): 111–137.

Power, Arthur. *Conversations with James Joyce*. London: Millington, 1974.

Pratt, R. 'The Order of the Canterbury Tales.' *PMLA* 66:6 (1951): 1141–1167.

Price, Richard, ed. *Maroon Societies: Rebel Slave Communities in the Americas*. Baltimore, MD: Johns Hopkins University Press, 1996.

Pugh, Tison. 'Chaucerian Fabliaux, Cinematic Fabliau: Pier Paolo Pasolini's I racconti di Canterbury.' *Literature/Film Quarterly* 32 (2004): 199–206.

Puhvel, Martin. 'The Wife of Bath's "Remedies of Love."' *Chaucer Review* 20:4 (1986): 307–312.

Rackin, Phyllis. *Shakespeare and Women*. Oxford: Oxford University Press, 2005.

Raitt, Jill. 'The "Vagina Dentata" and the "Immaculatus Uterus Divini Fonti."' *Journal of the American Academy of Religion* 48:3 (1980): 415–431.

Ramazani, Jahan. 'Black British Poetry and the Translocal.' In *The Cambridge Companion to Twentieth-Century English Poetry*, edited by Neil Corcoran, 200–214. Cambridge: Cambridge University Press, 2007.

Rawcliffe, Carole. 'Margaret Stodeye, Lady Philipot (d. 1431).' In *Medieval London Widows, 1300–1500*, edited by Caroline M. Barron and Anne F. Sutton, 85–98. London: Bloomsbury, 1994.

Renoir, Alain. 'Thebes, Troy, Criseyde, and Pandarus: An Instance of Chaucerian Irony.' *Studia Neophilologica* 32 (1960): 14–17.

Reynolds, P. *How Marriage Became One of the Sacraments: The Sacramental Theology of Marriage from Its Medieval Origins to the Council of Trent*. Cambridge: Cambridge University Press, 2016.

Richmond, Velma Bourgeois. *Chaucer as Children's Literature: Retellings from the Victorian and Edwardian Eras*. Jefferson, NC: McFarland, 2004.

Rickard, P. 'Anglois Coué and L'Anglois Qui Couve.' *French Studies* 7 (1953): 48–55.

Riddle, John. *Contraception and Abortion from the Ancient World to the Renaissance*. Cambridge, MA: Harvard University Press, 1992.

Riddy, Felicity. 'Mother Knows Best: Reading Social Change in a Courtesy Text.' *Speculum* 71:1 (1996): 66–86, 85–86.

Rigby, S. H. 'The Wife of Bath, Christine de Pizan, and the Medieval Case for Women.' *Chaucer Review* 35:2 (2000): 133–165.

Roberts, Jeanne Addison. 'Falstaff in Windsor Forest: Villain or Victim?' *Shakespeare Quarterly* 26:1 (Winter 1975): 8–15.

Robertson, D. W. *A Preface to Chaucer*. Princeton, NJ: Princeton University Press, 1962.

Robinson, Carol L. 'Celluloid Criticism: Pasolini's Contribution to a Chaucerian Debate.' In *Medievalism in Europe*, edited by by Leslie J. Workman, 115–126. Woodbridge: Boydell and Brewer, 1994.

Robinson, James. 'Hughes and the Middle Ages.' In *Ted Hughes in Context*, edited by Terry Gifford, 209–218. Cambridge: Cambridge University Press, 2018.

Rollins, Hyder E. 'The Black-Letter Broadside Ballad.' *PMLA* 34:2 (1919): 258–339.

Root, Jerry. *'Space to Speke': The Confessional Subject in Medieval Literature*. New York: Peter Laing, 1997.

Rowland, Beryl. 'On the Timely Death of the Wife of Bath's Fourth Husband.' *Archiv* 209 (1972–1973): 273–282.

Ruddock, Alwyn. *Italian Merchants and Shipping in Southampton*. Southampton: University College, 1951.

Salih, Sarah. *Versions of Virginity in Late Medieval England*. Cambridge: D. S. Brewer, 2001.

Sands, Donald B. 'The Non-Comic, Non-Tragic Wife: Chaucer's Dame Alys as Sociopath.' *Chaucer Review* 12:3 (1978): 171–182.

Scattergood, John. 'The Love Lyric before Chaucer.' In *A Companion to the Middle English Lyric*, edited by Thomas G. Duncan, 39–67. Cambridge: D. S. Brewer, 2005.

Schein, Sylvia. 'Bridget of Sweden, Margery Kempe and Women's Jerusalem Pilgrimages in the Middle Ages.' *Mediterranean Historical Review* 14:1 (1999): 44–58.

Schibanoff, Susan. 'The New Reader and Female Textuality in Two Early Commentaries on Chaucer.' *Studies in the Age of Chaucer* 10 (1988): 71–108.

Schieberle, Misty. 'Rethinking Gender and Language in Stephen Scrope's Epistle of Othea 1,' *Journal of the Early Book Society for the Study of Manuscripts and Printing History* 21 (2018): 97–121.

Schwartz, Lewis M. 'Eccles Street and Canterbury: An Approach to Molly Bloom.' *Twentieth-Century Literature* 15:3 (1969): 155–165.

Schwebel, Leah. 'What's in Criseyde's Book?' *Chaucer Review* 54:1 (2019): 91–115.

Scott-Warren, Jason. 'Was Elizabeth I Richard II?: The Authenticity of Lambarde's "Conversation."' *Review of English Studies* 64 (2013): 208–230.

Seal, Samantha Katz, and Nicole Sidhu. 'New Feminist Approaches to Chaucer Introduction.' *Chaucer Review* 54 (2019): 224–229.

Shamsie, Kamila. 'Kamila Shamsie: Let's Have a Year of Publishing Only by Women—A Provocation.' *Guardian*. https://www.theguardian.com/books/2015/jun/05/kamila-shamsie-2018-year-publishing-women-no-new-books-men.

Shimomura, Sachi. *Odd Bodies and Visible Ends in Medieval Literature*. New York: Palgrave Macmillan, 2006.

Simpson, James. 'Chaucer as a European Writer.' In *The Yale Companion to Chaucer*, edited by Seth Lerer, 55–86. New Haven, CT: Yale University Press, 2006.

———. 'The Not Yet *Wife of Bath's Prologue and Tale*.' In *Gender, Poetry, and the Form of Thought in Later Medieval Literature: Essays in Honor of Elizabeth A. Robertson*, edited by Jennifer Jahner and Ingrid Nelson, 201–221. Bethlehem, PA: Lehigh University Press, 2022.

Smith, Warren S. 'The Wife of Bath Debates Jerome.' *Chaucer Review* 32:2 (1997): 129–145.

Sobecki, Sebastian. 'Wards and Widows: *Troilus and Criseyde* and New Documents on Chaucer's Life.' *ELH* 86 (2019): 413–440.

———. '"The writyng of this tretys": Margery Kempe's Son and the Authorship of Her Book.' *Studies in the Age of Chaucer* 37 (2015): 257–283.

Southern, R. W. *The Making of the Middle Ages*. New Haven, CT: Yale University Press, 1953.

Spearing, A. C. *Medieval Autographies: The "I" of the Text*. Notre Dame, IN: University of Notre Dame Press, 2012.

Staley, Lynn. *Margery Kempe's Dissenting Fictions*. University Park: Pennsylvania State University Press, 1994.

Stallybrass, Peter, and Allon White. *The Politics and Poetics of Transgression*. London: Methuen, 1986.

Strauss, Neil. *The Game: Penetrating the Secret Society of Pick-Up Artists*. Edinburgh: Canongate, 2007.

Strohm, Paul. *Social Chaucer*. Cambridge, MA: Harvard University Press, 1989.

Stuart, Donald Clive. 'The Source of Two of Voltaire's "Contes en Vers."' *Modern Language Review* 12:2 (1917): 177–181.

Summit, Jennifer. *Lost Property: The Woman Writer and English Literary History, 1380–1589*. Chicago: University of Chicago Press, 2000.

Sumption, Jonathan. *Pilgrimage: An Image of Medieval Religion*. London: Faber and Faber, 1974.

Sutton, Anne F. 'Two Dozen and More Silkwomen of Fifteenth Century London.' *Ricardian* 16 (2006): 1–8.

Swanson, R. N. *The Twelfth-Century Renaissance*. Manchester: Manchester University Press, 1999.

Swift, Helen. 'The Poetic I.' In *A Companion to Guillaume de Machaut*, edited by Deborah McGrady and Jennifer Bain, 15–32. Leiden: Brill, 2012.

Talbot Donaldson, E. *The Swan at the Well*. New Haven, CT: Yale University Press, 1985.

Teramura, Misha. 'The Anxiety of *Auctoritas*: Chaucer and *The Two Noble Kinsmen*.' *Shakespeare Quarterly* 63:4 (2012): 544–576.

Thompson, Ann. *Shakespeare's Chaucer: A Study in Literary Origins*. Liverpool: Liverpool University Press, 1978.

Thurston, Bonnie. *The Widows: A Women's Ministry in the Early Church*. Minneapolis: Thurston Press, 1989.

Tilley, M. P. 'Two Shakespearean Notes.' *Journal of English and Germanic Philology* 24:3 (July 1925): 315–324.

Treharne, Elaine. 'The Stereotype Confirmed? Chaucer's Wife of Bath.' In *Writing Gender and Genre in Medieval Literature: Approaches to Old and Middle English Texts*, edited by Elaine Treharne, 93–115. Cambridge: D. S. Brewer, 2002.

Turner, Marion. *Chaucer: A European Life*. Princeton, NJ: Princeton University Press, 2019.

Vaddi, Aarthi. 'Narratives of Migration, Immigration, and Interconnection.' In *The Cambridge Companion to British Fiction since 1945*, edited by David James, 61–76. Cambridge: Cambridge University Press, 2015.

Veale, Elspeth. 'Matilda Penne, Skinner (d. 1392–3).' In *Medieval London Widows, 1300–1500*, edited by Caroline M. Barron and Anne F. Sutton, 47–54. London: Bloomsbury, 1994.

Vermeule, Blakey. *Why Do We Care About Literary Characters?* Baltimore: Johns Hopkins University Press, 2010.

Vighi, Fabio. 'Pasolini and Exclusion: Žižek, Agamben and the Modern Sub-Proletariat.' *Theory, Culture & Society* 20:5 (2003): 99–121.

Wallace, David. *Chaucerian Polity: Absolutist Lineages and Associational Forms in England and Italy*. Stanford: Stanford University Press, 1997.

——. 'New Chaucer Topographies.' *Studies in the Age of Chaucer* 29 (2007): 3–19.

Walter, Melissa Emerson. *The Italian Novella and Shakespeare's Comic Heroines*. Toronto: University of Toronto Press, 2019.

Walters, Lori. 'Chivalry and the (En)Gendered Poetic Self, Petrarchan Models in the "Cent Balades."' In *City of Scholars: New Approaches to Christine de Pizan*, edited by Margaret Zimmerman and Dina de Rentis, 43–66. New York: Walter de Gruyter, 1994.

Watt, David. *The Making of Thomas Hoccleve's Series*. Liverpool: Liverpool University Press, 2014.

Watt, Diane. "Margery Kempe.' In *The History of British Women's Writing, 700–1500*, edited by L. H. McAvoy et al., 232–240. London: Palgrave Macmillan: 2012.

——. *Women, Writing, and Religion in England and Beyond, 650–1100*. London: Bloomsbury, 2020.

Watts, John. *Henry VI and the Politics of Kingship*. Cambridge: Cambridge University Press, 1996.

White, Hayden. *The Content of the Form: Narrative Discourse and Historical Representation*. Baltimore, MD: Johns Hopkins University Press, 1987.

Willard, Charity Cannon. *Christine de Pizan: Her Life and Works*. New York: Perseus Books, 1984.

Wimsatt, James I. *Chaucer and His French Contemporaries: Natural Music in the Fourteenth Century*. Toronto: University of Toronto Press, 1991.

Winstead, Karen. *The Oxford History of Life-Writing*. Vol. 1. Oxford: Oxford University Press, 2017.

Winton, Calhoun. *John Gay and the London Theatre*. Lexington: University Press of Kentucky, 1993.

Withingson, Phil. 'Putting the City into Shakespeare's City Comedy.' In *Shakespeare and Early Modern Political Thought*, edited by David Armitage et al., 197–216. Cambridge: Cambridge University Press, 2010.

Wright, Tom. *St Paul: A Biography*. London: SPCK, 2018.

Zanden, Jan Luiten van, Sarah Carmichael, and Tine de Moor. *Capital Women: The European Marriage Pattern, Female Empowerment and Economic Development in Western Europe, 1300–1800*. Oxford: Oxford University Press, 2019.

Zink, Michel. *The Invention of Literary Subjectivity*, translated by Davis Sices. Baltimore: Johns Hopkins University Press, 1999.

Index

Abbott, Diane, 223

'ABC to the Virgin' (Chaucer), 214

Abelard, Peter, 98–103

Acts and Monuments (Foxe), 167

Adversus Jovinianum (Jerome): on bestiality, 40; Christine de Pizan and, 106; on marriage and remarriage, 80, 81–82; in Wife of Bath's Prologue, 15, 18; women as metaphors for texts in, 31

Aesop's fables. *See* 'the man and the lion' fable

affect, 116–17

Affrikano Petro (African Peter), 234

Agbabi, Patience, 142, 227–28, 230–31, 233–34, 235–36, 237, 240, 241–44

Agnes Bookbynder, 58

Aldee, Edward, 154–55

Alisoun Sings (Bergvall), 142, 222–26

All's Well That Ends Well (Shakespeare), 172

Alnwick manuscript, 134–35

Amores (Ovid), 32

Ancrene Wisse, 29

Annales Rerum Anglicarum (Worcester), 63–64

Anne of Bohemia, 92

antifeminist literature: Chaucer and, 3; Christine de Pizan and, 106–8; on

marriage and remarriage, 80–82; in Wife of Bath's Prologue, 15–18, 40–41, 71, 106, 107–8 (*see also* 'book of wikked wyves'); working women and, 49–50. See also *Adversus Jovinianum* (Jerome); *La Roman de la Rose* (*Romance of the Rose*)

Arabian Nights (1974 film), 204

Aristophanes, 181

Arndt-Ober, Margarethe, 191

The Arrival of Brighteye and Other Poems (Breeze), 230, 232, 244. *See also* 'The Wife of Bath in Brixton Market' (Breeze)

Atwood, Margaret, 140–41

Augustine of Hippo, 23, 31, 79–80, 82–83, 114

Austen, Jane, 88

Avianus, 87–88, 90

Bailey's Café (Naylor), 228

Baker, David Erkine, 182

ballads, 7, 140, 142, 154–60, 163, *fig. 7*

Bally-Otes-Franck, Isabel, 4–5

Bamme, Adam, 74–75

Bardolf, Agnes, 118, 124–25

Barton, Anne, 181

BBC (British Broadcasting Corporation), 230

Remedia Amoris (Ovid), 221
Richard, Duke of York, 64
Richard II, King of England, 158–59
Richard II (Shakespeare), 158–59, 172
Richard of Ireland, 126–27
Richard of York, 75–76
Richeldis de Faverches, 116
Riddy, Felicity, 55
Roberts, Jeanne Addison, 173
Robertson, D. W., 3–4
Rolle, Richard, 94
La Roman de la Rose (*Romance of the Rose*): Christine de Pizan on, 18, 105; confessional discourse and, 23, 24; Heloise and, 98, 101–2; La Vieille in, 23, 30, 32, 35, 69–70, 106, 107
Roman de Thebes, 5
romances, 5, 22, 28–29, 30–31, 43–46, 246. *See also specific works*
A Room of One's Own (Woolf), 49, 53, 88
Roy, Arundhati, 223
Royal Shakespeare Company, 228
runaway slaves (maroons), 244–45
Rykener, John/Eleanor, 225

Sands, Donald, 27
Sarduche, Nicholas, 4–5, 65–66
Sawka, Jan, 208–9, *fig. 13*
Schibanoff, Susan, 148
Scrope, Stephen, 111
self and literary subjectivity, 3–5, 22–28, 32–33
Series (Hoccleve), 93–94
sexuality and sexual economy: Dryden and, 163–64; Heloise and, 98–101; *Ulysses* (Joyce) and, 215–16; Wife of Bath and, 163–64, 179, 215–16; women as travellers and, 119–20, 125–28, 130–31, *fig. 3*. *See also* marriage and remarriage

sexual poetics, 31
sexual violence. *See* rape
Shakespeare, William: Devereux and, 158–59; Fuseli and, 190; influence of Chaucer on, 7, 140, 142, 144, 166, 169–72; Wife of Bath's Prologue and, 174–76, 179–80, 182–88; Wife of Bath's Tale and, 172, 182–88. *See also* Falstaff (character)
Shakespeare, William, works of: *All's Well That Ends Well*, 172; *Henry IV Parts 1 and 2*, 174–83, 188; *Henry V*, 188; *The Merry Wives of Windsor*, 171–73, 180, 182–88, 189–90; *A Midsummer Night's Dream*, 170–71; *Richard II*, 158–59, 172; *The Taming of the Shrew*, 182, 183; *Troilus and Cressida*, 170
Shepherd, John and Alice, 129–30
Shipman's Tale, 85, 141
Shrek (2001 film), 43
Sidney, Philip, 166
Simpson, James, 252n13
sin, 22–23, 37
Sir Gawain and the Green Knight, 29
Sir Orfeo, 28–29
Skelton, John, 144, 153–54
slave labour, 53–54
Smerucci, Antonio, 269n37
Smith, Emma, 171
Smith, Zadie, 140, 142, 227–28, 231–34, 235–36, 237–46, *fig. 14*
social mobility, 13
Spenser, Edmund, 144, 166, 167
Squire (character), 32
Statutes of Labourers, 13
Stodeye, Idonia, 73
Stodeye, Joan, 75
Stodeye, John, 73
Stodeye, Margaret, 73–75, 83, 130